JN438071

한국수력원자력(주)
영광원자력본부

The 26th World Poetry Kaya Golden Crown Prize Winner(2012)

The Poetic Anthology Awarded 수상 시집 : **Living As Yearning** 내 이렇게 살다가

*Born at Uijeongbu, Kyunggido, Korea
*Graduated from Dept. of Creative Writing, Literal Arts College, Seorabeol Univ.
*Graduated from Dept of National Language and Literature, from Graduate School, Jungang University
*Made a Debut as a Critic(1962)-Writing "Poetry and the Poetic Theory"
*Retired from a Principal of Jukjeon Middle & High School
*Professor of Hanra University
*Additional Professor of Kyunggi University
*Representative Prof. of Kwangju Literal Arts University
*President of 'Kwangju Forum', Kwangju City, Kyunggido
*Member of Editorial Staff of 'Great Encyclopedia of Korea Poets'
*Member of the Korean Writers' Association
*Director of the Korean Poets' Association of Freedom
*Chief of Director of Hyundae(Modern) Poets' Association of Korea
*Received the main Prize of the Korean Poets' Association of Freedom
*Received the Prize of Kaya Golden Crown from the World Poetry Institute
*Poetic Anthology: "Weight of Yearning" with 8 Vol.

* 경기도 의정부 출생
* 서라벌예술대학 문예창작과 졸
* 중앙대학교 국문과, 동 대학원 졸
* 「詩와 詩論」으로 등단(1962년)
* 용인시 죽전중학교 교장 정년퇴임
* 한라대학교 전임교수
* 경기대학교 겸임교수
* 〈광주문예대학〉 대표교수
* 경기도 광주시 〈광주포럼〉 회장 역임
* 〈한국 시 대사전〉 편집위원
* 한국문인협회 회원
* 한국자유시인협회 이사
* 한국현대시인협회 중앙위원장
* 한국자유시인협회 본상 수상
* 세계시 가야금관왕관상 수상 외
* 시집: 〈그리움의 무게〉 외 8권

Strong Yearning To Brighten His 50 Years' Poetic Power

- The Warm and Serious Poetic World of the Poet, Jeong Song-jeon

The poet, Jeong Song-jeon's poems start from "a Yearning, or a Longing". His longing through a waiting and a watching, aims at embracing "us" combining you and I.

"The waiting and watching" in his poetic anthology "Weight of Yearning", being serious, they change to a sorrow, and become a miserable pain. Their root of the pains is so entangled, that we are sure bound to pile them up one by one in our mind. However, when the poet replaces "the pains" with "implanting objects", we surprise at the poetic art once and admire twice at such a poetic line as "papering a wall alone in spite of the severe pains". This expression is his poetic leap, that is to say, is a change of his specific conception.

But in a way he keeps his poetic silent tone even writhing in a desperate agony because of "a waiting and a yearning". In such poetic tones, we can't find a characteristic diction in his poems, but rather find to use an everyday words only. Therefore what his poetry has an animating power, namely, as a poetic spices, handling to finish his poems from the beginning, and in the middle, and to the last process in his poetic art.

Such everyday words in his life as 'flower and wind', 'heaven and earth', 'morning and evening', 'love and hate, and 'meeting and separation', if they are inserted in his poem, they have their own living power, relish their own deep flavor in the due positions. This is his own poetic art that he can do only.

I am sure his poetic power is due to his liberal, and flexible thinking on things. His roundabout and direct narrations originate in his stern, and mild character.

The following lines tell us with an air of innocence as "the tree standing at the yard falls down from the cliff, grasping me," "the mountains and the fields familiar to the eyes, stirring the loneliness,", "that the weak-eyed wife looked at, is not the flower, but may be an "I", and yet that makes me hesitate, I stand in the yellow flower petals as if taken by her hands". Here are the moving, strong power. When we turn our backs, his poetic lines have big reverberation pulling our minds. The poet has another poetic world we cannot aim with our sense, and this occupies our consciousness freely and expand it.

His firm and extinguished poetic power at last accomplished his will and purpose to the glorious place. We believe this is a little compensation for his firm and strong poetic spirit. <Gwon O-un(Poet, Prof. Dept. of Creative Writing, Jungang Univ.)>

시력 50년을 밝히는 견고한 '그리움'

-따스하고도 절절한 정송전의 시세계

정송전의 시는 '그리움'에서 출발한다. 그리고 그 그리움은 '기다림'과 '바라봄'을 관통하여 너와 나를 아우르는 '우리'를 '그러안기'에 이른다.

기다림과 그리움이 지독하면 서러움이 되고 그것은 곧 처절한 '고통'이 되게 마련이다. 그 고통의 뿌리는 깊고도 가열(苛烈)하여서 차라리 '내 안에 촘촘히 심어 놓고' 말게 된다. 그런데 이 '고통'을 '심는' 대상으로 치환시키는 기교에 우리는 한 번 놀라고, '혼자서 벽지를 바르는' 대목에서 또 한 번 놀라게 된다. 이만저만한 발상의 비약이 아닌 까닭이다.

그는 또 기다림과 그리움으로 서럽고 고통스러워 몸부림치면서도 한결같이 차분한 음성을 견지한다. 그렇다고 그가 독특한 시어(詩語)를 만들어 쓰는 것도 아니다. 어찌보면 지나칠 정도로 꾸밈 없는 일상어들 뿐이다. 그러면서도 시가 맛깔스럽게 살아나는 것은 평범한 일상어를 요리조리 시어로써 시치고 박음질하고 휘갑치는 기술이 뛰어나기 때문이다.

꽃과 바람, 하늘과 땅, 아침과 저녁, 사랑과 미움, 만남과 이별 따위의 일상어들이 그의 손을 타면 제자리를 찾아 들어가 한결 깊고 오묘한 맛을 내게 된다. 오로지 그만이 가능한 일이다.

이것은 또한 그의 사고(思考)가 유연한 까닭이기도 하다. 차근차근 귀엣말처럼 완곡하면서도 군더더기 없는 그의 직접화법은 냉엄하면서도 유화(柔和)한 그의 성품에서 우러나온다. '마당에 서 있는 나무가 나를 붙잡고 절벽으로 떨어져 내리'거나, '적막을 휘저어 눈에 익은 산과 들이 차창을 열고 들어오기'나, '시력도 좋지 않은 아내가 바라본 꽃은 꽃이 아니라 자기였을지 모르지, 아직도 헷갈리는 것은 노란 꽃잎 속에 손에 잡힐 듯 내가 서 있나 보다'처럼 시침 뚝 따고 내질러 놓는 식이다. 그런데 거기에는 강력한 힘이 있다. 돌아서면 잡아당기는 울림이 있다. 이렇듯 정송전의 시에는 가늠하기 어려운 냉엄한 또 하나의 세계가 있다. 그것이 자유자재로 우리를 넘나들고 있다.

이렇듯 50년을 한결같이 견지해 온 견고하고도 돌올한 그의 시력이 마침내 상찬의 자리에 오르게 되었다. 그의 뜨겁게도 확연한 시정신에 얼마만큼의 위안이 될 수 있으리라 믿는다. 〈권오운(시인 · 중앙대 문창과 교수)〉

The 26th World Poetry Kaya Golden Crown Prize Winner(2012)

The Poetic Anthology Awarded 수상 시집 : **Long Letters of A Crane** 학의 장서

*Ex-Chairman of Writer's Association at Gimjae Branch
*President at General Society of Arts of Korean Painting
*Member of Literary Men's Association of Korea
*Vice Chairman of Kirin Literature at Jeon-Buk
*Member of Literary Men's Association of Jeon-Buk
*A Compilation Committee of A Dictionary of Modern Poets in Korea
*Received Prizes:
- Chosen Four Times at The Nation-Wide Arts Exhibition of Byok-Gol
- Won the Prize of new Poet from "The Han-Kook Poetry" monthly
- Won the Great Prize from "The Han-Kook Poetry" monthly
- Won the Prize of Culture of Gimjae Citizens
- Won the Prize of Nosan Literature
*Publication:
- An Extra Star, Hanging in the Sky
- The Reason the Wind Sits on the Tree
- Now and Then, On Such A Day
- Long Letters of A Crane

* 김제 문인협회 전,지부장
* 한국화예총회 회장
* 한국문인협회 회원
* 전북 문인협회 회원
* 전북 기린문학 부회장
* 한국 현대시인사전 편찬위원
* 수상 경력
-전국 벽골미술대전 특선4회
-한국시 시인수상
-한국시 문학대상 수상
-김제시민의장 문화장 수상
-노산문학상
* 저서
- 여유별 뜨는 날
- 바람이 나무에 걸터앉은 이유
- 더러는 이런 날도
- 학의 장서

Winner 수상자 : Poet Jin Sang-soon 진상순(陳相順) 시인

The Lyricism, Awakened the Immortal Soul

The winner, Jin Sang-soon is a leading poetess and painter, and already has his own 4 books of the poetic anthologies: the First, "The Day The Wolf Star Rises",the Second, "The Reason Which The Winds Sit On the Tree", the Third, "Occasionall On A Day", " The Long Letters of A Crane".

The poetess was born in a peaceful family and has an original poetic power to describe and portray by nature.

As the poet, Rainer Maria Rilke referred,"the poetry is an experience", the poetess has experienced a long struggle against his diseases during his medical treatment, conquering them, and she has her own characteristic world due to her experience.

She pursues dualistic world balancing between eternity and nothing rooted in the metempsychosis and the language of Buddhism caused by an attitude of her earlier life.

Especially in her poem, "The Long letters of A Crane", We can find it that she wrote a world of longing projected from her delicate and right-minded life to the sublimated world.

We are proud of her strong merits to balance with lyrical intellect and so we would like to pay our tribute of praise to the poetess Jin Sang-soon who is recognized as the best Shijo poet. <Recommender: Kim Joung-woong, Yun Hae-kyu>

불멸의 혼을 일으킨 서정의 시심

수상자 시월(詩月) 진상순 시인은 화가이며 네 권의 저서 제1시집 "여우별 뜨는 날" 외에 "바람이 나무에 걸터 앉은 이유" "더러는 이런 날도" "학의 장서" 등 서정의 절정에 이르는 중견 시인이다.

수상자는 대체로 화목한 가정에서 태어나 선천적으로 자연을 음미하는 시의 창의력과 미적 묘사를 절묘하게 그려내는 독특한 여류 걸사이다.

독일의 시인 "라이너마리아 릴케가 시는 체험이다" 그랬듯이 수상자는 수없는 투병으로 사선을 넘나들며 고통의 늪에서 역경을 극복하여 불멸의 혼을 일으킨 자만이 시가 나올 수 있다는 체험의 긍지를 내보이기도 한다.

수상자의 작품은 불교적 윤회의 세계관과 언어에 의한 관념적 관찰로 압축시킬 수 있는 것은, 어렸을 때부터 자연 환경과 잘 조화하여 살았기에 자신의 시에 소멸성과 영원성의 교차를 통한 이원적 세계를 추구하고 있다.

특히 "학의 장서"에서는 그의 섬세하고 올곧게 살아온 삶의 촉각이 모정(慕情)의 빛에 투영되어 사모(思慕)의 세계로 모든 설움을 안으로 승화시켜 작품으로 나타내 었다.

서정의 본 모습을 지성적으로 지켜주고, 보여주는 진상순 시인이 우리 시조시단의 정점으로 우뚝 서서 문학사의 한 획을 긋고 있기에 왕관상을 주어 찬양하는 바이다.

〈심사 위원 : 김정웅 · 윤해규〉

The 26th World Poetry Kaya Golden Crown Prize Winner(2012)

The Poetic Anthology Awarded 수상 시집 : **The Earth Is Indisposed** 지구는 미령靡寧하시다

*Poet, Essayist
*Graduated from Graduate School of Jungang University
*Member of Korean Writers' Association
*Director of the World Poetry Institute
*Received the Prize of Kaya Golden Crown
*Received the Prize of President of the Korean Mothers' Society(Meeting)
-For Writing of an Impression on "Demian" by Herman Hesse
*Poetic Anthology: "The Earth is Indisposed (Unwell)"
*Essay Anthology: "Patchwork Wrapping Cloth"

*Address:142-8 Daehyun-dong, Seodaemun-gu, Seoul. Korea
*Tel: 02-362-6332/ 010-4762-6331
*E-Mail: nja6332@hanmail.net

* 시인 · 수필가
* 중앙대학교 대학원 졸업
* 한국문인협회 회원
* 세계시문학회 부회장
* 세계시 가야금관왕관상 수상
* 헬만헷세 〈데미안〉 독후감 대한어머니 회장상 수상
* 시집 : 〈지구는 미령靡寧하시다〉
* 수필집 : 〈조각보〉

* 주소 : 서울시 서대문구 대현동 142-8
* 전화 : 02-362-6332, 010-4762-6331
* e-mail : nja6332 @hanmail.net

Winner 수상자 : Poet No Jung-ai 노정애(盧貞愛) 시인

Poems of An Introspection About Life of Being
- Based on the Family History

In the preface of his poetic anthology, "The Earth Is Unwell" the poet refers to his housing site "A Salddemee" at his home town, and lots of the loveable landscapes basing on "A Salddemee" as if this site might prove for a fatal place to exist, are described with his lyrical pen. We can guess this is based on his poetic spirit which shows living style with an anxious mind for the necessary things to be in his living site at his home town. As if the sense of solidarity connected with delicate blood vessel like spider's web enclosing I and self, is his case, he puts it in the center of his poems and transforms into the poetic world the realistic things he watches through them. While he has lived, the experiential lumps he has undergone, are unavoidable psychological discords of his separation with families, sticking like moss from an archetype of a tragic life, showing his will to express the endless growing desire of affection to make up for them. Solidified as the desire of ego being latent in unforgettable consciousness, he figured them as poetic images.

Now with the mind, yearning for his home town left at the north, even though he recollects his appetite of home town's, taking a meal named "Chung-guk-jang" at a Tong-il-cheon restaurant near the Imjin river, the poet watches at the painful reality figuring the symbolic birds, that they have to fly to the south altogether again. Such his recognition for reality is rooted deeply in his mind together with painful agonies of his family's history, so the peace of world he has dreamed stays always at other shore, the actual world we face to exist, is so entangled with en inevitable

fatal restraint named "ties of blood", his being always shudders with fear and is confined himself in a melancholic consciousness. However, he has a strong prospect to the bright future for holding one grass or plant, one scene of the foreign landscapes in his bosom, and so I am sure his poems are dotted with a pathetic and bright color for the peaceful symbol. <Park Dong-kyu, Literary Critic, Publisher, "Monthly The Simsang: Image">

가족사를 바탕으로 한 존재의 삶에 관한 성찰의 시편들

그의 시집 〈지구는 미령靡寧하시다〉 서문을 보면, '살떼미' 라는 고향 집터가 나오고 '살떼미'를 중심으로 한 사랑의 풍경들이 마치 그가 살아가야 할 터전이었음을 증명이라도 하듯이 정겨운 서정의 붓으로 그려내고 있다. 이는 바로 잊지 못하는 고향 터전 안에 있어야 할 것들에 대한 안타까움을 가슴에 품고 살아가는 것을 보여주는 것으로서 그의 시적 정신의 바탕을 이루는 것임을 짐작할 수 있을 것이다. 그리고 그는 나와 자아라는 존재를 둘러싸고 있는 거미줄 같은 가는 핏줄의 연대를 마치 그가 가진 모든 것인 듯 시의 중심에 있게 하고 이를 통해서 그가 바라보는 현실의 세계를 시로 변용하고 있는 것이다. 따라서 그는 살아오는 동안 그가 겪은 모든 체험의 덩어리는 '살떼미'라는 고향을 떠날 때 지녔던 비극적 삶의 원형에서 이끼처럼 머물러 있는 가족과의 어쩔 수 없는 이별의 심정적 균열과 이를 메워보려는 가족에 대한 끝없는 애정의 성장적 욕망을 그려내려는 의지를 보여주고 있는 것이다. 이는 잊혀 지지 않는 의식의 잠재된 자아의 욕망으로 굳어져 이를 시의 형상으로 만들어 보고자 한 것이라 할 수 있을 것이다.

시인에게 있어서 북에 두고 온 고향을 그리는 마음으로 임진강가에 서 있는 지금 비록 통일촌 청국장 먹으면서 고향의 입맛을 회상하는 것이지만 남북을 오가는 상징적인 의미의 새를 그리면서 다시 일제히 날개를 펴 남쪽으로 날아들 수밖에 없는 현실의 아픈 상처를 바라보고 있음을 알 수 있다. 그의 이러한 현실인식은 모든 가족사의 뼈아픈 고통과 함께 내면에 깊숙이 자리 잡고 있어서 그가 꿈꾸는 세상의 평화는 항상 저 편에 있고 그가 안고 살아가는 현실은 핏줄이라는 피할 수 없는 숙명적 연대의 속박에 얽매여 있기 때문에 그의 존재는 항상 전율하고 침울해하는 의식의 세계에 갇혀 있음을 말해준다. 그러면서도 그는 오히려 밝은 내일에 대한 전망을 보다 강하게 가짐으로서 풀 한포기 외국의 풍경 하나도 그가 안아볼 수 있는 평화로운 삶의 표상이 되고 있어서 그의 시는 애절한 밝음의 색깔로 점철되어 있다고 할 수 있다. 〈박동규(월간 시 전문지 심상사 대표 문학평론가)〉

The 25th World Poetry Kaya Golden Crown Prize Awarding Ceremony
Commemoration Ceremony For Publication of The 29th Series of World Poetry

- 일시 : 2011년 11월 11일(金) 오후 6시
- 장소 : 대한출판문화회관

第25回 『世界詩 伽倻金冠王冠賞』 施賞式

第29輯(2011) WORLD POETRY(世界詩文學) 出版紀念會

- 主催 : 世界詩文學會 · 乙支出版公社
- 後援 : 光州 金病院 · 한국수력원자력(주)영광원자력본부

Winner 수상자 : Poet Jeong Jin-su 정진수(鄭鎭洙) 시인

*Serving at the National Tax Office(Present)
*Graduate from Dept. of National language of the Air and Correspondence College
*Member of the Association of Korean Writers
*Member of the Literary Circle in National Tax Office
*Member of the Association of the Literary Trend and Thought
*Member of the World Poetry Institute

* 현 국세청 근무
* 방송통신대학 국어국문학과 졸업
* 한국문인협회 회원
* 국세청눈우회 회원
* 세계시문학회 회원
* 문예사조문인협회 회원

The heart-aching emotional feelings touch deeply our mind unexpectedly
- The Poem, 'Walking Along the River'

The man is a warm-hearted and a cool-headed poet, who has served as one of the high ranking public officials, without being imbued with urban manners and tainted with vice, and keeping on human way as his own way.

In the above poem, he expresses the characters of his families very lively with a humanistic mind, as "the white hawkweed flowers split their hairs/ I take a walk with my wife along the riverside path.....// At the riverside path with rich chestnut flower's leaves scattered/ Our couple are left alone.....// They all would flow happily along the star's way in the river" What we all find in his poem is the original human soul rooted deeply and his own emotional attitude of life. The heart-aching emotional feelings touch deeply our mind unexpectedly.

<Recommender: Yun Hae-kyu, Kim Kyung-hee>

그의 정서는 우리에게 뜻하지 않은 포근함을 느껴
-정진수 시 '강물 따라 걷다'

국가공무원 고위직에 있는 그는 어수선한 현실에서 몸과 마음에 너무 쉽게 굳은살 박히지 않고 한길을 가고 있는 냉철한 머리와 가슴이 따뜻한 시인이다.

"하얀 조팝꽃 가르마 타는 / 강변길을 아내와 함께 걷는다......// 짙은 밤꽃 이파리 흥건한/ 강둑 길에 우리 부부만 남겨진다.......// 강물속 별길/ 따라 모두 행복하게 흐르고 싶다."라면서 가족들의 본모습을 그대로 간직한 채 생생하고 따뜻하게 나타내고 있다. 우리가 그의 시에서 발견할 수 있는 것은 정진수 시인만이 발견한 인간정신, 생활정서다. 글썽거리는 그의 정서는 우리에게 뜻하지 않은 마음의 포근함을 느끼게 해 주고 있다. 〈심사 위원: 윤해규 · 김경희〉

W.P 출판기념회 및 「세계시 가야금관왕관상」 시상식(2011)에 국민의례를 하고 있는 참석자들

세계시문학 출판기념회 및 「세계시 가야금관왕관상」 시상식(2011)에 참석한 내빈과 회원들

왕관상을 수상하고 있는
김계윤(光州 金病院 院長) 시인과

시상하고 있는
김정웅 본회 회장

GOLD CROWN WORLD POETS PRIZE AWARD

COMMEMORATION CEREMONY FOR THE PUBLICATION
ANTHOLOGY AND THE 25TH KAYA GOLD CROWN WORLD POETS PRIZE AWARDING CEREMONY
왕관상(王冠賞) : 시인.김계윤(金桂潤 Poet, Kim Kye-yoon) 受賞作 : 『꿈에 어린 황룡강』"A Dreamy Hwang-Ryong Rever"
"Qatar, Land of Blessing"

왕관상을 수상하고 있는
김일례 시인과

시상하고 있는
이상진 본회 前 총재

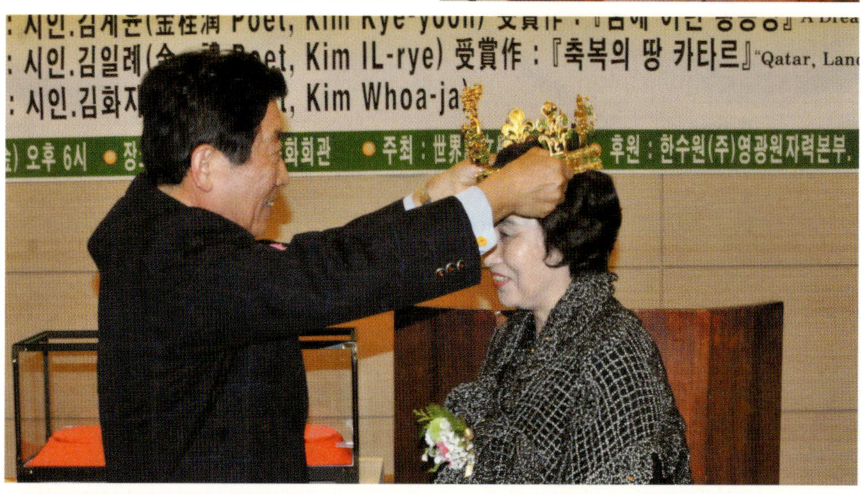

왕관상(王冠賞
왕관상(王冠賞)
문학상(文學賞)
2011. 11. 11

ANTHOLOGY AND THE 25TH KAYA GOLD CROWN WORLD POETS PRIZE AWARDIN
왕관상(王冠賞) : 시인.김계윤(金桂潤 Poet, Kim Kye-yoon) 受賞作 :
왕관상(王冠賞) : 시인.김일례(金一禮 Poet, Kim IL-rye) 受賞作 :
김화자(金花子 Poet, Kim Who
장소 : 서울대한출판문화회관

ANTHOLOGY AND THE 25TH KAYA GOLD CROWN WORLD POETS PRIZE AWARDING CEREM
왕관상(王冠賞) : 시인.김계윤
Poet, Kim Kye-yoon) 受賞作 : 『꿈에 어
"A Dreamy Hwang-Ryon
왕관상(王冠賞) : 시인.김일
受賞作 : 『축복의 땅
Land of Blessing"
문학상
: 시인.김화자

문학상을 수상하고 있는
김화자 시인과

시상하고 있는
김남웅 한국민족문학가협회
회장

: 시인.김일례(金一禮 Poet, Kim IL-
: 시인.김화자(
Poet, Kim Wh
오후 6시 ● 장소 :
화회관

祝
發

김화자(金花子 Poet, Kim Whoa
● 장소 : 서울대한출
● 주최
究會

Poet, Kim IL-rye) 受賞作
Poet, Kim
1

Poet, Kim
Poet,
2

Kim IL-rye) 受賞作 :
Kim
3

일시 : 2011. 11.
4

축
祝
5

1 축사를 하는 본회 김정웅 회장
2 축사를 하고 있는 김남웅 시인
3 시낭송을 하고 있는 고방규 시인
4 시낭송을 하고 있는 은요숙 시인
5 김귀례 시인 · 최기 교수 부부, 김정웅 본회 회장, 윤해규 시인 · 김효열 부부(좌부터)
6 심사 발표를 하고 있는 윤해규 을지출판공사 대표
7 사회를 보고 있는 오진환 시인
8 시낭송을 하고 있는 장현경(시인) 청계문학회 회장
9 정진수 시인 부부, 김경희 시인, 박귀근 시인(우부터)

6

7

8

9

1

『축복의 땅 카타르』"Qatar, Land
후원
광원자력본부,
2

일시 : 2011. 11.
서울대한출판문화회관
3

禮 Poet, Kim IL-rye) 受賞
花子 Poet,
hoa-ja)
주최 : 世界詩文學
4

im Whoa-ja)
文學研究會
5

문학상
6

1 시낭송을 하고 있는 황성이 시인
2 시낭송을 하고 있는 김경희 시인
3 시낭송을 하고 있는 홍양자 시인
4 시낭송을 하고 있는 강영덕 시인
5 시낭송을 하고 있는 김종분 시인
6 시낭송을 하고 있는 진명숙 시인
7 시낭송을 하고 있는 노정애 시인
8 시낭송을 하고 있는 국승윤 시인
9 시낭송을 하고 있는 최무자 시인
10 사진 촬영을 담당한 김돈영 시인
11 시낭송을 하고 있는 김미경 시인

Symposium of literary exchange between Korea and Mongol 韓蒙文學交流 심포지엄

Our institute attained a great success in a symposium of literary exchange between Korea and Mongol, in the occasion of the 30th anniversary of the foundation of the World Poetry Institution, held in the capital city, Ulanbator, Mongol, on the date 27~30 July, 2012.

본회는 2012년 6월 27일~30일까지 세계시문학회 창립 30주년 기념으로 한·몽 문학교류 심포지엄을 몽골에서 개최하여 대성황리에 국위 선양한 바가 있다. 참석자는 다음과 같다.

김정웅 시인, 임인철 시인, 김송배 시인, 여한경 시인, 박윤기 시인 부부, 전덕기 시인, 김희순 시인, 곽병수 시인 부부, 김미경 시인, 원응순 시인 부부, 정순자 시인, 김영미 시인, 강영덕 시인과 모친, 정지원 시인, 이상진 시인, 황성이 시인, 김소엽 시인, 김운중 시인

World Poetry

世界詩文學 세계시문학

Vol.30/2012

EDITOR : KIM JOUNG-WOONG
TRANSLATOR : WON EUNG-SOON

그림 : 조기현(시인·화가)

EulJi Publishing Company
을지출판공사
Republic Of Korea

WORLD POETRY 世界詩文學 세계시문학
Vol.30 / 2012
(price; $20)
EDITOR : KIM JOUNG-WOONG
TRANSLATOR : WON EUNG-SOON

Published by: Yun Hae-Kyu / 尹 海 圭
EulJi Publishing Company 乙支出版公社
〈등록번호 제 2-741호 1985. 2. 14 등록〉
394-81, Seogyo-dong, Mapo-gu, Seoul, 121-840, Korea
TEL (02) 334-4050 · 4090 FAX (02) 334-4010
e-mail : ejp4050@hanmail.net
Pubilshed on November 9, 2012. Printed on November 5, 2012

THE WORLD POETRY RESEARCH INSTITUTE
192-67, Eupnae-ri, Gochang-eup, Gochang-gun, Jeon-buk,
585-807, Korea
Tel. 82-63-564-4248, 82-63-564-6064 H.P 82-010-6318-4248

Founder President: Kim Young-sam. D.LITT.

CONTENTS

Symposium of Literary Exchange between Korea and Mongol
韓蒙文學 심포지엄

Mongol

KOREA

COLOMBIA

KOREA

RUSSIA

U.S.A.

World Poetry Translators

Names of Translators	Names of Translators
ADA AHARONI	HELLEN WONL PATTERSON
AILA O.COMES	HUCH MCKNLEY
ALAIN PIOTE CLAUDIA FLURY	IH MING-UH
AMY WAGNER	INGE DREYER
AN CHO-GEUN	JAIME GARCIA GARCIA
ANDRÉA DE PAULA SANTOS	JANE MAISKAYA
ANDRE BOUCHIER	JEANNE MAILLET
ANGELA PAIVA DE LUCIO	JEONG WI-JIN
ANTONIO AUGUSTO ULBUM	JIN CHEN-HUI
A.PAULA SANTOS	JN ARA DEADRLNS
A.S.DAWSON	JIN XUE-SHONG
A.SIMON DE SOUZA	JOANNE VARRICCHIO
BLACK EARL	JOHN ROBERTS
BETTINA HERR	JO MAN-HO
CARLA KRAUS	JO YUN-KYU
CHANG SOO-CHEOL	KANG SHIN-IL
CHANG SOON-BOK	KANG TONG-WON
CINDY CHILDO	KAPONE JULIE
CHOI SEI-KYUN	KAREN ALKALAY-GUT
CHONG YUN-BOM	KIM BYUNG-RIN
DAVID MACANN	KIM DONG-SOO
DENISE LEVERTOV	KIM DONG SUNG
DOLORES PEREDA	KIM JAI-HIUN
DOROTHEA	KIM IK-JE
ESTHER CAMERON	KIM IM-SUK
EVA SHALTIEL	KIM IN KYUNG
EVI PAPADIMA THEODORAKIS	KIM JOO-SENG
GE	KIM KWANG-BAE
FERNANDO ALONSO BARAHONA	KIM MAN-GON
G.PALUMBO	KIM MIN-SEONG
GUENI G.Z.AIMOF	KIM SANG-HWAN
HADASSAH HASKELE	KIM SENG-HUI
HAN IN-SOON	KIM YOUN-JAE
HAN SONG-SUN	KIM YOUNG-NAM
HANS-DIETER LUCKE	KIM YOUNG-SAM

Names of Translators	Names of Translators
KIM YUHN-BOK	ROBERTO MORAES PEREIRH
KOH CHANG-SOO	RO CHANG-SHIK
KIM YONG-SUN	RURIKO SUZUKI
KIM YUHN-BOK	RUTH PELDMAN
LEE BO-HEA	SEIJI HINO
LEE HEE-SEON	SHIM SANG-WOOK
LEE HE-YOUNG	SHIN MYONG-HO
LEE JONG-HWAN	SHIN TONG-CHOON
LEE JOON-YOUNG	SHIRA TWERSKY-CASSEL
LEE JUNG-KEE	SHULAMITS NARDI
LEE TAI-DONG	SONG IN-SOB
LEE YOUNG-GUL	SON SUCK-RIN
LI JAI-SIK	SON Y.S.
LI JONG WHAN	STEPHEN BADZIK
LIM HO-SOON	TAKEKAZY HISADA
LIM HYE-RYEON	SYM M.H.
LIVIA PAULINI	TAKESHI ISHIARA
LUIS A.SANCHEZ	TERESINKA PEREIRA
LUIS MUNIZ	TINA SALLEE
MAIA CIRCE	TUIS MUNIZ
MENTIRAS	VELTA SNIKERE
MIRABEL	VICKIE DIMITRIADON
MOHAMED SELMI	VICTOR OURIN
MOON SUL-CHANG	WAN HUA GOH CHAPOUTHER
NILSA Y.GARZA	WERMER MANHEIM
NOBUKO NAKAMURA	XIMENA CORTES
O.C.KIM PH.D	YEO HONG-SANG
OH CHEOL	YU JEONG-SUK
PARK JOOON-TAE	YOO YEONG
PARK SOON-WON	YOON CHONG-HIOK
PARK TAE-JIN	YOON GANG-WON
PARK YONG-JIN	YU IN-HO
PARK YOUNG-SU	ZEV DAVIS
RENE STREIFF	PARK, MEEN-HEUM
RIE LEIGH-LOOHUIZEN	KIM KWANG-OUP
ROBERT LEARNELY	WON EUNG-SOON

Winners of KAYA Golden Crown World Poets Award

Year	Country	Name of Winners
1986	KOREA	KIM IL-RO
1987	KOREA	LEE HAN-HO
	U.S.A.	ROSEMARY C.WILKINSON
1988	U.S.A.	VICTORY OURINE
	KOREA	MOON DEOK-SOO
	C. I. S.(RUSSIA)	DOLMA TOVSKY EUGINE
	ESPANA	TOMAS BEVIA ARANDA
	INDIA	D.K.JOY
1989	KOREA	SHIN DONG-JIP
	U.S.A.	ELLIS OVESEN
	YUGO(Sarajevo)	DR. AJSA ZAHIROVIC
	KOREA	JEONG KI-SEOK
1990	U.S.A.	DR. MARY J. BANERS
	KOREA	DR. KIM DONG-NI
	KOREA	DR. YUN JONG-HYOK
1991	JAPAN	UEMOTO MASAO
	KOREA	LIM JI-HYUN
	AUSTRALIA	JOY BEAUDETTE CRIPS
	KOREA	LIM HEON-DO
1992	KOREA	BAEK HAN-YI
	BRAZIL	ANGELA MARIA ROCHA BIASE
	KOREA	YANG SANG-WOOK
	CHINA P.R.	CHEN-HUI JIN
1993	KOREA	KIM JI-HYANG
	ISRAEL	ADA AHARONI
	JAPAN	JUNKO HAMAE
	KOREA	DR. KIM JOUNG-WOONG
	CHINA P.R.	Prof. LU JIN
1994	KOREA	CHOI YUN-YOUNG
1995	KOREA	LEE CHANG-HWAN
1996	KOREA	SON KI-SUB
	KOREA	KANG SHIN-IL

Year	Country	Name of Winners
1997	KOREA	KIM MIN-SEONG
1998	KOREA	KIM NAM-WOONG
	KOREA	KIM CHUI-KYONG
1999	KOREA	LEE JAE-HYUN
	KOREA	JUNG SOON-YOUNG
	KOREA	PARK KEUN-HOO
2000	KOREA	JIN EUL-JU
	CHINA	GE NAI FU
2001	KOREA	LEE KI-BAN
2002	JAPAN	JUN UENO
2003	KOREA	KIM CHANG-JIK
	KOREA	KIM JI-WON
2004	JAPAN	NATIKO WATANABE
	KOREA	CHUNG OK-IN
2005	KOREA	SEO JEONG-NAM
	KOREA	LEE JI-YOUNG
	KOREA	JUNG U-HA
2006	KOREA	OH MIN-PHIL
	KOREA	KIM SUNG-YOUL
	KOREA	LEE JONG-IL
2007	KOREA	SHIN SOON-AE
	KOREA	CHO KI-HYUN
2008	KOREA	CHOI SEUNG-BEOM
	KOREA	KANG HAE-KUN
2009	KOREA	SHIN DONG-MYEUNG
	KOREA	KIM JONG-WON
2010	KOREA	PARK MOON-JAE
	KOREA	LIM WON-SIK
	KOREA	EUN YO-SUK
2011	KOREA	KIM KYE-YOON
	KOREA	KIM IL-RYE
2012	KOREA	CHOUNG SONG-JUN
	KOREA	JIN SANG-SOON
	KOREA	NO JUNG-AI

An Address

To Become the Whole World as the Arena of Poetry

A flood of complimentary remarks have been given in which the exchange of lyrics among world-poets can make the consciences of the human spirit and eternity of the human beings while making the East and West, South and North harmonious. This institute, as a social gathering through a magazine, has been activated since 1982 by the late professor Poet Kim Young-sam whose idea was to exchange views on emotional aspects of mutual culture and intelligence. Certainly, exchange of lyrical poems was another institute, which intended to rise by way of necessary researches on World-poetry.

Years have passed since then, and a price of World-Poetry has been established by adopting trophy the ancient crown of King Su-ro of A.D. 42 who was the first King of Korean Land. The prize has been awarded to remember-poet of fame, and very well accepted, I believe.

This institute was well run by Professor Kim Young-sam From 1982 to 1993, then, I came to look after what he built up in relation to the institute. It has been my responsibility to publish this anthology and award the prize. Informatively, this anthology which donated nearly 4,000 copies to the university-libraries around the world contains over 800 poets' works from over 60 countries and aims their poetic exchange. Incidentally, the prize-awarding of Kaya Gold Crown Poets Award is a yearly since 1986, so awarding the prize is 26 times and the anthology is also published in 30 volumes until this year.

Our institute attained a great success in a symposium of literary exchange between Korea and Mongol, in the occasion of the 30th anniversary of the foundation of the World Poetry Institution, held in the capital city, Ulanbator, Mongol, on the date 27~30 July, 2012.

I believe that lyric poetry and cultural exchange between nations will continue through this institute. Incidentally, I once again give you my word of honor that I will administer this institute by using all my strength.

In conclusion, I hope the members of our institute will really enjoy every success and good luck.

Kim Joung-woong, President

온 세계가 시의 한마당이 되게 합시다

세계시문학회 회장 金 正 雄

본회는 세계 시인들의 정성 어린 서정시의 교류를 목적으로 하는 지상(紙上) 모임으로써 인간 정신의 양심을 東西와 南北을 화평하게 하면서 인류의 영원함을 가능케 할 것이라는 찬사가 답지되어, 1982년도에 김영삼 교수께서 세계적인 문화 정서와 인간 본연의 지성을 위하여 세계시문학을 연구 발표하면서부터 창립하였던 것입니다.

그 후 한국 최초의 왕 제도가 시행된 AD 42년 가야국 김수로왕이 착관한 가야금관왕관상을 World-Poetry상으로 제정하여 세계 저명한 시인들에게 시상케 되었습니다.

지금까지 60여 국 800여 시인들의 시문학 교류 및 작품 수록과 세계 유수한 대학교 도서관에 4,000여 권의 WORLD-POETRY를 기증하고 1986년부터 계속 세계시가야금관왕관상을 시상해 오고 있습니다.

1982년부터 1993년까지 김영삼 교수가 WORLD-POETRY를 주창해 오다 타계하므로 본인이 그 후임을 맡아 한 호도 빠짐없이 제30집 〈세계시문학〉을 출간해 오고, 제26회 세계시가야금관왕관상도 시상해 오고 있습니다.

본회는 금년 6월 27일~30일까지 W. P창립 30주년 기념으로 한 · 몽 문학교류 심포지엄을 몽골에서 개최하여 대성황리에 국위 선양한 바가 있습니다.

앞으로도 계속 세계시인들의 정성 어린 서정시의 교류와 문학창달의 궁극적인 정신을 통하여 세계를 하나로 시의 한마당이 되게끔 혼신을 다하겠습니다.

아울러 세계시문학회 회원 여러분의 건승과 문운이 함께하시길 빕니다

Statute of the World Poetry Research Institute

Chapter 1
General Provisions

Art. 1. Object

The object of this Institute shall be in interchanging the world poems, in promoting their friendly ties, in studying and improving the world poems as well as Korean poems, and in safeguarding its members' interests.

Art. 2. Naming

This institute shall be named The World Poetry Research Institute and World Poets Club.

Art. 3. This institute shall set up its headquarters in Seoul Korea:and it can set up its branch offices in every foreign country and in any parts of Korea where its members attend together.

Art. 4. Capacity of membership

This institute shall consist of world poets who agree on the object of this institute, and their capacity of its membership shall be deliberated and decided in the excutive meetings in its countries concemed and in all local branch offices in Korea.

Art. 5. Duties

Each member shall be oblighed to observe the provisions of this institute and shall pay his or her membership dues.

Chapter 2
Excutive Members and Their Duties

Art. 6. This institule's excutive members shall consist of as follows:

1) President:one person.

2) Vice president:Two persons from Korea, some persons from abroad.

3) Auditor:Two persons from Korea

4) Advisor:Some persons including one standing advisor.
5) Directors:Some persons from Korea and abroad.
6) Steering committee:Some persons.
7) Secretary-General:one person.
8) deputy secretary-General:two persons.

Art. 7. President and vice presidents shall be elected in the general meeting, president of a branch office in each country shall be elected in each own branch office in each foreign country as well as in some parts of Korea.

Art. 8. President shall represent the main institute and he shall exercise general control over all of this Institute affairs.

Art. 9. Vice presidents shall assist president and shall act for the president in case of his accident.

Art. 10. President of branch office shall represent all members of his or her own branch office.

Art. 11. Secretary-General and deputy Secretary-Generals shall be appointed by president and they shall get the approval of the general meeting, and they shall excute the Institute affairs.
1) Secretary-General shall attend excutive meeting and shall take charge of all of the Institute affairs.
2) The first deputy secretary-general shall take charge of the translations, finances and mail matters.
3) The second deputy secretary-general shall take charge of the edition of the publishing matters.

Art. 12. Directors shall be recommended by the presidents of the brach offices abroad and from Korea and shall be decided in the excutive meeting of the headquarters in Korea.

Art. 13. Cheering committee shall consist of not only poets but also any persons who shall agree on this institute's object and want to support this institute operation.

Art. 14. Auditor shall have the right of auditing over the general affairs excuted in the secretariat and financial management.

Art. 15. Advisors shall provide advices and suggestions as requested by the excutive members of the headquarters. This institute have a standing advisor and some other advisors.

Art. 16. The tenure of the excutive members shall be four years and just another one tenure may be relected or re-appointed.

Chapter 3
The Meetings and The Decision

Art. 17. The Meeting's Deliberative Organ shall consist of the regular meeting, the directors' meeting, the cheering committee meeting, and the extraordinary general meeting.

Art. 18. The regular general-meeting shall be summoned by president when the party in honor of the Publication of the WORLD POETRY and simultaneously the party in honor of conferring the Kaya Gold Crown World Poets Award are held, when the revision of the Institute regulations, the deliberation of budge bills, ballance-sheets, and other important affairs shall be excuted.

Art. 19. The extraordinary general-meeting shall be summoned by president as agreed by more than 1/3 members on the register or as requested in the directors' meeting.

Art. 20. Directors' meeting, excutive coucil and steering committee meeting shall be held more than once in a year and varous affairs shall be discussed and decided.

Art. 21. Some provisions may be revised and decided as agreed by more than half numbers of those present in the regular general-meeting.

Chapter 4
Projects and finances

Art. 22. This institute shall undertake such works as follows:

1) To publish THE WORLD POETRY Anthology annually.
2) To attend the World Poets Congress for the seminar.
3) To confer The World Poets Award.

4) And to do other necessary works.

Art. 23. Annual dues, earnings and donations, etc, shall be applied to the financial fund of this institute.

Art. 24. the amount of the annual dues shall be decided in the rgular general-meeting, and special fees or woking fund system shall be able to be set up.

Art. 25. We shall accounts in April every year.

Chapter 5
The Loss of the Capacity of admission and the membership

Art. 26. Any poet in more than one year career in the poetic circles in Korea and abroad shall be alllowed to become a member of this institute:and those supporters who agree on the object of the steering committee. When the application form is provided, recomendation by more than two regular members shall be requested. The new members approved shall pay the prescribed admission pay and shall cooperate for the operational affairs.

Art. 27. 1) The capacity of his or her membership shall be lost when he or she brings uniterestings to this Institute.
2) The decision of the loss of the membership shall be made in the directors' meeting ant the result shall be informed by president.

Supplimentary Povisions

Art. 28. Encouraged by the praise from the world poets for the first World Poetry(1982) in whose preface the author said: "This anthology will wake up our souls, will make East and West, South and North peaceful, and will make manking eternal, professor Kim Young Sam of Chungbuk National University established the World Poetry Research Institute. However, we did not make any definite constitution, and the posts of excutive council have not been clear since then. Therefore, the new constitution shall be in force from the date definately decreed on the Art. 30.

Art. 29. The details, not to be prescribed in this constitution, shall follow after the common practices or shall be decided by the decision made in the excutive council.

Art. 30. This constitution shall come into force from April 26, 1997.

President: Kim Joung-woong.

The World Poetry Research Institute
World Poets Club

192-67, Eupnae-ri, Gochang-eup, Gochang-gun,
Jeon-buk, 585-807, Korea
Tel. 82-63-564-4248, 82-63-564-6064 H.P 82-010-6318-4248

Detailed Regulations On the Steering Of the Kaya Gold Crown World Poet Award

1. This award shall be basically conferred on the day when publishing ceremony of the new World Poetry Anthology is held.
2. The Judge Committee for the Nominee
   1) This judge committee for the award nominee shall be consisted of less than 5 members.
   2) Commissions shall be entrusted by president after cosultation with excutive members and secretary-general. The List of the awrad nominee shall not be made public until the winners are determined.
3. The Qualification of the Award Nominee
   1)The nominee shall be qualified with several years of poetic career and with more than two poetry books issued.
   2) His or her contribution shall be proved to have made to the World Poetry.
   3) The poet or poetess already won the award shall not be renominated.
4. The Choice Of the Nominee
   1) It shall be made a rule that one nominee from foreign poet or poetess, another one from korean poet or poetess shall be nominated for the award. The number of the nominee shall be able to be a little increased or decreased in some cases.
   2) The award winners shall be determined by the mojority's of judge committee.
5. Awarding
   A diploma and a kaya Gold Crown shall be awarded to each winner.
6. This regulations shall come into force from Aprill 26, 1997.

President: Kim Joung-woong

Worldorld Poetry Research Institute
World Poets Club.

192-67, Eupnae-ri, Gochang-eup, Gochang-gun,
Jeon-buk, 585-807, Korea
Tel. 82-63-564-4248, 82-63-564-6064 H.P 82-017-318-4248

Member of World Poetry Research Institute (2012)

Nation	Name	Domicile	Position
Korea	Lee Ki-ban	11-301, Korong Apt, 1-ga, Pyeonghwa-dong, Wansan-gu, Jeonju-city, Jeon-buk, 560-779, Korea	Senior Counselor
Korea	Choi Seung-beom	361-8, Jinbuk-dong, Deokjin-gu, Jeonju-si, Jeonbuk, Korea	Senior Counselor
Korea	Lee Sang-jin	Director at the legal office, 458-88, Mangwon-dong, Mapo-gu, Seoul, Korea	Advisory Committee
Korea	Kim Joung-woong	192-67, Eupnae-ri, Gochang-eup, Gochang-gun , Jeon-buk, 585-807, Korea	President
Korea	Ahn Byung-don	145-3,Docheongmyeon, Buangun, Jeon-Buk, Korea.	
Korea	Ahn Jae-woon	102, Ga-dong, Geonyang Apt, 681-45, eupnae-ri, gochang-eup, gochang-gun, jeonbuk	
Korea	Ahn Jun-hee	609, mujigae Apt 3dong, seocho-dong, seocho-gu, Seoul city Korea	
Korea	Ahn In-sil	1306-1005, Jugong Apt, Chelsan-dong, Gwang myeong-si, Gyeonggi-do, 423-030, Korea	
Korea	Bae Myoung-sik	1th, 278-97, Sadang4-dong, Dongjak-gu, Seoul, 156-821, Korea	
Korea	Bae Young-suk	102-302, Dongseong Apt, Yeonhyang-dong Suncheon-city, Jeon-nam, 540-761, Korea	
Korea	Baek Bong-ki	103, 116dong, Hyundae apt, ajung-ri, Inhu1-dong Deokjin-gu, Jeonju-city, Jeon-buk, 561-781, Korea	
Korea	Baek Deok-sun		
Korea	Baek Han-yi	837-4, Hwagok4-dong, Gangseo-gu, Seoul, 157-014, Korea	
Korea	Bang Jung-sun	360, jaryong-ri, Sangha-myeon, Gochang-gun, Jeonbuk, 585-910, Korea	
Korea	Bark Il-so	603, 101 dong, wolgye 2 dong, nowon-gu, Seoul, Korea	
Korea	Chae Eun-sun Olive(미국 이름)	2012 Devonshire Dr Fort Collins, co 80526-2301 U.S.A	
Korea	Cho Keum-ja	191-15, Eupnae-ri, Gochang-eup, Gochang-gun, Jeon-buk, 585-807, Korea	
Korea	Cho Ki-hyun	102, 5-dong, Hanjung villa, Chun-chun-ri, Maesong-myeon, Whasong city, Gyeong-gi province	Advisory Committee

Nation	Name	Domicile	Position
Korea	Choi Byeong-ryun	204-703, Jugong Apt. Soosungdong, Jeongeup City, Jeon-Buk, Korea.	
Korea	Choi Hye-sook	305-804, Humansia Apt. Sangdong, Jeoneup City, Jeon-Buk, Korea.	
Korea	Choi Jung-sook	204-109, Myungcheon-Jugong Apt., Myungcheondong, Boryung City, Chung-Nam, Korea.	
Korea	Choi Jae-eon	201-1, Eupnae-ri, Gochang-eup, Gochang-gun, Jeon-buk, Korea	
Korea	Choi Kil-soon	19tong 7ban, #463-12, Myunmok 3-dong, Jungryang-gu, Seoul, Korea.	
Korea	Choi Moo-ja	Seohae Grangble Apt. 106-503, Geoman-dong, Seo-gu, Incheon City.	
Korea	Choi Yong-kwang	1701, Shinhyundae APT, Shiheung 5dong, Geumcheongu, Seoul	
Korea	Choi Yun-seon		
Korea	Choung Song-jun	201-201, Paradise Apt. #123-1 Songjeongdong, Gwangju City, Geonggido, Korea.	Advisory Committee
Korea	Chy Yang-hee	110-505, Yoosung 1st Apt. Jukjeongdong, Boryung City, Chung-Nam, Korea.	
Korea	Eun Hee-tae	17-5, Aenggok-gil, Gobu-myeon, Jeongeup-city, Jeon-buk, Korea.	
Korea	Eun Yo-suk	1638-5, Sinlim Bon-Dong, Gwanak-gu, Seoul,151-029, Korea	Vice President
Korea	Gwon O-un	2201-407, Moonlight Village, Whajungdong, Deokyanggu, Goyang City, Gyeonggido, Korea.	
Korea	Han Gwi-nam	2-61 Gyedong, Jongnogu, Seoul, Korea.	
Korea	Hong Chon-an	118-2106, Donga Chongsol Apt, Chang4-dong, Dobong-gu, Seoul,132-791, Korea	
Korea	Hong Seong-su	313-405, Myungcheon-Jugong 4th Apt., Myungcheondong, Boryung, Chung-Nam.	
Korea	Hong Kwang-seon	108-1302, Kanseok Pungrim Apt. A-dong, Kanseok-dong, 935, Namdong-gu, Incheon-city, Korea	
Korea	Hong Yang-ja	45-83, Muak-dong, Jongno-gu, Seoul, 110-813, Korea	
Korea	Hong Yun-pyeo	2238-1, Namsan-ri, Dang-jin-eup, Dangjin-gun, Chung-nam, 343-802, Korea	

Nation	Name	Domicile	Position
Korea	Hwang Seong-ee	307-907, Silver Light Apt. Sangge 1-dong, Nowongu, Seoul, Korea.	
Korea	Hwang Song-hae	101-502, Hangang Apt, Hyoja-dong, Wansan-gu, Jeonju-si, 560-891, Korea	
Korea	Jang Eun-hae	376-33, Hungnung 3rd-dong, Seongbukgu, Seoul, Korea.	
Korea	Jang Hyun-kyung	40-3, Joongkog 2nd Dong, Gwangjingu, Seoul, Korea.	
Korea	Jang Seong-yeon	102-504, Ujangsan Lotte Apt, 1148, Hwagok6-dong, Gangseo-gu, Seoul, 157-916, Korea	
Korea	Jeon Yu-yeong	102-206 Woosungsinsung Apt., Pyungwha 2nd-Dong, Wansangu, Jeon-Buk.	
Korea	Jeong Ji-ahn	Rm 207, 103-dong Hyundai Green Apt., Sigok-ri Dangjin-up Dangjin-gun Chung nam, 343- 753, Korea	
Korea	Jeong Ji-won		
Korea	Jeong Jin-su	4384, Singil 4-dong, Samsung Layan Apt. 106-301, Youngdeungpogu, Seoul, Korea	
Korea	Jeong Mi-na	Hand Phone: 010-4782-5881	
Korea	Jeong Soon-ja	247-162, Seokyodong, Mapogu, Seoul, Korea.	
Korea	Jeong Won-hwan	Seongnam-ri, Daesan-myeon, Gochang-gun, jeon-buk, 585-860, Korea	
Korea	Jeong Yeong-hwan	73-10, Gyochon-ri, Gochang-eup, Gochang-gu, Jeon-buk, 585-800, Korea	
Korea	Jin Myong-sook	805-102, Jugong Apt., Ha-An 2nd-dong, Gwang-myung City, Geonggido Korea.	
Korea	Jin Sang-soon	707, 101dong, Hyundae Apt, 315-1, Sinpung-dong, Kimje-city, Jeon-buk, 570-804, Korea	Directors
Korea	Jo Dal-ho	1093-23, Pyong-ri 3 dong, Seogu, Daegu megalopolls clty, Korea.	
Korea	Jo Hwa-hun	1301, Myeongji carat Apt, 535-5, Anyang6-dong, Manan-gu, Anyang-si, Korea	
Korea	Jun Duk-ki	147, Dongsomundong 4ga, Seongbukgu, Seoul, Korea.	
Korea	Jung Ok-im	5-305, Saneopin Apt., Gocheokdong, Gurogu, Seoul, Korea.	

Nation	Name	Domicile	Position
Korea	Jung U-ha	106, 105dong, Daewoo Apt, Yeonhyang-dong, Suncheon-city, Jeon-nam, 540-762, Korea	
Korea	Kang Chang-won	1205, Woojueunha Apt., 511-3, Sinjinri, Gwang choneup, Hongseonggun, Chung Nam, Korea.	
Korea	Kang Hae-kun	102-108, Kyunyoung apt, 72-3, Munjeong-dong, Songpa-gu, Seoul, 138-200, Korea	
Korea	Kang Jeong-ae	103, 203dong, Dongseong Apt, 35, Bundang-dong, Bundand-gu, Seonam-city, Gyeonggi-do, 463-747, Korea	
Korea	Kang Sang-ku	932-2, Duam 3rd-dong, Bukgu, Gwangju Metropolitan City, Korea	
Korea	Kang Young-duk	1-202, Daehan apt., 381-18, Hwagok7-dong, Gangseo-gu, Seoul, 157-885. Korea	
Korea	Kim A-lang	102-806, Chunggu Apt, shinbanpo, jamwondong, seochogu, Seoul, Korea	
Korea	Kim Ae-yeong	1109, 101dong, Sindonga Tower, Banyeol-dong, Haeundae-gu, Busan-city, 612-061, Korea	
Korea	Kim Baek-kyeong		
Korea	Kim Bok-nam	101-1205, Dongguk Apt, 1034-1, Jinbuk2-dong, Deogjin-gu, Jeonju-si, Jeon-buk, 561-782, Korea	
Korea	Kim Chong-ki	621, Sanghadong, Giheunggu, Yongin City, Suwon-dongmaeul Ssangyong Apt. 303-1701, Geonggido, Korea.	
Korea	Kim Don-young	311-13, Bulkwangdong, Metrotower 2206, Eunpyunggu, Seoul Korea.	
Korea	Kim Dong-ik	90-41, Junggyebon-dong, Nowon-gu, Seoul, 139-229, Korea	
Korea	Kim Eui-sik	328-7, Gildong 2nd-dong, Gangdonggu, Hanma eum-Jutaek 401, Seoul, Korea.	
Korea	Kim Gui-rye	1802, 301dong, 3th, Nueung Apt, Bongseon-dong, Nam-gu, Gwangju-city, 503-760, Korea	Directors
Korea	Kim Hak-jin	346, Yonggye-dong, Jeongeup-si, Jeon-buk, 580-230, Korea	
Korea	Kim Hee-soon		
Korea	Kim Hyung-chol	351, Bonghwang-ri, Dongjin-Myeon, Buan-gun, Jeon-Buk, Korea	
Korea	Kim IL-rye	E-mail : kimilrye@hotmail.com	Directors

Nation	Name	Domicile	Position
Korea	Kim Jae-kyun	1357-2, Yongbongdong, I-House 2nd Floor, Korea.	
Korea	Kim Ji-won	Gyeonseong grotto, San 3 Songneung 1-ri, Jinkeon-eup, Namyangju-city, Gyeonggi-do, 472-830, Korea	
Korea	Kim Ji-yeol	160, Ilsim-ri, Hwasun-eup, Hwasun-gun, Jeon-nam, 519-809, Korea	
Korea	Kim Jin-soo	401, Chungdam Park View, 61-11, Chungdam-dong, Gannamgu, Seoul.	
Korea	Kim Jong-hee	337-36 Seokyodong, Mapogu, Seoul, Korea	
Korea	Kim Jong-won	1083-23, Hwagok1dong, Gangseogu, Seoul, Korea.	
Korea	Kim Kwang-Ja	118-1805, kyongnam sunkyong Apt., 1448, haiwundaigu, Busan city, Korea	
Korea	Kim Kye-yoon	Kim Hospital, 161-2, Daemin-dong, Dong-gu, Gwangju-city, 501-030, Korea	Permanent Advisory Committee
Korea	Kim Kyung-hee	1269, Guro-Bondong, Gurogu, Jungang Apt., 10-1901, Seoul.	Directors
Korea	Kim Mi-kyoung	Boramaedong, Gwanakgu, Boramae Samsung Apt. 101-1502, Seoul, Korea.	
Korea	Kim Min-joong	442-2, Pyeongsa-ri, Sanoe-myeon, Jeongeup-city, Jeon-buk, 580-950, Korea	
Korea	Kim Nam-Woung	2430, 106dong, Dodeok Park Town, 625, Chulsan 4dong, Gwangmyeong city, Kyongki-do	Advisory Committee
Korea	Kim Sang-kyung	361-1 Hwagok 1-dong, Kangseo-gu, Hwagok Daelim Apt. 5-1504, Seoul	
Korea	Kim Sang-hyun	608-202, Hanguk Apt, 727-2, Sin-gok-dong, Uijeongbu-si, Gyeonggi-do, 480-787, Korea	
Korea	Kim Sang-soo	581-13, samcheondong-1ga, wansan-gu, Jeonju-si, Jeonbuk	
Korea	Kim Seok-ki	40-2, Jungangdong, Gwachun City, Geonggido, Seoul.	
Korea	Kim Seon-chul	489, Gesanmyun, Asanri, Kochanggun, Jeon-Buk, Korea.	
Korea	Kim Shin-jeong	567-3(1st floor), Hannamdong, Yongsangu, Seoul, Korea.	
Korea	Kim So-yeop	261, Chungsoodong ,Chunan City, Chung-Nam, Sunkyung Apt. 112-601.	Directors

Nation	Name	Domicile	Position
Korea	Kim Song-bae	112-44, naresilgil 40-1, yeonhee 1-dong, seodaemun-gu, Seou,l Korea	
Korea	Kim Sun	301 Ho, 105 Dong, Joyparkvill, 139-6, NamSan-ri, PaengSeong-eub, PyeongTaek-Si, Gyeonggi-do, 451-803, Korea.	
Korea	Kim Sung-youl	room 611-1103, dongmoon good morning Apt, Supsokkil maul, dongpe-ri 1687, kyoha-eup, paju si, Gyeonggi-do	
Korea	Kim Whoa-ja	487, Sajeong-dong, Joong-gu, Woonamstawon 101-801, Daejeon City.	
Korea	Kim Woon-jung	529-159 Bupyungdong, Bupyunggu, Palbangsan, Incheon City, Korea.	
Korea	Kim Young-mi	9-405, Boram Apt, Bondong, Gurogu, Seoul, Korea.	
Korea	Kim Young-mi	422-1 Sam-Lee, Gonjiam-Eup, Hyun-yeunrip B-dong, #103, Kwangju City, Kyunggi-do, Korea	
Korea	Ko Bang-kyu	463, Okjeri, Gochanggun, Jeon-Buk, Korea.	Vice Director of Executive office
Korea	Ko Seon-ok	102-1704, Hyundae Apt. Sukyori, Gochangeup, Gochang gun, Jeon-Buk, Korea.	
Korea	Koo Soon-ja	384-28, Mangwondong, Mapogu, Seoul, Korea.	
Korea	Koo Ja-cheol		
Korea	Kuk Mi-na	Hand Phone: 010-6799-3949. E-mail: kuk8989@naver.com	
Korea	Kwak Byung-soo	1704-102dong, Deokhyeon Apt, 808, Gyomun2-dong, Guri-city, Geonggi-do, Korea.	
Korea	Lee Byeong-chang	462, Shindeok-ri, Shindeok-myeon, Limsil-gun, Jeon-buk, Korea	
Korea	Lee Byung-Suk	#138, Chojangdong, Seogu, Jogejong Chunyong Temple, Busan, Korea.	
Korea	Lee Chang-hwan	176-3, Seobu-dong Yeongyang-Eup Youngyang-gun Kyeongbuk 764-800 Korea	
Korea	Lee Chung-hee		
Korea	Lee Deok-Sang	Geumgan Venturetel #1704, 1108 Bisandong, Dongangu,Anyangsi,Gyeonggido	
Korea	Lee Eun-hyeop	6-4, Daejodong, Eunpyeonggu, Seoul, Korea.	

Nation	Name	Domicile	Position
Korea	Lee Ji-soo	101-1205, Haeju Apt, 55, Sangha-ri, Hongnong-eup, Yeong-gwang-gun, Jeon-nam, 513-884, Korea	
Korea	Lee Ji-young	Rm 1002, 311-Dong Dongah Apt Dream Town, Pyungchon-dong, Dongan-gu, Anyang-City Gyeonggi-do, Korea	
Korea	Lee Kyeong-hwa		
Korea	Lee Jong-il	205, Anam apt. 9, Macheon2-dong, Songpa-gu, Seoul, 138-120, Korea	
Korea	Lee Jun-sil	691, Sangyedong, Nowongu, Jugong Apt. 718-1302, seoul Korea.	
Korea	Lee Kang	502, na-dong, Daemyeong Apt, Seoseohak-dong, Wansan-gu, Jeonju-city, Jeon-buk, 560-130, Korea	
Korea	Lee Kyu-sae	514-801, Jugong Apt, 702, Haan1-dong, Gwang myeong-si, Gyeonggi-do, Korea	
Korea	Lee Moon-ho	410, 101dong, Hyundai Apt, 785-1, Daerim3-dong, Yeongdeungpo-gu, seoul, 150-073, Korea	
Korea	Lee Sang-mok	954, 2nd Floor, Dogok-dong, Seoul, Korea.	
Korea	Lee Sin-kang	108-4, dunchon 2dong, gangdong-gu, Seoul, Korea	
Korea	Lee Su-jung	14 floor- 1, 102dong, Hyundai Apt 203-6, Deokgei-dong, yangju city, Geongkido	
Korea	Lim In-chol	707-1003, Mokryun Woosung Apt., Beomgyedong, Dongangu, Anyang City, Geonggido, Korea.	
Korea	Lim Won-sik	933-4, Wolsan 4-dong, Namgu, Gwangju Metropolitan city, Korea.	
Korea	Min Byung-hyu	101-1005, Namhae Onetteu vill, 508, Unrim-dong, Dong-gu, Gwangju-si, 501-200, Korea	
Korea	Min Suk-young	Apt 401, 490-5, Wolpi-dong, Sangrok-gu, Ansan-city, Gyeonggi-do, 425-070, Korea	
Korea	Nam Byung-geun	930, Baeseokdong, Cheonan City, Brownstone Apt 108-301, Chung-Nam, Korea.	
Korea	Namgung Yeon-ok	722-2, Gongheung the 3rd-ri, Yangpyung eup, Yangpyungun, Geonggido, Korea.	
Korea	No Jung-ai	142-8, Daehyun-dong, Seodaemon-gu, Seoul, 120-170, Korea	Vice President
Korea	Oh Hui-chang	202, 1402dong, Mokdong Apt, 329, Sinjeong6-dong, Yangcheon-gu, Seoul, 158-076, Korea	

Nation	Name	Domicile	Position
Korea	Oh Jin-hwan	2-202, Kyeong-nam Apt, 1-8 Banpo-dong, Seocho-gu, Seoul, 137-765, Korea	
Korea	Oh Keum-ja	31-3, Seongju 5-ri, Seongjumyeon, Boryung City, Chung-Nam.	
Korea	Oh Min-phil	45-1, Hakseong-dong, Jung-gu, Ulsan-city, 681-822, Korea	
Korea	Park Eun-seok	101 Daseong Villa, #173-6, Sonpa 2nd-dong, Songpagu, Seoul, Korea.	
Korea	Pak Ky-tae	102, Na-dong, Gwangjin Apt, 213-2, Hyojadong1-ga, Wansan-Gu, Jeonju-si, Jeon-buk, Korea	
Korea	Park In-ae	Reside in Dallas City, Texas, US	
Korea	Park Keun-hoo	449-4, Sang-dong , Jeongeup-city, Jeon-buk,. 580-801, Korea	Advisory Committee
Korea	Park Moon-jae	417-1 Songbaek Village, Mokwangri, Yangseo myun, Yangpyunggun , Gyeonggido, Korea.	Permanent Advisory Committee
Korea	Park Youn-ki	322-90 Chosan-ri, Habuk-myun, Yangsan City, Kyung-nam, Korea	
Korea	Park Sam-suk	1411, 103dong, Jungheung Apt, Yongbong-dong, Buk-gu, Gwangju-si, 500-070, Korea	
Korea	Seo Jeong-il	31-10 dongilro 104, 212 changamdong, euijeongbu city, keongkido	
Korea	Seo Jeong-nam	531-29, Sinrim-dong, Kwanak-gu, Seoul, Korea	
Korea	Shim Eui-pyo	990-22, Siheung I-dong, Keumcheongu, Jeongdo Twinville 101-801, Seoul. Korea.	
Korea	Shin Dong-myeong	601, Hyundae Apt, 171-61, Bulgwang2-dong, Eunpyong-gu, Soeul, 123-042, Korea	
Korea	Shin Hyun-sook	309-504, Jugong the 3rd Apt. Myungcheon dong, Boryung City, Chung-Nam, Korea.	
Korea	Shin Soon-ae	695-3, Ahyeon2-dong, Mapo-gu, Seoul city, 121-861, Korea	
Korea	Son Soon-ja	178-2, Sangyeon 1st-dong, 25 Setgolgil, Dongdoocheon, Geongigido, Korea.	
Korea	Song Kyung-deok	102-704, Eongbu-Centreville, Wolgyedong, Gwangsangu, Gwangju City.	
Korea	Song Yeon-ju	101-608, Hyundae Apt. Muakdong, Jongnogu, Seoul, Korea.	

Nation	Name	Domicile	Position
Korea	Tae Dong-chul	741-7, Oeri, Youngheungmyeon, Ongjingun, Incheon Metropolitan City, Korea.	
Korea	Won Eung-soon		Permanent Advisory Committee
Korea	Yang Ah-rim		
Korea	Yang Chi-joong	13 Sudong-gil, Daegu-myun, Kangjin-gun, Jeon-Nam, Korea	
Korea	Yang Hai-wan	508, 101dong, Hangang Apt, Hyoja 3ga-dong, Wansan-gu, Jeonju-city, Jeon-buk, 560-243, Korea	
Korea	Yang Seung-bon	836, Sanghyeon-dong, Suji-gu, Yongin-si, Gyeong-gi-do, 448-130, Korea	
Korea	Yeo Han-kyung	505, wubang town 5dong, 240, hwanggeum 1dong, suseong-gu, Daegu city	
Korea	Yeom Hae-sook	154-1, Rongseong1-dong, Seo-gu, Gwangju-city, 502-810, Korea	
Korea	Yoo Hee-bong	Tel: 02-6412-0702/ 010-6412-0702	
Korea	Yoo Hee-Jeong	104-405, daerim Apartment 57, umyeon-dong, seocho-gu, Seoul, Korea	
Korea	Yoon Hyoung-soon	Hyundae Prime Apt. 207-501, Sinjeong-maeul, 2-dong, Pungdeokcheon, Suji-gu, Yongin City, Gyeonggi-do, Korea	
Korea	Yoon Jae-myung		
Korea	Yoon Sang-hyun	713 Sungsa-dong, e-Pyeonhan-Sesang 117-1301, Deokyang-gu, Goyang City, Kyunggi-do	
Korea	Yun Hae-kyu	394-81, Seogyo-dong, Mapo-gu, Seoul 121-840, Korea	Permanent Advisory Committee
Korea	Yun Mu-jee	202-705 Yulgok-Ro, Yonkron-dong, Jaeil Office-Tel, Jongno-gu, Seoul	Directors
Korea	Yun Seok-tae	441-1, Seongduri, Gochangeup, Gochanggun, Jeon-Buk, Korea.	
Korea	Yun Sa-weol	Keongsusa, seodangchon, yeonhwari, syimwon-meon, gochanggun, Jeonbuk	
Korea	Yun Su-a	115-902, Hyundae HillState, 155, Onsudong, Gurogu, Seoul, Korea	

Nation	Name	Domicile	Position
Algerie	El'm Chalbedera	Cité les 160 logements Bât. D3,n 21 2700 Mostaganem Algerie(Africa)	President of Algerie Branch office
Angola	David Mestre	Caixa Postal 10.719 Luanda-Angola(Africa)	President of Angola Branch office
Austaralia	Joy Beadette Cripps	3 Mill St.Aspendale 03 580 415P Australia	President of Australian Branch office
Argentina	Viorginia Rhodas	Rivadavia 2284-1034-Buenos Aires Argentina. Tel.952-2625.(Sud America)	President of Argentina Branch office
Brazil	Olga de Brito	Rua Minas Gerals 65 Jardim Taruma 13200 Jundiai São Paulo, Brazil(Sud America)	President of Brazil Branch office
Brazil	Angela Maria Rocha de Biase	Endereço Av. Silvio Sciumbata, ne 596-Interlagos 04789-010 Såopoulo/Brazil	Vice President of WPRI (charged in South America)
Bulgaria	Dr.Gueni G.Zaimof	(P.E.N)(W.P.S.I) Cokiehe 5 Sofia 1421 Bulgaria(East Europe)	President of Bulgaria Branch office
Bosnia and Herzegovina	Ajsa zahirovic.	Str.Kranjcevica 41/3 Sarajevo 71000, Republic Bosnia and Herzegovina(East Europe).	President of Bonia&Herzegovina Branch office
Canada	Stephen Gill	Box 32 932-2135 Cornwall, Ontario K6H 5129 Canada(North America)	President of Canada Branch office
Chille	Desenka Vucasovic de Drasler	Casilla 247. Enap. Cerro Sombrero. Pcia de Tierra del Fuego.X Ⅱ. Region de Magallanes y Antartica Chilena. Chile(Sud America.)	President of Chille Branch office
China P.R	Prof. Lu Jin	Chinese New Poetry Research Insistute South-West-China Normal University Beibei, Chonquing 630715. P.R. China	President of China P.R. Branch office
Colombia	Enrique Osorio Beltran	Calle 131 #45-55 Bogota, D.C., Colombia Tel. (57) (1) 258-01-84	President of Colombia Branch office
Czecho-Slovakia	Vladimir Kostiha	Sekaniny 10805/70800 Ostrava-Poruba Slovakia(Czchoslovakia) (East Europe)	President of Czecho Slovakia Branch office
Denmark	Esther Gress	Ny Strandvej 27 3050 Humlebaek Denmark(Europe)	President of Denmark Branch office
England	Dame Stella Browning	2 Highfield Sussex Road. New Romney, Kent TN 28 8DS England. (Europe) Tel. 0797-363819	President of England Branch office
France	René Streiff	"Close Jean" 1.Rue Marc de Saint-Hilaire/ 83200 Toulong, France. Tel. 94 24 38 94 (Europe)	President of France Branch office
France	Paul Cariage	34. Chemin de Malpeigne 84000 Avignon, France.(Europe)	Vice President of WPRI(charged in Euprope

Nation	Name	Domicile	Position
Germany	Tily Boesche Zachrow	Launinsteig 14 a W-1000 Berlin 28 Germany(west). (Europe)	President of Germany Branch office
Ghana	Larweh Tereson Cofie	C/O The Mirror Graphic Corporation P.O.Box 742. Accra, Ghana, West Africa	President of Ghana Branch office
Grecce	Nickolas Moshovos	Pausania 21, ANO Tumpa GR-54352 The saloniki Greece	President of Greece Branch office
Guatemalak	Cesar Augusto de Leon Morales	Apdo Postal Num 22 13901 Huehretenango Guatemala Central America	President ofGuatemala Branch office
Italy	Giulio Palumbo	M.Cipoia 48 90123 Palermo Italia	President of Italy Branch office
Israel	Dr. Ada Aharoni	57 Horev Haifa Israel 34343 E-MAIL:ADA@ TX.Technion. Ac.IL Israel/Tel-Fax:972-4,824-3230	Vice President of WPRI(charged in Middle East)
Japan	Eiji Kuroha	653-8 Higashigoiso, Oiso-machi Naga-kun kanagawa-Prefequre Japan	President of Japan Branch office
Japan	Uemoto Masao	1-14-34 Kuninobu Umeda-cho Hiroshima-ken Angei-gun 736 Japan	Vice President of WPRI(charged in Asia)
Japan	Yoshifumi Sakura	3-50-8, Koinaka, Nishi-ku, Hiroshima, 733-0813, Japan	
Kwait	Oormila Vijayakrishnan	C/O. K.V. Vijayakrishnan Mechanical Engineer Kwait Fire Service Directorate Serveces Dept. Workshop Complex P.B.No 22228 Safat 13083-Safat, Kwait (Middle East Asia)	President of Kwait Branch office
Latvia	Janis Medenis	Latvian Center P.E.N Box 498 S-10126 Stockholm, Sweden (Europe)	President of Latvin Branch office
Malasia	Chew Khing-Hong	202-A, Jalan Junid, 84000 Muar, Johar, Malaysia. Tel. 06-9511643	President of Malasia Branch office
Malta	Amante Buotempo	J.U.O., Adv. S.R.R. 55st. Paul Street, Valleta VLT 07 Malta. Tel. 22 4082	President of Malta Branch office
Mexico	Elia Domenzain	Prolongacion 5 De Mayo 11 Pueblo San Pedro Martir, Tlalpan 14650, Mexico	President ofMexico Branch office
NewZealand	Anandathana Veronica Haunhey	2B, 'Waikite' Flats,255, the Terace, Wellington, New zealand.	President ofNew Zealand Branch office
Pakistan	Anandaghana Aripirala Viswam	3-6-415/2, 111 Floor, Street-4 Himalyatnagar, Hyderabad-500 029 P	President of Pakistan Branch office
Peru	Mario Rulz De Castilla J.R.	Urbanizacion Magisterial Segunda Etapa-"G" N°.8.Ciudad del Cusco Peru-South America.	President of Peru Branch office
Poland	Bogumil Wtorkievcz	Karczowkowska 12m. 127, 25-019, Kieke, Poland.	President of Poland Branch office

Nation	Name	Domicile	Position
Portugal	Luis Filipe Soares	Apardado 21 208-1131 Lisboa Codex, Portugal.	President of Portugal Branch office
Puerto Rico	José O. Colon Ruiz	P.O.Box 1373 Eaguas Puerto Rico 00626	President of Puerto Rico Branch office
R.O.C	Tin-Wen Chung (R.O.C)	(Continental Regent & Parnasian Jurist respectively) P.O.Box No.58508. Taipei, R.O.C.	President of R.O.C Branch office
Romania	Florentin Smarandache	The Paradoxist Movement P.O.Box 42561 Phoenix, AZ 85080 USA. Tel. (602)436-3862	President of Romania Branch office
Russia	Dr. Adolf P. Shvedchikov	4317 Petit Avenue Encino CA 91436-3516, U.S.A.	Russian Scientist, Poet and translator
Singapore	John L. Chin	# 05-315 Block 978 Jurong West St. 93 Singapore 2264. Tel. 02-7918382	President of Singapore Branch office
Sweden	Martin Allwood	Anglo-American Center S-56532 Mullsjo, Sweden USE.	President of Sweden Branch office
Switzerland	Charles P. Marie	78 Chemin de la Montagne, 1224 Chene-Bougeries, Geneve, Switzerland.	President of Switzerland Branch office
Tunis	Dr. Mohamed Selmi	Villa XYILigue Fu 17 XY, rue Mohamed Beyram 5, 1.004 El-Menzah 5 Tunis	Vice President of WPRI(charged in Africa)
Thailand	Montri Umavijani	14/18 Soi Amporn 6. Gardenhome Village Pabolyothin K,M,26,Bangkok 12130. Thailand	President of Thai Branch office
Uruguay	Alma Vasconcellos	Carlos de la Vega 4383 C.P.11.900 Montevideo Uruguay-Sud America	President of Uruguay Branch office
U.S.A	Park, Meen-Heum	2980 Valentine Ave # 307, Bronx NY 10458, U.S.A	English version Translator
U.S.A	Panos Demetrios	University of Toledo, Toledo, Ohio 43606 U.S.A.	President of U.S.A Branch office
U.S.A.	Teresinka Pereira	P.O.Box 352048 Toledo, OH 43635-2048, U.S.A.	Vice President(char-ged in North America
Venezuela	Max E. Perez	Calle Sucre No. 40 San Fernando-Apture Venezuela (Sud America)	President of Venezula Branch office

Do Not Cross The River

Do not cross the river, I pray.
But should you dare, my dear,
To plunge into water and to death,
What can I do, alas, my dear?

* This song, written in Old Chosun, is known as Konghu-in, a song accompanied by the Konghu, a string instrument. It is said that its author, Yeo-ok, wife of Kwakri-Jago, wrote it from a tale told by her husband.

麗 玉 / 韓國(古朝鮮)

公無渡河歌(箜篌引)

公無渡河
公竟渡河
墮河而死
公將奈何

— 古今注(晋 · 崔豹)所載 —
— 海東繹史記載 —
麗玉 = 津吏 · 霍里子高妻
— 白首老人隨河而死, 麗玉悲感作詩歌 —

공무도하가(공후인)

임은 건너지 말 것이지
임은 물을 건너다가
물에 빠져 죽으시니
임은 마침내 어이하리오

李 白 / 中國(唐)

公無渡河歌

黃河西來決昆崙
咆哮萬里解龍門
波滔天,
堯咨嗟

大禹理百川
兒啼不窺家
殺湍煙洪水
九州始蠶痳
其害乃去 茫然風沙

披髮之搜狂而痴 淸晨徑流欲奚爲
旁人不惜
妻止之老
公無渡河
苦渡之墮

虎可搏
河難恁
公果溺死流海湄邽
有長鯨白齒若雪山
公乎公乎挂罥于其間
箸箸所悲竟不還.

樂府詩 - 公無渡河歌 -

China/Li Bai
(AD. 701-762)

公無渡河(임이여 강을 건너지 마오)

黃河강 西로 흘러 昆崙산을 덮치며
萬里 포효로 龍門에 이른다
파도는 하늘에 닿고
堯임금도 탄식하네

禹왕은 百강을 다스리노라
아이가 태어나도 집을 돌볼 줄 모르네
물살을 잡아 洪水를 멈추니
아홉 州는 누에 치고 麻를 심었네
그 水害는 가고 모래바람 자욱하여라

머리 풀어헤친 미친 老人이
새벽 강물에서 뭘 하는고
주위 사람들은 가만 있으나
妻는 老人을 말리네
임이여 강을 건너지 마오
老人은 건너다 빠졌네

범은 때려서 물리칠 수 있으나
강물은 어찌할 수 없네
임은 드디어 빠져 죽어 바다로 흘러가네
雪山같이 커다란 고래이빨
오오 임은 무서운 이빨에 엮어지고
공후소리만 구슬프구나.
임은 돌아오지 않네

ПУНЦАГИЙН БАДАРЧ
Puntsagyn BADARCH

He was born in Bayanjargalan soum of Tuv province on August 17, 1939. He began to write poems in 1960. He became a merited worker of culture in 1999 won D.Natsagdorj literary prize in 1988 and People's writer in 2005.

ЯТГА

Онон Хэрлэн хоёрыг булаг байхад гэнэ
Ороо найман шаргыг унага байхад гэнэ
Ятга хөгжим, ялдамхан бүсгүй байжээ
Ялдамхан бүсгүй, ятга хөгжим болжээ
Аян дайнд донтой эр нөхрийнхөө энгэр налан
Амраг минь дахиж, дайнд бүү яваач дээ гэж
Янаг сайхан бүсгүй өнжин шөнөжин гуйгаад
Явна гэх догшин эрийнхээ үгийг сонсоод
Эрх цагаан согоо шиг энхрий танхил бие нь
Эр нөхрийнхөө өвөр дээр тэр чигээрээ хөшиж,
Эгмээ нөмрөн урссан, хар мяндас гэзэг нь
Эгээ л байсан янзаараа утас болон царцаж
Өнчин тогорууных шиг дуу нь ээдрэн ганганаад
Өвдөг дэрлэсэн бүсгүй – ятга болон хувилжээ.
Аяа! Эр хүн чи эгнэгт бүү омогш
Авилгач догшин дүрээр зүрхээн бүү тахь!
Өнгөлөг сайхан гэргий чинь үүнд л гомдож
Өвөр дээр чинь утас хулсханд хувилж
Өрөөлийн гараар л үглэж дуулах төдийхөн
Өдгөө энэ ятга болуужин гэж ай!
Онон Хэрлэн хоёрыг булаг байхад гэнэ л
Ороо найман шаргыг унага явахад гэнэ л
Ятга хөгжим, ялдамхан бүсгүй байжээ
Ялдамхан бүсгүй ятга хөгжим болжээ

야트가*

어넌 헤르렌 두 강이 작은 샘이었을 때였네
길들여지지 않는 담황색 말이 망아지였을 때였네
야트가, 감성적인 아가씨가 있었네
귀여운 아가씨, 야트가가 되었네
전쟁에 중독된 님의 가슴에 기대어
님이시여. 다시는 전장에 나가지 마소서 라고
사랑스러운 아가씨 밤낮으로 애원하고
가겠다 고집하는 님의 말에
응석부리는 하얀 암사슴처럼 온화하고 다소곳한 몸은
님의 품에서 그대로 굳어지고
어깨에 흘러내린 검은 명주 다발은
같은 모습으로 가는 현이 되어 얼어버리고
외두루미의 것 같은 노래는 우아함이 뒤엉켜
무릎을 베고 누운 아가씨-야트가가 되었네
아아! 남자여 늘 거만하지 말고
욕심부리고 몰인정한 모습으로 용기를 맹신하지 말아라
아름다운 너의 아내는 이것만이 불만이고
너의 품에서 현과 몸통으로 변하여
타인의 손으로만 소리내어 노래하는
지금의 야트가 되었다네
어넌 헤르렌 두 강이 작은 샘이었을 때였네만
길들여지지 않는 담황색 말이 망아지로 다녔을 때였네만
야트가, 아주 예의바른 아가씨가 있었네
예의바른 아가씨 야트가가 되었네

* 야트가: 14현의 가야금같이 생긴 몽골 전통 악기

- Translated into Korean by T. Otgontuul(Ph.D) Ha in hua(MA)

ТАНГАДЫН ГАЛСАН
Tangadyn GALSAN

He was born in 1932 at Zag soum of Bayankhongor provcince and graduated from the National University of Mongolia. He has the literature prize 'D.Natsagdorj', merited worker of culture and People's writer.

ӨГСҮҮР ЗАМЫН ДУУ

Онхол цонхолгүй вандан ширээ говийн
Оонон халиун толгод минь намайгаа өршөө
Олонцог элээгээгүй дэгдээхэй насандаа би чинь
Олон бор толгодоо уул гэж эндуурч явжээ

Оцор цацар довцгууд дундаа сүмбэр
Очир хэлбэрт уулс минь намайгаа өршөө
Отгонтэнгэрийн зулайг гишгэхээсээ урьд би
Оргил өндөр гэж уулсаа андуурч явжээ

Овоо тахилга нь бэлийн чулуугаар өндөрлөсөн
Отгонтэнгэр хайрхан минь намайгаа өршөө
Отго жинстэй Алтай давахаасаа өмнө би
Огторгуйн багана гэж таныг эндуурч явжээ

Он цагийн түүхийг мөнх цасандаа ботилсон
Онгод билгийн их Алтай минь намайгаа өршөө
Од зүлгэдэг Гималайг харахаасаа урьд би
Орчлонгийн зулай гэж таныгаа бишрч явжээ

Онхол цонхолгүй вандан ширээ говийн
Оорцог тоорцог толгод минь намайг бүү өршөө
Оосор бүчгүй сансрын уудмаас халиахад
Оргил бүхний оргил нь нутгийн минь
толгод л байж шүү дээ

언덕의 노래

평평한 긴 책상같은 고비의
암갈색 수양 언덕이여 나를 용서하라
안장에 얹은 방석이 닳지 않은 나이일 때 나는
많은 갈색 언덕을 산이라고 잘못 알고 다녔다

작은 천막 언덕들 중의 숨베르
뾰족한 산들이여 나를 용서하라
어트겅탱게르의 정수리를 밟기 전에 나는
정상이 높다고 산들을 잘못 알고 다녔다

어워 제단은 사면에 돌로 높였고
성스러운 나의 어트겅탱게르여 나를 용서하라
작은 구슬이 달린 알타이를 넘기 전에 나는
창공을 기둥이라고 당신을 잘못 알고 다녔다

세월의 역사를 만년설에 담아낸
신들린 나의 거대한 알타이여 나를 용서하라
별을 연마하던 히말라야를 바라보기 전에 나는
세상의 정수리라고 당신을 축복하며 다녔다

평평한 긴 책상같은 고비의
개개의 둥근 언덕들이여 나를 용서하지 마라
끝 없는 속세에서 방황할 때
모든 정상의 정상은 나의 고향의 언덕뿐이구나

- Translated into Korean by T. Otgontuul(Ph.D) Ha in hua(MA)

ШАРАВЫН СҮРЭНЖАВ
Sharavyn SHURENJAV

He was born on Avdarbayan soum of Tuv province. He graduated from the National University of Mongolia in 1963 and Gorky Literature Institute in Moscow in 1981. He wrote poems and scenarios. He became the National Literature Laureate in 1988 and people's writer in 1999.

ТЭНГЭРЭЭ

Чи яагаад мөнхийн дув дуугүй ширтэнэ вэ?

-Тэнэгүүдийг хараад хэлэх үг олддоггүйдээр тэр

-Од мичдээ чи яагаад зөвхөн шөнөд л цэцэглэдэг юм бэ?

-Охид хүүхнүүд шөнөд л гэрэлтдэг

Болохоор тэр

-Гол усаа чи яагаад дандаа

-Яаран шуугин урсана вэ?

-Хаая би чинь урсгалаа зогсоож

Хөлддөг шүү дээ

-Яагаад?

-Хүмүүст миний тухай бодох зав өгөх гэсэндээ тэр

-Тэнгэрийн шувуухай чи хаах нь суудгаад намайг харж байна вэ?

-Тэндээс чинь миний төрх чиний нүдээр харвал ямархан харагдах бол?

-Хоёулаа байраа соливол чамд ямар санагдах вэ?

- Хоёр хөлт хүний энэ суудал тэнгэрийн хавцгайд чинь таарах болов уу?

하늘이여

너는 왜 영원히 말없이 보고만 있는가?
—바보들을 보며 할 말을 찾을 수 없어서 그러네
—별들이여 너는 왜 오직 밤에만 피어나는 것인가?
—아가씨들이 밤에만 빛나기 때문에 그러네
—강물아 너는 왜 항상 급하게 흐르는가?
—가끔 흐름을 멈추면 얼어버리잖아
—왜?
—사람들에게 나에 대해 생각할 시간을 주기 위해서 그러지
—하늘의 작은 새는 어디에 앉아서 나를 보고 있는가?
—거기서 너의 눈으로 보는 나의 모습은 어떠한가?
—둘이 바꿔보는것을 너는 어떻게 생각하는가?
—두 다리를 가진 사람의 자리는 하늘의 벽에 닿을 수 있을까?

- Translated into Korean by T. Otgontuul(Ph.D) Ha in hua(MA)

ДАМБЫН ТӨРБАТ **DambiinTURBAT**

Damba Turbat was born in 1955 in Dundgobi province and in 1981 graduated from the Mongolian State University in the profession og journalism. In 1986 he graduated from the Institute of International journalist Institute in Budapest city of Hungary. He wrote 12 novels. He received S.Buyannemekh price, received state prize of Mongolia. He is a representative member of the Academy of Mongolian Literature.

БҮРГЭД

Үхэх, сэхэх нь оньсого
Үүлэн чанадын сарьдагаас
Унах, нисэх нь таавар
Уйтгарт саарал хавцал руу

Төрүүлсэн эхээрээ
Түлхүүлж, жигүүрээ дэлгэдэг
Тэмүүлсэн тэнгэртээ
Тэнцэж чадахгүй бол үхдэг

Бүхнээс төгөлдөр
Бүргэдийн хууль
Бүгдэд нь
Бүтэн заяадагтаа
Хөөрхий сонсохгүй жаргадаг
Хөхрөгчөө ээзгнэж эргэдэг.

독수리

죽고 사는 것은 수수께끼
구름 저쪽의 만년 설산
넘어지고, 나는 것은 예측불허
슬픈 회색 협곡으로

낳아준 어미로
밀어내면, 날개를 편다
열망했던 하늘에
어울리지 못하면 죽는다

모든 것에서 완전한
독수리의 법.
모든 것에서는
운명 지어진 것 전부에
불쌍하게도 듣지 못하고 지고 만다
하늘을 지배하고 돌아다닌다

- Translated into Korean by T. Otgontuul(Ph.D) Ha in hua(MA)

ХҮСЭЛ

Эрвээхэйтэй хөөцөлдөн төөрч буусан
Эгшиглэнт охин тэнгэртэй хөтлөлцөн
Хаяа манасан заяа юунаас зугтаж
Хар нялхын чулуун гэртээ очихсон.
Тулга тойрсон сэтгэлээсээ холдож
Туулайн бүжин шиг өвөрт нь хярж
Хөмөрсөн бумба шиг хөхөнд нь наалдаж
Хөмсөг зангидсан зангаа мартахсан
Гурваар дарсан гэзгий нь сүлжиж
Гунигаа мартаж өвдгий нь дэрлээд
Нойтон сэвлэгтэй жаахан амьтан шиг
Нойрондоо дийлдээд нам унтахсан
Үнэгэнд хууртаад цочиж сэрэх юмсан
Үнэрлүүлж тайтгараад буцаж унтахсан
Үхэж зүүдлээд уйлж босох юмсан
Үнсүүлж тайтгараад ахиж нойрсохсон.

소원

나비와 함께 놀다 돌아 내렸다
얀질함*과 손잡고 다니다
선율에 따라 노래하는 소녀는 신에게 이끌려
하야*를 덮은 운명에서 도망가
어릴 적 놀던 돌로 만든 집에 들어갔으면...
톨가*를 두른 마음에서 멀어져
새끼 토끼처럼 품에 숨어들어
뒤집힌 사발처럼 가슴에 달라 붙어
눈살을 찌푸렸던 습성을 잊어버리기를...
세 갈래로 머리를 땋아
외로움을 잊고 무릎을 베고 누운
젖은 머릿단의 작은 아이처럼
졸음을 이기고 깊이 잠들어 버리기를...
여우에 속아 놀라서 깨어나기를...
향기에 취해 마음놓고 다시 잠들기를...
죽는 꿈에 울며 일어나기를...
입맞춤 당하고 진정하기를 반복하며 잠이 들기를...

* 얀질함: 불교에서 시와 예술을 주관하는 여래불
* 하야: 몽골 전통가옥인 겔(Ger)의 벽을 두른 펠트의 아랫부분
* 톨가: 옛날 전통 난로

- Translated into Korean by T. Otgontuul(Ph.D) Ha in hua(MA)

ШАГДАРЫН ДУЛМАА
Shagdaryn DULMAA

Was born in 1931, in Aldarbayan soum of Tuv province. She graduated from the National University of Mongolia and University of Journalist in the Soviet Union. She has published over 20 books of poems. She won a Award of Mongolian Writer's Union the Prize of Natsagdorj honored Art worker.

ХАРЦ

Харц харц учиртайхан харц

Хан хорвоод мөнх амьдрах харц

Халуун сэтгэлийн хайрыг шингээж

Хаанаас ч гэсэн даллах харц

Харц харц учиртайхан харц

Хайлган уярааж сөгдөөн биширүүлэх харц

Элэг зүрхийг сум шиг нэвтлэн

Энэ ертөнцөд жаргал бэлэглэх харц

Орчлон дэлхийд хүний харц шиг

Очтон гэрэлтэх юм хаана байха вэ?

Хонгорхон бүсгүйн ухаалаг харцанд

Хорвоо бүхлээрээ багтнам биш үү?

눈빛

눈빛 눈빛 이유가 있는 눈빛
왕이 세상에 영원히 사는 눈빛
사랑의 열정을 담아
어디에서라도 손짓하는 눈빛
눈빛 눈빛 이유가 있는 눈빛
마음을 녹이고 감동시키려
무릎 꿇고 유혹하는 눈빛
심장을 꿰뚫는 화살처럼
이 세상에 행복을 선물하는 눈빛
우주 만물에 사람의 눈빛처럼
빛나는 것이 어디 있을까?
귀여운 아가씨의 영롱한 눈빛에는
세상 전부를 담고 있는 것이 아닌가?

- Translated into Korean by T. Otgontuul(Ph.D) Ha in hua(MA)

ДАМДИНСҮРЭНГИЙН УРИАНХАЙ
Damdinsurengiin URIANKHAI

Born in 1940. he went to Moscow to study the State Economic Institute, from 1959-1964. After graduation he began to take part in a High course Gorky Literature Institute in 1977 for three years. He became a prize winner of 'Union of Mongolian Writers, Bolor Tsom and 'the university of knowledge'.

ИНЭЭД ШИГ ХУУЧИН ХҮНИЙ АМЬДРАЛД...

Инээд шиг хуучин хүний амьдралд
Нулимс шиг халуун байх!
Маргааш шиг ойрхон байх!
Магад ирэх Үхэл шиг
Давтагдахгүй байх!
Нулимс шиг хуучин хүний амьдралд
Мөрөөдөл шигээ гэгээн байх
Хайргүй хүндээ ч хайр шагнах
Харагдахгүй Бурханы хутаг олох!
Мартагдахгүй гомдолдоо
Уйлахгүй тэсэхээр цайлган байх!

Гомдол шиг хуучин хүний амьдралд
Харагдахгүй Бурхан шиг ил байх!
Өнөөдрийнх шиг уйтай өдрийг
Дахиад яасан ч тэвчихээргүй
Тэсрэмтгий байх!

Өчигдрийнх шиг,
Уржигдрийн шиг,

Утгагүй тарчилгах удаан өдрөөс
Яасан ч дахиад амьд үлдэхээргүй
Тэрсүүд байх!
Тэгээд яасан ч ийм
Тэнэг шүлэг бичихээр
Дахин төрөхгүй байх
Инээд шиг хуучин...
Нулимс шиг хуучин...
Гомдол шиг хуучин...
Харагдахгүй Бурхан шиг
Хүний амьдралд
"Байхгүй юм "шиг нь
Үргэлж шинэ байх!
"Байгаа" бүгдээс нь
Мөнхөд өөр байх!..

웃음 같은 노인의 삶에...

웃음같은 노인의 삶에는
눈물처럼 뜨거움이 있다!
내일처럼 가까움이 있다!
반드시 찾아오는 죽음처럼
되풀이되지 않는다
눈물같은 노인의 삶에는
꿈과 같은 밝음이 있고
사랑없는 사람에게도 사랑의 상을 주고
보이지 않는 신의 축복을 찾는다
잊혀지지 않는 불만을
울지 않고 견디는 고운 마음이 있다!

불만 같은 노인의 삶에는
보이지 않는 신처럼 분명함이 있다
오늘날처럼 비탄의 날을
어떻게든 다시 참아내지 않고
폭발하기 쉬움이 있다

어제처럼,
그제처럼,

이유없이 괴로워한 오랜 날들에서
어떻게든 다시 목숨을 부지하려하지 않고
비뚤어져 있다!
그래서 어찌되었던 이런
바보같은 시를 쓰려고
다시 태어나지 않는다
웃음처럼 늙은...
눈물처럼 낡은...
불만처럼 오래된...
보이지 않는 신처럼
인간의 삶에
“없는 것” 같은 것은
항상 새롭게
“있는” 모든 것은
영원히 다른 모습으로 있기를!...

- Translated into Korean by T. Otgontuul(Ph.D) Ha in hua(MA)

ӨЧИГ

Орчлонд би олон ч биш, ганц ч биш,
Огторгуй дор үүрд ч биш, зуурд ч биш!
Хүн байтугай чулуу бууралтдаг хорвоод
Хүслээ нөмөрч л жавар хаадаг нүцгэн хөөрхий!

Нуусан хайр минь хийсэн алдаа шигээ илээ,
Нулимс инээд хоёр минь ч үнэн болохоор илээ!
Манан бүсэлсэн хангай шиг хааяа дүнсийдэг ч
Магнайн гурван үрчлээндээ нар хонуулан дүнхийдэг ээ

Өд сөдөө ч зулгаан зулах жигүүртэн сэтгэлд минь
Өрөвдөхийн халуун л шатан, нойргүй хонуулдаг аа
Ганихрах гунихрахын цагт нөхөр үгүйлэх сүүрс
Гарааны морьд шиг цанхаалан, цээжинд цамнадаг аа!

Олон дунд өнчрөөд, мөрөөссөний урам хугаравч
Орой намрын навчистай адилыг нь бодон нөмөрлөдөг өө
Загийн үндэс шиг хайр минь чулуу мөргөвч
Зам муруйлгүй зүтгэсээр ард түмнээ л зорьдог оо!

Нүд хужирлах өнгөнд хөл алдахад нь зовниж
Нүцгэн биенд нь гал зурснаар дулаацахгүйд нь энэлж
Нүргээн дунд замхрах өнчин хонхон дуу
Нүүдэл удмын болор шүлгэндээ гунигаа юүлдэг ээ!

Салхи шиг хуугиа бага наснаасаа би
Сайранд ургасан шарилж , бутаа ч эвийлэн харж
Санахын зовлонд дэвтсэн эгшиглэнт бясалгалаар
Санчиг, зулайгаа агийн толгой шиг цайлгасан!

Орчлонд би олон ч биш, ганц ч биш!
Огторгуй дор үүрд ч биш, зуурд ч биш!
Амьдыг байтугай үхсэнийг элээдэг хорвоод
Аз заягаар туйгаагүй минь хохь ч биш, зол ч биш ээ!

고백

우주에서 나는 하나도 아니고 여럿도 아니다
하늘 아래 나는 연원하지도 순간적이지도 않다
인간도 돌마저도 회색으로 변하는 이 세상에서
나는 전라의 몸, 나의 희망으로 덮어서 추위를 견뎌내는 맨몸의 나약함

나의 숨겨진 사랑은 내가 저질렀던 실수만큼이나 명백하고
나의 눈물과 웃음은 그들이 진실하기에 명백하다
안개 낀 항가이처럼 때때로 조용해져도
이마의 세 주름에는 해가 지는 고요함이여

깃털까지 뽑아 자리를 까는 새들, 내 마음의
아픔 뜨겁게 불타오르는 불면의 밤이여
우울할 때 친구를 찾는 한숨
출발선 상에 서 있는 말처럼 서투르고, 앞서는구나

무리 속에 혼자가 되고 바라던 꿈이 꺾였지만
늦가을의 잎사귀처럼 생각하고 마음에 가둔다
jng* 뿌리처럼 내 사랑은 돌이 머리를 때릴지도
길에서 벗어나지 않고 곧 바로 민중을 향해 나아간다

눈으로 바라만 보는 색만에 가볍게 생각하고
벌거벗은 몸에 불을 피워도 따뜻함을 느끼지 못하고
소음 속에 사라지는 외로운 종소리
유목민 사정의 두명한 시에 슬픔을 비운다

바람처럼 지나간 어린 시절에 나는
강변에 자란 집술과 덤불도 다정하게 바라보고
그리움의 고통에도 부드러운 음소로 기원하여
양옆과 가운데 머리는 agi*의 꽃봉오리처럼 하얗게 되었구나

우주 속의 나는 단수도 복수도 아니다
하늘 아래 나는 연원하지도 아니고, 순간적이지도 않다
행복이 가득하지 않은 것은
운이 좋은 것도 나쁜 것도 아니다

* jag: 고비에서 자라는 뿌리가 돌처럼 단단한 식물
* agi: 식물

- Translated into Korean by Choi Dong-guen(Ph.D, Prof), T. Otgontuul(Ph.D)

АРЛААНЫ ЭРДЭНЭ -ОЧИР
Arlaan ERDENE-OCHIR

Born in 1972, Education: Graduated from the Mongolian Pedagogical University by the profession of literary worker. Now he works as Editor of the magazine "Tsog". First prize at the poetry festival "Bolor tsom" /Crystal Cup/, Prize of the Union of Mongolian Writers in 1998, Prize of the D.Natsagdorj 2006.

АЯЛАГХАН ЗАЛУУ НАС МИНЬ

Ханилсан нөхрөө би
Халтирахад нь түлхэж явсангүй
Амьтны урдуур орж
Алдрын хаалгаар чихэлдэж байсангүй
Аяа, миний аялагхан залуу нас минь

Жаргах цагтаа наргиж, зовох цагтаа гуниж явнаа
Жамт хорвоогоос харин нуугдах газар эрж байсангүй
Жавар салхинаас бусдыг нөмөрлөх сэтгэлтэй явж
Жаахан чамайгаа уйлахад нулимсыг чинь арчиж байснаас,
амталж явсангүй

Дарсны хатууд халамцаж, хүүхний сайханд дурлаж байснаас
Дайсан нөхрөө ялгах гэж сэтгэлээ эвдэж явсангүй
Давааны өндрийг мартаж, хүлэг морио гуядаж
Даамай алсын замдаа бусдын унаанд дайгдсангүй

Аар саархан зовлон зүрх тархийг идэж
Алдар хүндийн золионд бусдын үхэхийг үзэж
Амьтны үрийг өрөвдөж өр цээжээ барсаар
Амьд явахад шаналан шиг хүнд ачаа үзсэнгүй ээ.

나의 감성적인 청춘

나의 벗을 나는
미끄러울 때 밀지 않았고
사랑 앞에 나서서
명성의 문으로 떠밀지 않았다
아아, 감성적인 나의 청춘이여

행복할 때에 즐기고, 괴로울 때에 슬퍼한다
법도 있는 세상에서 숨을 곳을 찾지 못했다
찬 바람 말고는 다 감싸주는 마음을 가지고
네가 울 때 눈물을 닦아주었지 울리지 않았다

독한 와인에 취하고, 멋진 아가씨를 좋아했으며
적과 동지를 구분하려고 마음을 깨지 않았다
언덕의 높음을 잊어버리고, 준마를 채찍질했었고
먼 길임을 알고도 남의 말〔馬〕*에 편승하지 않았다

사소한 고민은 심장과 뇌를 먹고
명예의 희생에 다른 이들이 죽는 것을 보았으며
인간의 후예를 불쌍히 여기고 가슴에 원한을 품고
살면서 괴로움 같은 무거운 짐을 보지 못했다.

*yhaa(오나): 모든 교통수단을 일컫는 오나라는 단어를 말〔馬〕로 번역하였음

- Translated into Korean by T. Otgontuul(Ph.D) Ha in hua(MA)

ГОМПИЛДООГИЙН МӨНХЦЭЦЭГ
Gompildoogyn MUNKHTSETSEG

G.Munkhtsetseg was born in Dornogobi province. She won the first place of Bolor Tsom poetry competition in 2001. She published poetry books as 'Blue Sky', 'Omen birds are red' and others. She awarded Best Cultural Worker of Mongolia in 2008 and Polar Star Order, High State Award in 2009.

БИТГИЙ УРВААРАЙ МИНИЙ ХҮҮ

Хаанаас ирсэнийг нь мэдэхгүй
Хачин янзын амьтан минь
Хүзүүндээ зүүж эрхлүүлсэн
Хуруун чинээхэн бурхан минь ээ
Үсээн цайтал хүлээсэн хөгшид
Үр минь чамайг авчрах гэж холын холд одоцгоосон
Гоёхон насаа өөрөөсөө ч харамласан ижий минь
Ганцхан өглөөний нарнаар л эмээ болж угтсан юм шүү
Чарлахаас өөрийг мэдэхгүй ирсэн чамайг
Цас бороо бүгдээрээ сонссон юм шүү
Цамцны минь цаанаас унах гэж яарсан өдрүүдээ
Чамлаж л битгий урваарай миний хүү
Чийгтэй хөх өвс яаж уйлдагийг харуулах гэж
Чинийхээ хөлийг шүүдрээр угааж өгсөн юм шүү
Цэцэг тасалж эрхлэхгүй уяхан болгох гэж ээж нь
Чихэн дээр чинь тонгойн шүлэг аялсан юм шүү миний хүү
Торгон ногоон дэвжээг хотойтол дэвсэн аав нь
Тоглох газрын чинь хатууг зөөллөх гэж
Торгоор гоёсон зодгоороо
Тоосыг нь хааяа арчиж босдог юм шүү миний хүү
Томоо болсныг чинь шалгах гэж
Тоостой орчлон хайртай бүхнийг чинь булаалддаг юи
Тогтохын дээдээр тогтсон хүлгийн нуруунаасаа
Тохсон эмээлээ сольж өөрөөсөө битгий урваарай
Бүгдээрээ чамайг жаргаах гэж
Бүсгүй болгон царайлаг төрдөггүй юм шүү
Бүгээн хонгор нулимсаа эр хүн нууж унагадаг юм
Бүсээн нэвчтэл ганцаардахад чинь хэрэг болно тэр чинь
Ивэлээн сүүгээ эгштэл асгаруулж
Цээжээ хатгал өөрийгөө шингээлээ ижий нь чамд
Цагийн цагт холын холд ч
Цадатлаа хөхсөн хүний л үнэрээс минь битгий урваарай миний хүү
Бүсийг чинь задалж хуурайлцсан
Аавынх нь энгэр шиг дулаахан
Бүгдээрээ зүхсэн ч Монголоосоо
Бүүр ч битгий урваарай миний хүү

변덕 부리지 마라 내 아들아

어디서 왔는지는 모르겠다
내 귀여운 강아지
목에 걸쳐 응석부리는
손가락만한 나의 신이여
백발이 되기까지 기다린 노인들이
너를 데려오려고 멀고 멀리 떠나버렸다
아름다운 나이를 스스로도 아까워한 나의 어머니는
단 하루의 아침 햇살만으로 할머니가 되어 맞이했었단다
고함치는 것 말고는 아무것도 모르고 온 너를
눈 비 모두가 들었었단다
내 몸 밖으로 나오려고 서둘렀던 날들을
불만스럽게 여기지 말고 변덕부리지 마라 내 아들아

물기 머금은 파란 풀이 어떻게 우는지 보여주려고
너의 발을 이슬로 씻어 주었단다
꽃을 꺾지 않는 성품의 아이가 되었으면 하는 어미는
너의 귀에 대고 노래를 불러주었단다 내 아들아
초록 비단 뎁제*를 가라앉을 때까지 밟은 아버지는
단단한 네 놀이터를 부드럽게 해주고
비단으로 멋을 낸 저덕*으로
가끔씩 먼지를 쓸어주려고 일어났었단다 내 아들아
네가 자라는 것을 확인하려고
먼지나는 세상은 네가 사랑하는 모든것을 빼앗아 가곤 했단다
사람을 태우게 된 말 등에서
덮은 안장을 바꾸듯 자기 자신에 대해 변덕 부리지 마라

모두 너를 행복하게 하려고
아가씨들마다 예쁘게 태어나는 것은 아니란다
사나이는 뜨거운 눈물을 남몰래 흘리는 것이다
네가 허리띠에 스며들 만큼 외로울 때 그것이 도움이 된다
남는 젖을 말려 쏟아버리고
가슴이 마르도록 자신을 너에게 주었단다 어미는
시간 시간마다 멀고 먼 곳에서도
배부르도록 젖을 먹인 나의 냄새를 맡고 변덕부리지 마라 내 아들아

너의 기저귀를 갈아준
아버지의 품처럼 따뜻하고
모두가 욕해도 몽골 사람으로서
정말로 변덕 부리지 마라 내 아들아

* 초록 비단 뎁제: 씨름 경기하는 장소의 풀
* 저덕: 1.씨름선수가 입는 옷 2. 시베리아에서 나는 두꺼운 나무껍질

- Translated into Korean by T. Otgontuul(Ph.D) Ha in hua(MA)

СОЛОНГОСЫН ХОЙГ

Ази тивийн зүүн хэсэг рүү
Алхам алхамаар дөхөн очивоос
Авсаархан жижиг Солонгосын хойгийн төгсгөл
Алтан наранд гялбанхан үзэгдэнэ

Уужим тал өргөн говийн эх газараас
Бүх дэлхийг морин тууриагаар тамгалсан
Их монголын Чингис хааны гэрчүүд

Хойд далайн эрэг
Алтан уул усны үзэгсгэлэнтэй манай улсад
Монгол хөх толбоор батлаад өгөх юм

Аа! Уран шүлгийн тугаа намируулж
Дэлхийн соёл шүлгийн гайхамшигт тал дээр
Солонгос Монголын яруу найргийн үрийг цацан
Ахан дүүсийн найрсаг харилцааг билэгдэн байна

Ким Жон Үн

태양 빛에 어린 한반도
—세계시문학회

아세아의 동쪽으로
기웃기웃 올라가면
아담한 한반도의 끝
태양빛에 눈이 부시다

사막과 허허벌판 대륙에서
온누리에 말을 달리며
세계를 포효하는
몽골의 징기스칸

서해의 연안을 타고
금수강산 화려한 나라에
몽골반점의 증표로
이어주고 있다

아! 서정시의 깃발을 날리며
세계의 문화 언어 평화
한-몽문학의 씨를 뿌려
친선의 가교가 낭랑히 들려온다.

ЧИ БОЛ БИ, БИ БОЛ ЧИ

-Даяаршиж буй ертөнцөд илгээх захидал –

Сэтгэл болон нүдээ томхон нээгээд харваас
Чи бид гэдэг чинь яахын аргагүй
нэг л оршихуй

Царс мод ганцаар үндэслэн ургах нь
Цаглашгүй энэ ертөнцийн жам юм
Байгаль ертөнц бүхнийг захирагч хүн гэдэг
Байж чадах уу ганцаараа
Барж чадах уу энэ амьдралыг

Хайраар нэгдэж хоорондоо
Аз жаргалыг хоорондоо бэлэглэхэд
Баяр жаргал амар амгалангийн цэцэг дэлбээлэх нь
Багахан энэ хорвоогийн ёс юм

Дөрвөн зүг найман зовхисыг дээрээс нь тольдон ажих
Дөлгөөхөн цагаан үүлс батлаад өгнө үүнийг
Уул нугаар тэнүүчлэн явсаар
Ус ихт далайд цутгах
Урсгал голууд хэлээд өгнө бас
Бид бүгд л нэг оршихуй
Бие биенээсээ салахын аргагүй гайхамшиг

Ёо Хан Гён

나도 너이고 너도 나이고
―한 지구촌을 위한 메시지

눈을 크게 뜨고도 작게만 보는 사람 있듯이
눈을 작게 뜨고도 크게 본다면 우린 하나다
나도 너이고 너도 나이고

흙 속으로 뿌리 박은 푸나무들 이야기 자연의
따라 홀로도 살아간다지만
만물을 지배하고, 만물을 다스려야 하는
만물의 영장인 인간들이야 그어찌
세상을 홀로만 갈 수가 있다더냐

주고받고 서로가 보듬으며 서로가
사랑으로 하나 될 때, 거기에
기쁨이 꽃피고, 평화가 꽃피고
지혜가 꽃피고, 이것이 섭리라고

사방 팔방을 살피며, 높은 하늘을 떠가는
저, 흰구름이 말해주지 않더냐
계곡을 조잘대며 바다로 나아가는
저, 시냇물이 말해주지 않더냐
우린 하나다, 나도 너이고 너도 나이고
아니, 삼라만상이 하나다

СҮНС

Хүн гэдэг амьтан чинь
Сүнс бие хоёртой байж л
Сүүдэр гаргаж амьдардаг гэнэ

Халуун цус нь урсахаа больж
Хар үхэл ирэхэд
Хайчдаг юм болоо энэ сүнс маань

Мэдэх аргагүй энэ асуултын
Хариулт нь зөвхөн ...<биенээсээ гарах>...
Хийсвэр ертөнцийн эхлэл ч юмуу

Бүр мэдэх аргагүй учир
Бүтэн биений минь төгсгөлийг
Бүлээн цус зогсох тэр л агшин гэж
үзэхээс дээ би

Үхсэний дараа болох хийх зүйл
Хэрэв чамд байгаа бол
Энэ шүлгийн доороос цувуулаад бичээрэй та
минь

Жон Дог Ги

Бичгийн нэр <Хаврын бороо>

영혼

사람은 영혼과 육신
두 가지로 삶을 유지한다

사람은 피가 멎으면 죽음인데
육신의 장막 떠난 후
그 영혼은 어찌되나?

못내 알 길 없는
정답은 내 권한 밖
오직 창조주의 영역일뿐

더 알 수 없으니
생명의 한계는
피가 멎을 때라

죽음 이후 스스로의 의지로
생각하고 행동하는 것 있으면
여기 열거해 보라고

НАГДУН МӨРНИЙ ЭРЭГ ДЭЭР

Үүрийн туяа

Яг л чам шиг үзэсгэлэнтэйгээр туяарна

Салаалдаггүй гол зам шиг л урссаар

Ганцаар алхах чиний дэргэд дуусах юм

Чиний төлөө

Сэтгэлээ шүр шиг улайлган байж

Сэмхэнээр залгих нулимсандаа

Өнөөдрийг хүртэл живүүлээд

Хагацалд аяндаа бэлдэх сэтгэлээ

Харуусан өрөвдөх юм би

Дэргэд минь тогтолгүй яваад л өгсөн чиний сурагийг

Усны шувуудаас хүртэл горьдох юм

Эргэж ирээд хажууд минь

Хацар юугаан улайлган байгаад

Энэ тэр сониныг ярьж суугаа юм шиг

Өчигдөрхөн нутгийн минь дундуур урсан өнгөрсөн

Нагдун голоо сайн байна уу?

Пак Юн Ги

낙동강에서

노을
그 속내만큼 아름답게
다 젖도록 타오르는 외길속
혼자 걷는 그대 곁에 선다

그대 위해
마음 붉은 상주처럼
목마다 넘치는 갈대들의 눈물에
어느새 가득 찬 오늘도
빈 걸음으로 준비한 이별은
어둠에 젖고

철새들이
간이역 지나
몰운대로 가는 그대를
언제 또 찾아와
호롱불처럼 부끄러울 날 있으랴
이런 저런 안부 속에
엊그제 고향 다녀온 그대여
낙동강이여!

УСАН ЗАМ

Алтан утаст цэцэг мөнх цэцэгтэй баглаа болж
Ариухан насанд очих замыг даллана
Зөрөг цэцэг даган хөвөрсөн сэтгэл
Зүүдний сайхан руу одох жим болно

Салхи, турьхан мөчирийг чичирээж
Оршин буйгаа зарлана
Шувуудын жиргээн салхин морь унан ирж чихэнд минь хургана
Цэцэгс дэлгэрч гуниглах дуун сонсогдох шиг
Амраг хосуудын сэтгэлээ илчлэх шивнээнд
Тэнгэрийн хаяа, нар жаргах туяатайгаа чийг даах шиг үзэгдэнэ

Өндөр хурд, сүүлийн үеийн технологи
Өнөөдөр дэлхийг захирч байгаа хүмүүс
Бие сэтгэл нь агуу боловч
Байгаль эхийг өмнө юутай жижигхэн юм

Сарны туяа сүүн замыг татуулан
Саяхан мэндлэх шинэ амьдралыг угтана

Ким Ми Гён

수경길

금계국 망초꽃 어우러져
유년의 길 끌어온다
곡선의 길따라 곡선의 마음들이
순수로 돌아가는 길

바람은 초록이파리 흔들어 존재 알리고
새들의 노랫소리 바람 타고 귓전에 머무네
꽃이 피고 지는 소리 들린 듯
깊은 늪의 잉태하는 생명 보일 듯
연인들 마음 열리는 소리
석양 노을에 젖는다

초고속첨단 기술 편리함 누리며
시원의 자연 갈망하는 현대인
몸과 마음 거대하게 자랐지만
공허함에 순수를 갈망하는 곳

열정과 평화 하나 되는 곳
달빛 머금어 생명의 싹
꿈틀거린다

БУГА БА НУУР

Тогтуухан дөлгөөн нуурын эрэг дээр
Торомгор нүдтэй буга иржээ
Хөх тэнгэрийн хэсэг газарт буучихав уу гэмээр энэ нуурт
Хөнгөхөн үүлс нь хүртэл хөвөн харагдах юм

Нуур бас бугыг ажина
Нууран дундах ганц бугыг түүний нүднээс харна
Хөвөн цагаан үүлс
Хөх тэнгэрийн хэсэг болсон өөртэйгээ бас харна

Бугыг нуур дахин ажина
Нуурын тусгалд харин буга сүрэгээрээ мэт харагдана
Олуулаа харагдах тэр хөх тэнгэрт
Үүлс хөлөглөсөн сүрэг буга хөвөн айсуй

Нуур бугыг бас дахин ажина
Нуурын ажих бугын нүдэнд
Сүрэг буга тогтуун нуур тэр чигээрээ багтана
Хөвөн үүлс хөлөглөсөн бугын сүрэг
Хөх тэнгэрээр дүүрэн бэлчинэ
Эцэс төгсгөлгүй аниргүйн дунд
Нуур ч бас аниргүй...

Ким Жун Хи

사슴과 호수

사슴이 호숫가에 와서 호수를 들여다봅니다
잔잔한 호수 속에는 하늘이 가득합니다
그 하늘 위로 흰 구름이 떠다닙니다

호수가 사슴을 봅니다
사슴의 눈동자에는 홀로 서 있는 사슴과
떠다니는 흰 구름과
푸른 하늘 가득한 호수가 있습니다

사슴이 호수를 다시 들여다봅니다
호수는 온통 사슴으로 가득합니다
사슴으로 가득인 푸른 하늘에
사슴을 가득 실은 흰 구름 떠다닙니다

호수가 사슴을 다시 봅니다
사슴의 눈동자에는 사슴으로 가득한 호수와
사슴을 가득 싣고 떠다니는 흰 구름과
사슴으로 가득인 푸른 하늘이 있습니다
그러나 한없이 고요합니다
호수도 그러합니다

ГАНЦ ХОЁР ХУНДАГА ДАРСНЫ ДАРАА

(Уушийн газарт)

Модон торхонд мэлтэлзэх

Мянга нэгэн мишээсэн цэцэг

Ганц балган сэтгэлээ норготол

Үнэрт нь согтон мансуурах шиг

Цэцгийн дэлбээ хагас дэлгэрэхдээ л үзэсгэлэнтэй байдаг шиг

Цэнгэлт мансуурал хэтрээгүй үед бүр жаргалтай

Дарс хэмжүүрийн аягыг цэцэгт навчаар хийжээ

Дахиад ганц хундага хийгээч ..

Цүл цүл дугаран хундагалагдах шүлэгийн шимэнд сэтгэл минь гэгэлзэнэ

Ганц хоёр хундага дарсаар гоёж аваад

Ганган зуны шүлгийн замд гаръя даа өнөө орой...

Ким Хи Сун

두어 잔 술에

새우젓 항아리에
만개한 웃음꽃

한 모금 가슴 적시니
취기가 돌아난다

오래 전 주인장이 마련한
화개반주미취*

또 한 잔
됫박* 만든 연잎 위로

그득 그득 따라주는 시 한 수
귀가 트인다
두어 잔 술로 치장하고
길 나서는 여름 한때

* 화개반주미취: 꽃은 반쯤 피었을 때가 보기 좋고 술은 약간 취했을 때가 기분 좋다.
* 됫박: 되를 대신하는 바가지.

ЭРДЭНИЙН ЧУЛУУ

Санаж л явна чамайг

Гэхдээ энэ бол нууц

Далдын далд нуусан эрдэнийн чулуу юм

Эрдэнийн чулуу гялалзана

Эргэж чамайг хараагүй байхад ч гялтганана

Үүр цайхад ганцаар үлдээд анивалзах од шиг гялалзана

Ким Хаг Жин

보석

그립습니다
비밀입니다
깊이 숨겨둔 보석입니다

보석은 빤짝입니다
그대가 봐 주지 않아도 홀로 빛나는
여명의 샛별처럼 빤짝입니다.

ДОЛДУГААР САРЫН ЦЭЦЭРЛЭГ

Нүдээ нээтэл цэцэрлэг угтлаа
Ногоон хилэн хөвсгөр зүлэг нь
Миний сэтгэл шиг цэнхэр униартай юм

Дугуйран хүрээлэх нил өнгөт хонгорзулын
Дотносон шивнэлдэх нь сонсогдох ч шиг
Борхон сэвхтэй ичингүйрэн ягаарсан алтанзул

Өнөөдөр яагаад ч юм бүх сэтгэлээ уудална гэнэ
Өнгө өнгийн цэцэгсийн наадам үргэлжилэнэ
Өнөө шөнө тэд дэлбээгээ хумихгүй гэцгээнэ

Дээгүүр нь эргэлдэх эрвээхэйнүүдтэй
Дэндүү дотносон аальгүйтэх гэнэ
Сарнай цэцэг өнгө өнгөөр алаглах нь дэндүү тансаг
Салхит бороо намдсан цэцэрлэгт шүүдэр үлдэн нүд
гялбуулна

Зуны зочин хүр хорхойн дуу царгиж
Зандан модны үнэр өвөрт минь л үнэртээд байна

2011.8.12

Жон Сүн Жа

7월의 정원

이중창 열어
정원을 내려다보니
연둣빛 융단 고운 잔디
내 마음의 푸르름 담아내는 것 같아

빙 둘러선 영산홍 철쭉
힘차게 약동하고 있네
검은 딱지 다닥다닥 주황 빛나리꽃

오늘따라 속내를 다 내보이고
흰백합 노랑백합 축제가 한창이네
연보랏빛 도라지꽃 흰 도라지꽃

흰나비 맞이해 희희낙락거리고
장미 색색이 피어 화려하게 장식하네
긴 비 걷힌 뜰엔 햇살도 눈부시며

여름 손님 매미들 합창도 우렁차고
향나무 향기 퍼져 뜰에 가득하네

- 2011. 8. 12

УХААРАЛ

Улааран туяарах хойд зүгийн тэнгэрийн хаяа

Наран шингэх намуухан чимээг

Чи сонссон уу?

Хорвоод,

Уусан алга болдог зүйлс нь ч үзэсгэлэнтэй сайхан байх юмаа

Хөөрхий модны мөчир чичирэн туялзана

Хөөж үлээж буй тэрхүү салхийг

Чи олж харав уу?

Өнгөрөөд явчихсан хойно нь дурсан санах нь

Хорвоогийн жам юм уу?

Амьдралд,

Сонсогдох ч үгүй харагдах ч үгүй мөртлөө

Минийх гэхээр зүйлс

Магад их байдаг бололтой

Куак Пён Сү

무심

서쪽 하늘 붉은 노을
해 넘어 가는 은은한 소리
그대는 들어보았는가
세상은
사라지는 것조차 아름다운데

바람에 흔들리는 나뭇가지
스치며 흔드는 바람을
그대는 보았는가
지나가는 것들도 그리운데

세상에
들리지도 않고
보이지도 않는 것이
나에게는 너무도 많구나.

БУЯНЫ ҮЙЛСТЭН

Эрдэнэ мэт хоёр гар нь
Хайрлаач гэж л залбирна

Эцэст нь хүрсэн ч тайлагдашгүй амьдралын
Энгийн сайханыг нь л тэд гэрчилдэг

Дэргэд нь байхад л нулимс цийлэгнэж уярмаар
Дэнс цэцэг дэлгэрэх амьдралын хаварыг хамтдаа хүлээдэг
Тэдний нэр нь буяны үйлстэн

Хайр гэдэг үгэнд мэлмий нь хаагдаж
Хамтдаа гэсэн үгэнд сэтгэлээ булаалгасан
Холын холд цаг хугацаа одсон ч
Хосгүй хайрын төгөлд л сэтгэлээрээ тэд үлддэг

Ким Ён Ми

1.Буяны үйлстэн: (цалин хөлсгүйгээр бусдын төлөө сайн үйлс бүтээгчид)

자원 봉사자

언제나 한결같이
두 손 모으는 비손은
오로지 사랑하게 하소서입니다

가도 가도 알 수 없는 세상이지만
냉정한 미소만 있는 것이 아니라고
온몸으로 말하는 이들이 있습니다

눈물 머금은 이의 곁에서
함께 울고 웃으며
찬란히 꽃피울 봄을
함께 기다리는
그들의 이름은 자원봉사자입니다

사랑이란 이름에 눈멀고
동행이란 글자에 마음 빼앗겨
강물 같은 시간이 흘러도
사랑의 늪에서만 살아갑니다

ОН ЖИЛҮҮД

Яаж ч гуйж учирласан ч
Гарцаагүй сайн нөхөр минь байж
Ганцхан эргээд л яваад өгөх юм
Явах мөрөөрөө явчихгүй
Явдал дундаа эргэн эргэн харсаар
Ядарсан намайг уйлуулах юм

Тас тэврээд явуулмааргүй байсан ч
Та нэг л мэдэхэд арилаад өгөх юм
Бодол сэтгэлээс минь түрүүлэн давхих
Жолоо нь алдарсан морь ч юмуу?

Өдөр өдөрт харц тулгаран
Чимээгүйхэн дэргэдээ суулгачихаад
Чимх чимхээр жолоог нь суллаж баймаар
Аниргүйн дундах амраг минь чи он жилүүдээ..

Кан Ён Дог

세월

떠나려 하여도
쉽게 보낼 수 없는
단짝 같은 친구이건만
끝내 이별을 고하고
뒤돌아서서
아쉬운 눈시울 적시는 그림자

품어도 꼭 껴안아도
어느새 빠져나와
늘 나의 의지보다
앞장서서 달리기만 하는
고삐 풀린 말

소중히
하루하루와 입맞춤하며
조용히 내 곁에 두고
조금씩 서서히
풀었다 낚았다 하고 싶은
침묵의 동반자

ДУГУЙН УРАЛДААН

Үүрийн гэгээ туяарахад

Үзэсгэлэнт сайхан Хан мөрний эргийн

Зурайн үргэлжлэх торгон замаар

Дөрөө жийн хурдална би

Хоёр дугуйнд амиа даатган

Хоёргүй амьдралын дөрөөнд хүч нэмэн хурдална

Сөүл хотын дугуйн уралдааны энэ өдөр

Канхуа хаалганаас Хан мөрнийг гатлан арваад бээрийн холд жийнэ

Зургаан том гүүрийг дамнан

Зураг мэт үзэсгэлэнт Хан мөрний

Сэрүү татсан агаараар амьсгалангаа

Сайхан мэдрэмж энэ л чигээрээ

Амар амгалангийн цэцэрлэгт хүрчих юмсан

Хан, Кым, ЁнСан голыг гатлан Нагдун мөрөнг чиглэх

1592 км үргэлжлэх дугуйчдын давалгаан дунд

Дөрөө жийн хурдлан давхиад л баймаар

Дөрвөн салаа дугуйн зам нь

Эрүүл ногоон ертөнц рүү хөтлөх болтугай.

ИСанЖин

자전거 여행

이른 새벽
한강변의 실크로드를 따라
페달을 밟으면서 달린다

두 바퀴에 몸을 맡겨
삶의 페달을 밟는다
오늘은 '하이 서울 자전거 대행진의 날'
광화문 광장에서 한강대교를 건너
10km가 넘는 한강변을 달린다

여섯 개의 큰 다리를 지나면서
탁 트인 한강, 시원한 강바람을 마시면서
노을 공원을 지나 평화의 공원까지

이제는 한강, 금강, 영산강을 넘어 낙동강까지!
1,592km 자전거의 새물결
자주, 더불어 더욱 멀리 달리고 싶은 임진년의 희망
4대강 자전거길이 녹색 성장을 이끌 바람이 되길!
더불어 국태민안의 큰 길을!
이미 후천개벽이 시작했음을, 세상의 큰 길이 열렸음을!

ОЧИРБАТ

Чингисийн морин цэрэгийн
Чичиргүүлж явсан толгодод
Чиглүүлж байсан одоо

Урал Алтайн нуруу
Ургац арвин амуу нь
Дэлхийн өврөөр дэлгэх эсгий мэт

Наран мандаж шингэх
Тэнгэр газрын хаан Очирбат
Шинэ улсын
Шинээр томилсон албат

Гар гараа барилцсан
Эхийн дулаан хамжлагатай
Монгол хөх толбот оо

오치르바트

칭기스 말 달리던
구름 너머엔
은하 지킨 별빛

알타이 우랄 등성
이고 잔 풀밭
지구별 양탄자

햇별 쬔
하늘 땅 칸
오치르바트*
새 나라 새 머슴

손에 손 마주 잡은
어머니의 피
몽골리안 반점

* 오치르바트: 1993년 민주화 직전 초대 대통령

ШИНЭ ЗУУНЫ НАР САР

Шинэ зууны шинэ өглөө
Шилэн бөмбөлөг шиг тунгалагхан
Шинэ зууны шинэ өглөө
Молор эрдэнэ мэт гялтаганана
Мөрөөдөл нээгдэнэ

Хуучин зууны хөх цэнхэр нууын усанд
Хамаг муу сэтгэлээ угааж
Анхны хайрын эзэн хүү шиг ариухан сэтгэлтэй болохсон
Хуучин зуунд миний сэтгэл нулимс үргэлжилсэн уртаас урт үзэн ядалт байсан бол
Дэргэд минь өнгөрөх мянган жилд

Дээрхи муу сэтгэл минь
Дээд тэнгисийн номин цэнхэр усаар угаагдаасай
Эцэг өвгөдийн хайр шингэсэн бүлээхэн хөрст өвөрт
Эгэл хүнийг хайрласан хайрын сэтгэлийг үрслүүлэхсэн

Нэг өвөг дээдэс нэгэн эхээс улбаалсан ахан дүүсийн хайрын үрийг бас суулгахсан

Энэ бие минь шороо болж
Энэ мянган жил ч шороо болоход
Таван өнгөт цэцэг жимс болон эргэн төрөөд
Шинэ мянганы хүн төрөлхтний хайрын үндэс болдог юм билүү?
Орчлон хорвоог гэрэлтүүлэгч нарны туяа ч болдог юм билүү!
Сарны цэнхэр туяа
Сайхан үүрийн гэгээ ч болон төрдөг юм билүү..
Шинэ зууны шинэ өглөө

Хуан Сон И

새 천년의 해와 달

새 천년의 새 아침에는
유리알같이 맑고 투명한
선사 시대가 열리리
새 아침에는
수정같이 맑고 투명한
태고의 꿈이 열리리

파르란 선사 시대의 이끼 푸른 연못에는
20세기의 오염된 나를 벗고
20세기의 아픈 허물일랑 고이 벗고
한 점 두려움 없는 옛사랑 심으올까
한 점 다툼없는 옛꿈을 심으올까

옛 천년이 내 가슴 피눈물로 이어내린
기나긴 마음과 회한의 정일랑
아스라이 스쳐가는 정겨운 꿈의 천년
파아란 남해의 쪽빛 바닷물에 띄우고

선조님이 미소 짓는 따사로운 흙의 품엔
우호의 빛으로 아롱진 이웃사랑 심으올까
한 조상 한 어머님의 겨레 사랑 심으올까

이 몸이 흙이 되어
새 천년 흙이 되어
오색과 실향 나무로 거듭 다시 태어나서
새 천년 인류 위한 사랑의 열매로 맺히올까나...
대자연 우주 밝히는 태양의 숨결로 되살아날까나...
달님의 파아란 그림자로 되살아날까나...
새 아침 새 샛별로 되살아날

A Sketch on A Winter Night

In a winter night
He drew close like cello to me.
I don't remember his face,
But only he produces a cello tone.
With being touched deeply, its tone is melted in blood.
After passing a few years as if forgetting it,
Suddenly in a winter night,
In the aroma of coffee emitting from an unknown coffee house,
The Air on the G-string is melted.
His tone was flowing as one of cello.
When I came to a stop for a while,
Time was passing between it.

- Tr. by Won Eung-soon

어느 겨울밤 스케치

어느 해 겨울밤에
그는 첼로처럼 다가왔다.
나는 그의 얼굴을 모른다
다만, 그에게선 첼로음이 나왔다.
깊은 감동에 젖어 그 음音은 피에 녹았다.
몇 년을 잊은 듯이 지내다가
어느 겨울밤, 문득
이름 모를 찻집에서 풍기는 커피 내음 속엔
G 선상의 아리아가 녹아 있었다.
그의 음성이 첼로음으로 흐르고 있었다.
잠시 걸음을 멈추었을 때엔
그 사이로 세월이 지나가고 있었다.

ЗУРГИЙН ЦОМОГ

Хэдэн хуучин гэрэл зургаа цэгцэлэн үзэж сууна

Хичнээн ч жил өнгө зүсээ алдан, хэцүүхэн байсан тэр цаг хаалганы цаана үлдэж дээ

Намайг орхиод явчихсан эгэл амьдралын минь хагацал

Намрын гандуу салхины үнэр шиг л сэттэлд шингээстэй

Угааж цэвэрлэсэн өнөөх л хэдэн зурагнаас маань

Урагдан сэмрэн гээгдэх нь гээгдэж алга болсон ч

Учирч явсан түүний минь инээмсэглэлд шингэсэн

Үүрийн туяа, оддын гэрэл, солонгын өнгө нь сэтгэлээс минь яахин гээгдэх билээ

Чиг Чиг Чиг Чиг

.. Эргэж учралгүй амьдралын минь гэрч

Энэхүү алга дарам хар цагаан дүрс

Эцэст нь цэгцэлж боломгүй гуниг ганцаардлыг үлдээх юм

Цомгоо цэгцлээд дууслаа

Болзоот салхи цаг хугацааг дуудна

Улирал аа даган гандсан цэцэгс

Учраад одсон сайхан мөчийг минь санах ч үгүй биз дээ

Ким Сун Бэ

사진들을 정리한다

빛바랜 채 닫혀 있던 시간의 문 앞에서
간혹 먼저 떠난 이생의 인연들도
그냥 바람으로 남아 있다

인화된 애환들을 한 장씩 버린다
더욱 환한 피사체의 미소에 서린
무지갯빛 노을빛 별빛들은
아직도 지울 수가 없다

찰깍찰깍
...한이 세상의 흔적들
확인하지 못한 치의 여백 때문일까
끝내 정리할 수 없는 그리움 하나

사진첩을 덮는다
다시 무상의 바람이 시간을 부른다
철 지난 꽃들이
무채색의 인연들을 기억하지 않는다

■ The Thematic Address:

The Living Power of Metaphysical Poetics in the Age of Post Modernism

by Prof. Won Eung-soon Ph.D.

1

In the early 21 century, one of the famous critics, H.J.C. Grierson gave a definition on the 'metaphysical poetry' as follows:

The mataphysical poetry, in the full
sense of term, is a poetry which, like that of the Divina Commedia, the De natura Rerum, perhaps Goethe's Faust, has been inspired by a philosophical conception of the universe and of the role assigned to the human spirit in the great drama of existence.(metaphysical lyrics, xiii)

And again he explained:

Passionate thinking is always apt to become metaphysical, probing and investigating the experience from which it takes its rise. All these qualities are in the poetry of Donne, and Donne is the greatest master of English poetry in the seventeenth century.(Ibid., xvi)

Therefore, it was a reasonable thing for T.S. Eliot to find the best answer in the so-called "Metaphysical Poetry" of John Donne in the 17 century, as the mechanism of sensibility, that is to say, 'unification of experience' rooted in the literary tradition of his poetic theory. And again the poet, Eliot says about the motive he was infatuated with John Donne's poetry like this:

A thought to Donne was an experience; if modified his sensibility. When a poet's mind is perfectly equipped for his work, it is constantly amalgamating disparate experience; the ordinary man's experience is chaotic, irregular, fragmentary. The latter falls in love, or reads Spinoza, and these two experiences have nothing to do each other, or with the noise of the typewriter or the smell of cooking; in the mind of the poet these experiences are always forming new wholes. (SE, p. 287)

And the critic, G. Williamson, in his analyzed book, A Reader's Guide to T.S. Eliot explains he devoted himself to Donne's poetry as follows:

This method may be summarized as the assumption of an ironic mask or attitude, mock-heroic in effect and wit, expressing a mixed, often by dramatic means. It indulges in self-mockery or ridicules serious feeling; it represents mixed reactions to things, the subjective mocked by the objective, the discrepancy between appearance and reality. It sees boredom and horror, the frustration or derision of latent feeling, the shams of modern life; it dissimulates sympathy for their victims. (Ibid., p. 51-52)

However, the comment on John Donne's poetry in his age is as rough as his poem's cadence. First of all, John Dryden criticized harshly like this:

Donne too much affects the metaphysics---and perplexes the minds of the fair sex with nice speculations of philosophy, when he should engage their heartand entertain them with the softness of love.(Smith, John Donne, The Critical Heritage 1:13)

But Dryden commented again, "he is the greatest wit, though not the best poet in our nation." And Alexander Pope also said, "he has nice wit, but without cadence(poetic rhyme).

2

Now let's examine some distinguished characteristics shown in Donne's poems. At approaching to 20 century, first, the critic Grierson commented on the Songs and Sonnets of John Donne, 1921, and so did John Heywood, 1929, and Helen Gardner, 1965.

One of his characteristics is the "conceit" known well as the principal one of metaphysical poetry, and was an art of versification distinguished from Petrarchan Style poetry. First, 18c critic, Dr. Samuel Johnson commented on the defects of John Donne's poetry, but the reverse was the case of explaining "conceit" exactly:

a kind of discordia concors, a combination of dissimilar images, or discovery of occult resemblances in things apparently unlike.

This critique of his poetry was an exact comment on the external feature of "conceit" of the metaphysical poets. H. Gardner explained on the "conceit" of the poetic metaphor again:

A conceit is a comparison whose ingenuity is more striking that its justness, or at least, is more immediately striking. All comparisons discover likeness in things unlike: a comparison becomes a conceit when we are made to concede likeness while being strongly conscious of unlikeness. (Metaphysical Poets, p.15)

T.S. Eliot explained this comparison of "conceit" as his poetic theory "objective correlative". He pointed exactly that the English poetry raised the dissociation of sensibility seriously between 19c and 20c. He declared the subversive theory on the definition of poetry:

Poetry is not a turning loose of emotion, but an escape from emotion; it is not the expression of personality, but an escape from personality. But of course, only those who have personality and emotions know what it means to want an escape from these things.

That is to say, the above 'poetic theory of objective correlative' is the same one of the poetic technique of 'conceit'.

Let me look into a poem "Valediction: Forbidding Mourning" of John

Donne's poetry:

If two souls therefore, which are one,
  Though I must go, endure not yet
A breach, but an expansion,
  Like gold to airy thinness beat.

If they be two, they are two so
  As stiff twin compasses are two:
Thy soul, the fixed foot, makes no show
  To move, but doth, if the other do; (6-7stanza)

In the above poem, the valediction means 'a breach'. But the paradox that can't divide or break off between the lover's relation, makes it possible the following two parables, "Though I must go, endure not yet/ A breach, but an expansion/ Like gold to airy thinness are two" and also "If they be two, they are two so/ As stiff twin compasses are two". These parables are the surprising conceits.

The second characteristic of his poetry is a style of a dramatic monologue which was influenced by the blank verse of W. Shakespeare's drama, a kind of baroque style, in dramatic expression through European countries at that time. Therefore John Donne could expressed the delicate emotions between lovers through the baroque imagination:

The dramatic, indeed the theatrical, is perhaps the major constituent of the baroque imagination. (Frank J. Warenke, John Donne, p. 10)

The third is an expression of 'paradox and irony'. According to Brook's opinion, This two words are explained as same meaning. In his book, The Well-Wrought urn: The language of Paradox, Cleanth Brook expresses John Donne's poem,"The Canonization" as a structure of the paradox and irony:

Call us what you will, we are made such by love;

Call her one, me another fly,
We're tapers too, and at our own cost die,
And we in us find the eagle and the dove.
The phoenix riddle hath more wit
By us: we two being one, are it,
So, to one neutral thing both sexes fit,
We die, and rise the same, and prove
Mysterious by this love. (3 stanza, 1-9 line)

We can die by it, if not live by love,
And if unfit for tombs and hearse
Our legend be, it will be fit for verse; (4 stanza, 1-3 line)

The intrinsic metaphor in the above subject already gives us a clue of a sort of the paradox. Because in his poem he imprudently deals a low love as if it were a holy one. So we know that the above third stanza is no longer the threadbare Petrarchan conventionalities; they have sharpness and bite. Furthermore the last one, the likening of the lovers to 'the phoenix', is fully serious, and with it, the tone has shifted from ironic banter into a defiant but controlled tenderness.

What the two lovers is compared to the 'pheonix' is skilfully connected with other two parables, one is that the lovers is regarded as "tapers", the other is as "eagle and dove". And the poet says the phoenix is a bird, and the tapers burns, so this two images skilfully fusing into a kind of paradoxical structure in the poem. Because it makes the contradiction become harmony by means of the creative imagination beyond the science and the commonsense. An explanation on this point, the critic S.T. Coleridge backs up the above:

It(Unity)reveals itself in the balance or reconcilement of opposite or discordant qualities: of sameness, with difference; of the general, with the concrete; the idea, with the image; the individual, with representative; the sense of novelty and freshness, with old and familiar objects; a more than usual state of emotion, with more than usual ... .

Again Cleanth Brooks expresses it with Alexander Pope's lines from "The Essay on Man":

In doubt his Mind or Body to prefer;
Born but to die, and reas'ning but to err;
Alike in ignorance, his Reason such,
Whether he thinks too little, or too much....

Created half to rise, and half to fail;
Great Lord of all things, yet a prey to all;
Sole Judge of Truth, in endless Error hurl'd;
The Glory, Jest, and Riddle of the world!

Above, it is true, the paradoxes insist on the irony, rather than the wonder.

Lots of poems of T.S. Eliot, which are influenced by the symbolic poet, Jules Laforgue, are expressed as a poetic method of 'irony', and he emphasized that it is one of the metaphysicality in the new age:

Laforgue had an innate craving for order:
that is, that every feeling should have its intellectual equivalent, its philosophical justification, and that every idea should its emotional equivalent, its sentimental justification. The only world in which he could have satisfied himself, therefore, was a world such as Dante's. The disintegration of the intellect, in Laforgue, had reached a much more advanced stage than with Donne: for Laforgue, life was consciously divided into thought and feeling; but his feelings were such as required an intellectual completion....and the philosophical systems which he embraced were so much felt as to require a sensuous completion. they did not fit, hence the metaphysicality of Laforgue reaches in two directions: the intellectualising of the feeling and the emotionalising of the idea. Where they meet, they come into conflict, and Laforgue's irony, an irony

always employed against himself, ensues. (The Varieties of Metaphysical Poetry, p. 212-13)

The heroes' self scorn and gloominess from Laforgue's poetry, are expressed in a mocking tone seriously with wearing masks without falling down to completely the world of sadness. That is to say, the heroes in the poetry are divided mentally and the objective self refuses or ridicules the subjective self. We can read many lines in T.S. Eliot's poetry written in the poetic method of 'irony'.(Refer to The Love Song of J. Alfred Prufrock)

3

Since Eliot began a new literary movement, the so-called "modernism", many groups of the literary coteries have appeared to oppose it through this age of postmodernism, that is called "Anti-modernism". The American critic, Delmore Schwartz in his book, The present State of Poetry criticized strongly on Eliot, that our poets had taken walks in a silent park full of the afternoon's sunlight at an agreeable summer, breaking through 'the tomb of thought' decorated by Eliot. Again Schwartz insisted on that the modernism's poetics as the poetics of reason, the revival of unification, the realization of metaphysical semantic system, the pursuit of the closed form based on the presence of Logos or transcendental symbol, only had led a comfortable life to the postwar generations and had not given the real sensibility to the Americans in the age of postmodernism since 1950.

Then considering what is the so-called post-modern sensibility, I think it will be an abnormal rebellious spirit against 'reason and rationality'. So they build up their 'revolution of the word', and there are lots of the literary coteries such as the experimental groups: Olson's "the Black Mountain Group" for projective poetics; Ginsberg and Snyder's "Poets of Beat Group"; Lowell and Roethke's "the Confession Group"; and Ohara and Ashberry's "New York Group"(Harvard graduates), etc.

In conclusion, though lots of poets of post-modern poetics denounce 'the theory of unified sensibility' based on 'the poetics of reason' through their experimental poems, and dissolve the established poetical world, they only debased poetic quality, not breaking bounds of the poetics of modernism or new criticism(J.C. Ransom or Allen Tate). Therefore I dare assert that the only poetic principle based on the metaphysical poetics among many poetic theories has maintained its living power lively even in this post-modernism. (*I ask your consent for not having enough time to explain on the literary subject to you)

Thanks to you all.

■ The Brief Record on the Speaker

*Won Eung-soon(元應淳)
*Born in Seoul, Korea.
*Graduated from Dept. of English Literature, Yonsei Univ.(Degree of B.A. & M.A.)
*Graduated from Graduate School, Sungkyunkwan Univ.(Degree of Ph.D.)
*Lecturer at English Dept. Yonsei Univ., & Prof. of Kyung Hee Univ.
*Exchange Prof. of Yale Univ.
*Recommended as a Poet, 1972.
*Received A Great Prize of Racial Literature of Korea, 2009.
*Present: Poet, Emeritus Prof. of Kyung-Hee Univ., Chief Editor of the Christian Literature(quarterly magazine), Committee of the World Poetry Research Institute.

■ 한국 · 몽골 문학 심포지엄 강연

포스트 모던 시대에 있어서 형이상 시학의 생명력

원 응 순
(시인, 경희대 명예교수, 영문학 박사)

"친애하는 몽골의 시인 여러분, 한국의 세계시문학회에서 활동하시는 시인 여러분, 그리고 내외 귀빈 여러분, 오늘 저녁 두 나라 시인들이 모여서 시문학 세미나를 진지하게 갖게 된 것을 기쁘게 생각하며, 이 자리를 통해 서로의 우의를 다지고 우리들의 시문학 세계가 더욱 발전하는 기회가 되기를 간절히 소망하며, 비록 짧은 강연이지만, 여러 시인들의 내면세계에 깊은 울림이 되었으면 합니다."

1

20세기 초에 영국의 비평가 그리어슨(H.J.C. Grierson)은 형이상학시에 대한 정의를 다음과 같이 내렸다:

형이상학 시는 단테(Dante)의 '신곡', 루크레티우스(Lucretius)의 '자연론'이나 괴테(Goethe)의 '파우스트'처럼, 우주에 관한 철학적인 개념과 위대한 존재의 연극 속에서 인간정신이 해 낼 수 있는 임무에 대한 구상에 의해 영감을 받은 것이다. (17세기 형이상학 서정시 평전, xiii)

Metaphysical poetry, in the full sense of term, is a poetry which, like that of the Divina Commedia, the De natura Rerum, perhaps Goethe's Faust, has been inspired by a philosophical conception of the universe and of the role assigned to the human spirit in the great drama of existence.(Metaphysical lyrics, xiii)

그리고 그리어슨은 다시

형이상학파 시인들의 열정적인 사고는 항상 형이상학적이 되기 쉬우며 체험이 나타나는 곳을 탐색하고 면밀히 조사하게 되는 것이다. 이모든 요소는 존 던의 시에 편재해 있고 그러므로 존 던은 17세기 영시의 대부이다. (위의 책, xvi)

Passionate thinking is always apt to become metaphysical, probing and investigating the experience from which it takes its rise. All these qualities are in the poetry of Donne, and Donne is the greatest master of English poetry in the seventeenth century. (Ibid., xvi)

다시 엘리엇(T. S. Eliot)이 그의 시 이론의 전통성에 바탕한 '체험의 통일성'이라는 감수성의 메커니즘으로써 17세기 영국의 존 던(John Donne) 일파의 소위 '형이상학 시'(Metaphysical Poetry)에서 그의 가장 이상적인 해답을 찾으려고 한 것은 당연한 일이었다. 그리고 이처럼 엘리엇이 존 던의 시에 심취하게 된 동기에 대해 다음과 같이 말하고 있다:

존 던에게 사상은 체험이었다. 그것이 그의 감수성을 수정했다. 시인의 마음이 일을 할 준비가 되면 잡다한 체험이 융합된다. 보통 사람의 체험은 혼란스럽고 불규칙적이고 단편적이다. 반면에 시인이 사랑에 빠지거나 스피노자의 책을 읽을 때 이 두 가지 체험은 서로 관련이 없다. 혹은 타이피스트의 소음이나 요리냄새도 마찬가지이다. 이러한 잡다한 체험들이 시인의 정신 속에서 항상 새로운 전체로 형성된다.(SE, p. 287)

A thought to Donne was an experience; it modified his sensibility. When a poet's mind is perfectly equipped for his work, it is constantly amalgamating disparate experience; the ordinary man's experience is chaotic, irregular, fragmentary. The latter falls in love, or reads Spinoza, and these two experiences have nothing to do with each other, or with the noise of the typewriter or the smell of cooking; in the mind of the poet these experiences are always forming new wholes. (SE, p. 287)

한편 윌리암슨(G. Williamson)은 엘리엇 시를 분석한 책, "엘리엇 시 안내서"(A Reader's Guide to T. S. Eliot)에서 시인이 형이상학 시에 몰두하게 된 이유를 다음과 설명하고 있다:

이 형이상학시의 방법은 혼합된 무두(mood)를 극적인 방법으로 묘사하여 아이러닉한 가면 것은 진지한 감정을 자조하거나 웃음거리로 만든다. 그리고 직관에 의해 조롱당하는 주관성, 현상과 실재 사이에 간격 등, 사물에 대한 반응도 복합적이다. 권태와 공포, 감정의 좌절 혹은, 현대생활의 허풍을 본다. 그것은 희생자들에 대한 연민을 감춘다.(p. 51-52)

This method may be summarized as the assumption of an ironic mask or attitude, mock-heroic in effect and wit, expressing a mixed mood, often by dramatic means. It indulges in self-mockery or ridicules serious feeling; it represents mixed reactions to things, the subjective mocked by the objective, the discrepancy between appearance and reality. It sees boredom and horror, the frustration or derision of latent feeling, the shams of modern life; it dissimulates sympathy for their victims. (Ibid., p. 51-52)

하지만 존 던의 시대의 그의 시에 대한 비평은 그렇지 않았다. 우선 드라이든(John Dryden)나 포우프(Alexander Pope)의 경우를 들면, 드라이든은 존 던의 시작품들은 "보통의 언어로 쓰인 깊은 사상들이지만, 거칠은 운율"(deep thoughts in common language, though rough cadence)이라고 혹평을 하면서, 다시 던은 형이상학을 너무 많이 사용을 하여--- 여성의 마음을 사랑의 감미로움으로 즐겁게 해 주어야 할 때, 지나치게 철학적 사색으로 여성의 마음을 난감하게 만든다 "(Donne too much affects the metaphysics---and perplexes the minds of the fair sex with nice speculations of philosophy, when he should engage their hearts and entertain them with the softness of love. Smith, John Donne, The Critical heritage 1:13)고 했다. 그러나 다시 "우리나라 영

국의 최고의 시인은 아니지만 가장 위대한 기지의 시인"(the greatest wit, though not the best poet of our nation)라고 칭찬도 아끼지 않았다. 포우프도 "던은 기지는 있으나 운율이 없는 시인"라고 드라이든과 같은 견해를 나타냈다.

2

이제 존 던의 시에 나타난 특징들을 잠시 살펴보자. 20세기에 접어들어 먼저 존 던의 연가인 The Songs and Sonnets에 대한 비평서를 먼저 그리어슨이 1921년에, 존 헤이워드(John Heyward)가 1929년에, 그리고 헬른 가드너(Helen Gardner)가 1965년에 각각 내 놓았다.

존 던의 시의 특징들 중 첫 번째 특징은 형이상시의 주요한 특징으로 알려진 '기상'(conceit)이라는 이전 시대의 '페트라르카풍의 시(Petrarchan style poetry)와는 완전히 구별된 작시법을 사용하였다. 먼저 18세기 새뮤얼 존슨(Samuel Johnson)은 형이상학 시인들의 특징을 정확하게 지적했다:

일종의 부조화의 조화, 서로 같지 않는 심상들의 연결, 확실히 상이한 사물 속에 은밀히 숨어있는 유사성을 발견하는 일.

a kind of discordia concors, a combination of dissimilar images, or discovery of occult resemblances in things apparently unlike.

이 평가는 적어도 형이상학 시인들의 기상(conceit)이라는 외형적 특징을 정확하게 표현했다. 가드너(H. Gardner)는 이 '기상'이라는 시적 비유를 다음과 같이 설명했다:

기상이란 정확성보다는 재능이 더 돋보이거나, 최소한 보다 더 직접적으로 뚜렷하게 눈에 띠는 비유(사물간의 비교)인 것이다. 모든 비유는 닮지 않은 사물들 간의 유사성을 발견하고, 우리가 그 닮지 않은 것들을 강하게 의식하면서도 그 유사성을 시인하게 될 때 기상(conceit)이 이루어진다.(형이상학 시인들, p.15)

A conceit is a comparison whose ingenuity is more striking that its justness, or at least, is more immediately striking. All comparisons discover likeness in things unlike: a comparison becomes a conceit when we are made to concede likeness while being strongly conscious of unlikeness.(Metaphsical Poets, p.15)

엘리엇은 이 같은 컨시트(conceit)의 시법을 '객관적 상관물'(objective correlative) 이론으로 설명했다. 그는 18세기와 19세기를 거치면서 영시는 심하게 감수성의 분열을 일으켜 돌이킬 수 없게 되었다고 보고 시의 본질은 감정의 해방이 아니라, 감정이나 정서로부터 도피라고 주장하면서 시는 사상이나 정서를 생경하게 그대로 나타낼 수 없으므로 그 사상이나 정서에 상응하는 등가의 사물의 이미지나 장면을 찾아 표현해야 한다고 '전통과 개인의 재능'( )에서 주장했는데, 이 시법은 '기상'(conceit)의 시법과 동일한 것이다.

존 던의 다음의 시 '고별사: 슬픔을 금하며'(Valediction: Forbidding Mourning)을 살펴보자:

우리 두 영혼은 그러므로 하나여서
  비록 나는 가야하지만, 단절이
아니라 확장을 겪은 다오,
  공기처럼 가늘게 쳐 늘인 금박처럼.

만일 우리 영혼이 둘이라면, 둘이라오,
  마치 뻣뻣한 콤파스 다리가 둘인 것처럼,
당신의 영혼은 고정된 다리여서, 움직일 기색도
  안 보이지만, 다른 다리가 움직이면 움직인 다오. (슬픔을 금하며, 6-7연)

If two souls therefore, which are one,
  Though I must go, endure not yet
A breach, but an expansion,
  Like gold to airy thinness beat.

If they be two, they are two so
As stiff twin compasses are two:
Thy soul, the fixed foot, makes no show
To move, but doth, if the other do; (Forbidding Mourning, 6-7stanza)

위의 시에서 이별은 단절(breach)을 나타낸다. 그러나 진실하게 사랑하는 연인들의 관계는 분리나 단절이 있을 수 없다는 역설이, 곧 둘이 아닌 한 몸을 쪼개어 나누는 것이 아니라, 마치 공기처럼 가늘게 쳐서 늘리는 금박이라는 비유라든가(Though I must go, endure not yet/ A breach, but an expansion/ Like gold to airy thinness beat), 두 연인의 이별의 관계를 콤파스의 두 다리라는 놀라운 이미지(If they be two, they are two so/ As stiff twin compasses are two)로 표현하는 비유법은 'conceit'의 좋은 예라 할 수 있다.

두 번째 특징은 '극적 대화체' 형식이다. 이 시풍은 물론 엘리자베스조朝에 무운시(Blank verse)로 된 셰익스피어의 드라마(Shakespearian Drama)의 영향을 받은 것으로, 당시 유럽에서 풍미한 일종의 바로크(baroque)풍의 극적 표현양식이다. 존 던은 이 같은 바로크풍의 상상력을 통해 연인간의 사랑의 미묘한 감정의 변화를 표현할 수 있었다.(The dramatic, indeed the theatrical, is perhaps the major constituent of the baroque imagination. Frank J. Warnke, John Donne, p. 10)

세 번째 특징은 '역설'(paradox)과 '아이러니'(irony)의 표현이다. 브룩스(C. Brooks)의 견해를 따르면, 역설과 아이러니를 동일한 의미로 해석하고 있음을 본다. 그는 그의 '역설의 언어' The Well-Wrought Urn: The language of Paradox)에서 존 던의 시 '시성諡聖 "The Canonization"를 역설과 아이러니의 구조로 설명하고 있다:

우리를 그대들 마음대로 부르시오, 사랑으로 이렇게 되었으니;
그녀를 한 마리의 날 파리라고, 나 또한 그것이라고 부르시오.
우리는 촛불이어서, 우리 스스로 태워 비용을 치르며 죽는다오.
그리하여 우리 속에는 독수리와 비둘기가 들어있고,

불사조의 수수께끼는 우리로 인해
더욱 의미를 갖는다오; 하나이며 둘인 우리가 바로 그것이므로,
그러니 우리 양성은 중성이 되고,
우리는 죽어서 같은 것으로 부활하여, 이 사랑으로
신비스러운 것으로 판명된다오.(3연 1-9행)

우리는 사랑으로 살 수는 없어도 죽을 수는 있소.
우리의 사랑의 이야기가 비명이나
명정銘旌거리는 못되어도, 시에는 어울리리라;(4연 1-3행)

Call us what you will, we are made such by love;
Call her one, me another fly,
We're tapers too, and at our own cost die,
And we in us find the eagle and the dove.
The phoenix riddle hath more wit
By us: we two being one, are it,
So, to one neutral thing both sexes fit,
We die, and rise the same, and prove
Mysterious by this love. (3 stanza, 1-9 line)

We can die by it, if not live by love,
And if unfit for tombs and hearse
Our legend be, it will be fit for verse; (4 stanza, 1-3 line)

위 시의 제목에 내재해 있는 메타포(metaphor)에서도 이미 반영하고 있지만, 이미 일종의 역설을 암시하고 있다. 왜냐하면 시인은 뻔뻔스럽게도 비속한 사랑을 마치 성스러운 사랑인 것처럼 다루고 있기 때문이다. 위의 시의 비유는 더 이상 페트라르크풍(Petrarchan style)의 진부한 시법에서는 볼 수 없는 예리함과 통렬함이 스며있다. 더욱이 연인들을 불사조(phoenix)에 비유하는 마지막 이미지는 매우 심각할 정도이다.

두 연인을 '불사조'에 비유하는 것은 그 이전에 두 개의 다른 비유

와 교묘하게 관계된다. 즉 하나는 연인을 촛불(tapers)로 보는 것이고, 다른 하나는 연인들을 독수리(eagle)와 비들기(dove)로 보는 것이다. 그리고 다시 '불사조'는 '새'라는 것이고, '촛불'은 '탄다'는 것으로 두 이미지는 교묘하게 융합하여 다시 살아나는 역설의 구조를 형성하게 되는 것이다. 이처럼 이는 두 가지 요소를 창조적인 상상력이 작용하는 결합의 한 메타포로 역설의 언어를 사용하는데 성공하고 있다 이 것은 과학과 상식을 초월하여 부조화의 모순을 동시에 결합하고 있기 때문이다. 영국의 낭만주의 비평가이며 시인인 콜리지(S.T. Coleridge)의 설명이 이를 뒤받침하고 있는 것이다:

서로 반대되거나 모순되는 성격의 균형 또는 융합 속에서 제 모습을 드러내는 것이다. 즉 서로 이지적인 동시에 동질적이며, 구체적인 동시에 일반적이며, 이미지인 동시에 관념이며, 개체이면서 전형적인, 오랫동안 익숙한 동시에 새롭고 신기한 지각이며, 일상적 질서 이상의 것인 동시에 일상적 정서 이상의 것이다.

It(Unity) reveals itself in the balance or reconcilement of opposite or discordant qualities: of sameness, with difference; of the general, with the concrete; the idea, with the image; the individual, with the representative; the sense of novelty and freshness, with old and familiar objects; a more than usual state of emotion, with more than usual....

브룩스(C. Brooks)는 다시 포우프(Alexander Pope) 시인의 '인간론'(Essay on Man)을 역설(paradox)의 구조를 갖고 있는 시로서 오히려 아이로니(irony)를 강조하고 있다고 설명한다:

인간의 마음을 택할까 육체를 택할까 망설이며,
태어나지만 죽고, 합리적 사고를 하지만 오류에 빠진다.
그의 이성이 이 정도니, 너무 적게 생각하거나
너무 많이 생각하거나, 무지하기는 매한가지...

일어났다가 넘어지게 창조되었고,
만물의 영장이면서, 만물의 제물.
진리의 유일한 재판관이면서, 끊임없는 오류 속에 내 던져지니,

세상의 영광이요, 웃음거리요, 수수께끼로다!

In doubt his mind or body to prefer;
Born but to die, and reasoning but to err;
Alike in ignorance, his Reason such,
Whether he thinks too little, or too much....

Created half to rise, and half to fall;
Great Lord of all things, yet a Prey to all;
Sole Judge of Truth, in endless Error hur'ld;
The Glory, Jest, and Riddle of the world!

프랑스 상징주의 시인, 줄 라포르그(Jules Laforgue)의 영향을 받은 시인 엘리엇(T.S. Eliot)은 그의 대부분의 시는 아이러니(irony)로 나타나는 것으로, 새로운 시대의 형이상성(metaphysicality)이라고 강조하였다:

라포르그(Jules Laforgue)는 질서에 대한 선천적 갈망을 가지고 있었다. 다시 말하면, 그 모든 갈망이 그것의 지적 등가물과 철학적 정당화를 가져야 하고 모든 생각이 그것의 정서적 등가물과 감정적 정당화를 지녀야 한다는 것이다. 따라서 그가 스스로 만족할 수 있는 유일한 세계는 단테와 같은 것이었을 것이다. 라포르그에 있어서 지성의 분열(disintegration of the intellect)은 존 던 보다 훨씬 더 진행된 단계에 와 있었다. 그의 경우에 삶은 의식적으로 사상과 감정으로 나뉘어져 있었다. 그러나 그의 감정은 지적 완성을 요구하는 그런 것이었고.... 그가 품었던 철학세계는 감각적 완성을 요구할 정도로 느껴지는 것이었다. 그 사상과 감정은 어울리지 않았다. 따라서 라포르그의 형이상성形而上性은 감정의 지성화知性化와 관념의 정서화情緖化라는 두 가지 방향에 이르게 된다. 그들은 서로 만나는 곳에서 충돌을 일으키고 여기서 라포르그의 아이러니(irony), 항상 자신에게 역방향으로 작용하는 아이러니가 발생한다. (형이상시의 다양성, 212-13)

Laforgue had an innate craving for order: that is, that every feeling should have its intellectual equivalent, its philosophical justification, and that every idea should its emotional equivalent, its sentimental justification. The only world in which he could have satisfied himself, therefore, was a world such as Dante's. The disintegration of the intellect, in Laforgue, had reached a much more advanced stage than with Donne: for Laforgue, life was consciously divided into thought and feeling; but his feelings were such as required an intellectual completion....and the philosophical systems which he embraced were so much felt as to require a sensuous completion. They did not fit. Hence the metaphysicality of Laforgue reaches in two directions: the intellectualising of the feeling and the emotionalising of the idea. Where they meet, they come into conflict, and Laforgue's irony, an irony always employed against himself, ensues. (The Varieties of Metaphysical Poetry, p. 212-13)

라포르그의 대부분의 시의 주인공들은 자조와 우울이 완전한 비애의 세계로 떨어짐 없이 가면을 쓴 채 진지한 감정을 희롱조로 표현하는 아이러니의 수법이 많이 나타나고 있음을 볼 수 있다. 다시 말하면, 시 속의 주인공이 심리적으로 분리되어 객관적 자아가 주관적 자아를 부정하거나 희롱하는 그런 수법을 사용되는 특징을 갖고 있는 것이다(T.S. Eliot: 프루프록이 연가, The Love Song of J. Alfred Prufrock 참조)

3

엘리엇 이후 소위 포스트모더니즘(postmodernism) 시대를 거치면서 여러 시인들의 동인 구룹들이 나타나 반 모더니즘(Anti-Modernism) 운동을 전개하게 되었다. 이 시대의 문학정신을 델모어 슈와르츠(Delmore Schwartz)는 그의 '시의 현재의 정신상태'(The Present State of Poetry)라는 글의 표현대로, 엘리엇(T.S. Eliot) 등이 장식해 놓은 '생각의 무덤' 속으로 새어드는 "쾌적한 한 여름 오후의 햇살이 가득한 한가로운 공원에서 산책하고 있었다"고 평하고, 다시 그는 엘리엇의 모더니즘 시학은 이성시학理性詩學으로, '통합의 재현, 형이상적 의미체계의 구현, 닫힌 형식의 추구, 로고스의 존재와 초월적 상징 과

해석 등을 바탕으로 하는 시학으로서 전후세대들을 안주시켰을 뿐, 1950년대 이후 미국시의 포스트모더니즘 시대의 미국인들의 진정한 감수성을 담아내지 못했다고 주장했다.

그러면 포스트모던적 감수성의 출발은 무엇일까 고려해 보면, 아마도 '이성과 합리성'에 대한 병적인 반항심리가 아닐까 합니다. 이들은 소위 '말의 혁명'(revolution of the word)을 전개해 나갔는데, 이 시대에 나타난 동인들의 시론그룹들은 실험적인 성격을 띤 것으로, 올슨(Charles Olson) 중심의 '투사 시론'(projective poetics)을 주장하는 '블랙마운틴 그룹 시인들', 알랜 긴즈버그(Allen Ginsberg)와 게리 슈나이더(Gary Snyder) 중심의 '비트파 시인들', 로월(R. Lowell)뢰트키(T. Roethke)의 '고백파 이인들', 그리고 오하라(Frank O'Hara)나 애쉬베리(John Ashberry)이 중심이 된 '뉴욕파 시인들(하버드 대학 출신 시인들) 등이었다.

결론적으로 아직도 이 포스트모던 시대의 여러 시인들이 실험 시들을 통해 '통합시론'을 바탕으로 하는 형이상시론을 소위 '이성시학'으로 매도하고 해체시키지만, 모더니즘 시학이나 신비평 시학원리(랜섬 J.C. Ransom, 이나 앨런 테이트 Allen Tate 중심의)를 넘어서지 못한 채 시의 질적 저하를 초래하게 되었다. 따라서 본인은 지금까지 나타난 수많은 시론이나 시작법들 중심에 흔들림 없이 오랜 세기를 견디고 지속적으로 굳건히 그 생명력을 활발하게 나타내고 있는 것이 존 던의 형이상학 시학의 원리라고 감히 주장하는 바이다. 따라서 오늘 우리 시인들은 이 형이상 시학원리를 보다 더 발전적으로 연구하여 확산시켜 나가야 하는 것이 우리 시인들의 한 의무이고 사명이라고 생각합니다. (본 주제 강연이 20분이라는 시간제약으로 충분하지 못한 점 양해를 구합니다) 감사합니다.

■ 참고문헌

* Brooks, Cleanth, The Well Wrought Urn: in the Structure of Poetry, New York, 1971.
* Clements, A. L. ed. John Donne's Poetry, New York: W.W. Norton. 1966.
* Grierson, H. J. C. ed. Metaphysical Lyrics and Poems of the Seventeenth Century. Oxford, Clarendon Press, 1958.
* Eliot, T. S. The Varieties of Metaphysical Poetry, Faber and Faber, 1993.
  ______, Selected Essays. London: Faber and Faber, 1980.
* Gardner, Helen, ed. The Metaphysical Poets. new York: Penguin, 1982.
* Mahood, M. M., Poetry and Humanism, New Haven: Yale University Press, 1950.
* Redpath, Theodore. The Songs and Sonnets of John Donne, London: Methuen, 1956.
* Ransom, John Crowe, The new Criticism, New York, 1941.
* Richards, I. A., Principles of Literary Criticism, London, 1924.
* Simpson, E. M., ed. John Donne: Essays in Divinity, Oxford, The Clarendon Press, 1952.
* Tate, Allen, On the Limits of Poetry: Selected Essays, 1928-48, new York, 1948.

* 강연자 약력

* 원응순(元應淳) Won, Eung-soon
* 연세대학교 영문과 졸업(B.A. 및 M.A. 학위)
* 성균관대학교 대학원 영문학 전공(Ph.D. 박사학위)
* 연세대학교 영문과 강사, 청주대학교 영문과 조교수
* Yale 대학교 교환교수
* 경희대학교 영문과 교수, 학생처장, 외국어대학 학장 역임
* 논문 및 저서: John Donne 시에 나타난 Caritas 연구 외, 현대 영미시 및 작가 연구, 번역서 다수
* 한국민족문학대상 수상(번역문학부문)
* 현재: 시인, 경희대 명예교수, 한국 크리스천 문학 편집주간, 한국 형이상 시회 편집위원, 세계시문학회 상임이사 및 번역위원, 서울 동숭교회 장로.

HORAS AUSENTES

Las horas que se van
son como los sueños
que para siempre vanamente se agotan.

Las horas que ya nunca estarán
son como esas espigas quebradas
ya para siempre por el viento.

Y solamente en este bosque espectral
una voz del pasado;
amada voz, amada ilusión,
podría rescatarte
de tan vano presente.

ENRIQUE OSORIO BELTRAN / Colombia

*Born in Bogota, Colombia, in 1958.
*Writer, Poet, Philosopher and Astronomer.
*Member of several international associations.
*His poems are in several anthologies of many countries.
*Received 3 st. Prize, XII Concurso de Poesia "El paisaje", Aranguren, Vizcaya, Spain, 1983; 1 st.Prize, Concurso Poetico "Nirvana Populi", Segovia, Spain, 1983. Titles: Titular Academico, Vizcaya, Sapin, 1978; Academico Benemerito ad Honorem, Felgueiras, Portugal, 1981; Honorary Appointment to "The research Board of advisors, 1999, American Biographical Institute, USA. President for Colombia of World Poetry Research Institute of Korea.
*Address: Calle 131 #45-55 BOGOTA, D.C., COLOMBIA
* Tel: (57) (1) 258 01 84 / H.P.(Celular): 3204764752
*E-mail: enosbe@hotmail.com

QUIMERAS Y FANTASMAS

Todo cuanto construimos para el futuro,
que es una quimera,
halla sus cimientos en el pasado,
que es un fantasma.
Y como ni el uno ni el otro
existen más allá de lo mental,
la única realidad posible
es la del brevísimo presente,
el cual no es más
que esa impetuosa corriente
que se establece,
desde que el ser es Ser,
en el espacio-tiempo
entre lo quimérico y lo fantasmal.

BUSQUEDA

¿ De quién es aquella voz
que entre náyades entumecidas
canta y canta;
voz hechizada de silencios
cual espejos rotos
sobre caderas en pleamar?

Toda búsqueda es causa
de sí misma,
y todo dolor procede
de la indagación errática
en una playa rocosa y sie arena.....

SORTILEGIO

¿ Queda algún rumor?
En ese silencio de la noche,
profundo vuelo indetenible
del alma, aún hay planicie?
¿ Qué nos queda
luego de perder el rumbo
entre las algas del dolor?
¿ Acaso la penumbra es sol?
¿ Quién ha visto a la mariposa
desnuda o al viento sin pasión?
El círculo se cierra
y en torno al fuego
alguien danza y despetala muertos.
La hora es fecunda
en hadas de sortílego traje
que se esfuman tan rápido
como aparecen sobre
la mohosa superficie del tiempo.
Entonces, ¿ todavía queda un espacio
para desnudar el no vivir?

The Season's Face

The winter, the end of seasons,
Hiding its face sticking out slightly
Between the heavy overcoat,
Inhabits together with intimate spring
Exposed its inside flesh lightly.

With a light green colored weakness
It changes into a freshness,
And the firm life
Is wiggling from within.

If the wind becomes good friend,
A southern news in its arms,
To the place where the northern wind is driven,
They exult over it
By an exciting gesture,

The nutritious elements into soil
Received from the sunbeams in the air
And united together as one,
We would like to be a mature summer
With a face of new nativity.

- Tr. by Won Eung-soon

Ahn Byung-don/Korea

* A poet, essayist
* A professor at Shinsung Univ.
* A director of Taechon Educational Culture Foundation (a body corporate).
* A director of the Korea Administration Institution (a body corporate).

계절의 얼굴

끝자락 계절의 겨울
두꺼운 외투 사이로
뾰족이 내민 얼굴 숨길까
속살 살짝 드러낸
친근한 봄

연두색 연약함으로
청순한 옷 갈아입고
안으려 알찬 삶이
꿈틀대고 있다.

북풍 몰아낸 자리로
남쪽 소식 안고
바람이 친구 되면
흥겨운 몸짓으로
신이 나고

하늘의 빛살 받아
땅속의 자양분이
하나로 함께하니
새로운 탄생의 얼굴
성숙의 여름 되고파라.

I Confess An Ignoramus

My ignoramus
I am not ashamed of much,
Thinking it as the pain of our Time.

It would have gone well with me
To do a little slowly, asking it
When I am illiterate.

One day,
I realized it(ignoramus) sad
After my kith and kin left home all.

My age, being 50 years old plus 20 years,
I learn to write our basic alphabet
Regarding a pencil as a weeding hoe,
And a notebook as a rows in the field.

Supposing at the bank window
To save for myself,
And to decode a written notice for payment of tax,

I hear my heart
Beating 'Plumps'
From my weak and fragile body.

- Tr. by Won Eung-soon

Bae Young-suk/Korea

* Born in Sooncheon, Jeonnam.
* The manager of Soonchеon branch office, A teacher at Kwangyang middle school.
* Published two Poetical Anthologies: 'The Poor Seoul', 'Yearning is Hanging down from White Cotton Curtain'
* baenara@hanmail.net * -http://blog.daum.net/baenara

까막눈을 고백하다

까막눈을
시대의 아픔이라 여기며
많이 부끄러워하지 않았다

모르면 모른 대로
물어가면서
조금 천천히 가면 될 일이었다

어느 날 살붙이가 모두
집을 떠나고서야
까막눈이 슬퍼졌다

내 나이 쉰하고 스물
호미를 연필 삼고
밭이랑을 공책 삼아
가갸거겨를 쓴다

은행창구에서
입출금을 하고
고지서를 해독할 날을
생각하니

푸석푸석한 몸에서
쿵쾅쿵쾅
심장 뛰는 소리가 난다.

A Forest Path of Acacia Flower

While we are living for a week,
As if forgot all entirely,
Pictures blocking the front of us blankly,

Opening vernal path,
The white flowers, depicting in space, overflow at every branch.

The coldest year, sprouted from its deep bosom
Makes the sea of green waves,
Pouring out its green memory,

When the white flowers sway and scatter in the sky
Designing patterns silently,
Being tossed about by the soft wind,
The wood's breathing becomes hot and emit fragrance in a mountain pass.

The living things, hungering for its fragrance
Move busily for a day of the forest path.

- Tr. by Won Eung-soon

Baek Bong-ki/Korea

* Manager of the Central council of agricultural cooperated association in Gochang District.
* Address : 103, 116dong, Hyundae apt, ajung-ri, Inhu1-dong, Deokjin-gu, Jeonju-si, Jeon-buk, 561-781, Korea.

아카시아 숲길

일주일을 살다 보면
까맣게 잊은 듯
무표정으로 앞을 가로막는 그림들,

봄날의 길 열며 허공에 그려진 하얀 꽃이
가지마다 넘친다

깊은 품속에서 돋아난 혹한의 세월은
푸른 기억을 쏟아내 초록 물결 넘치는
바다를 이루고

숨결 부드러운 바람에 밀려
하얀 꽃이 하늘에 그린 문양들 소리 없이
흔들이다가 흩어질 때
숲의 숨결은 뜨거워지고 산길에 번지는 향기

아카시아 향기 따라 허기를 채우려는 생명들
숲길의 하루가 분주하다.

Father's Camellia Tree

In the white garden of father's house
I planted one camellia tree and came,
Which would laugh and weep longer than I.

The dream tree of that day, growing in my heart,
And on the empty place that all left,
Lying down on the sky's roof alone
How a couple of years, or some years have I passed?

The hot hand as soon as I crossed over the hill,
Ran out faster than father,
Dyeing with gloaming in the smiling flower's bud,
So I portrayed a face that I wished to do,
I touched, and held it in my arms.

Embracing a sadly falling blossom,
In my hot breast,
I opened the heaven's door and buried it.

- Tr. by Won Eung-soon

Baek Deok-sun / Korea

* Born at Yeosu, Jeonnam, Korea.
* Made her debut as a poet in the monthly magazine "Han-Maek Literature", 2004.
* A Member of Writers' Association of Korea; of Progress Forum of Korean Literature; of Korean Writers of the Mountain; of "Sungnam Tancheon Literature"; and of Reciting Poetry Club; of Screen Reciting "The River of Lit."
* An Auditor of the U-dang Literary Society.
* A Committee of the Han-Maek Literary Society, of the Kang-Seo Literary Society, and of the Buddhist Literature.
* The 25 vol. of Joint Poetical Works of Poet' s Town.

아버지의 동백

아버지의 집 하얀 정원에
나보다 오래 웃고 울어줄
동백나무 한 그루 심어두고 왔어요

가슴에 놀던 그날의 꿈나무
모두 떠나버린 빈자리
하늘 지붕 아래 홀로 누워
한 해 두 해 몇 해가 지났는가

재 넘어서자 뜨거운 손길
아버지보다 먼저 달려나와
벙글거리는 꽃망울 속에
황혼빛으로 물들어 가는
보고 싶은 얼굴 하나 그려넣고
만져보고 안아보고 했어요

서럽게 떨어지는 꽃송이
붉어진 가슴 안에 품고 와
하늘 문 열고 묻어 두었어요.

A Silkworm's Life

A silkworm takes a meal(mulberry leaves) giving from nature,
Grows and is awakened from second sleep after first sleep,
His life draws near to an end,
And has to set the burden down
From his moment's journey.

He ceases to have taken the leaves
To preserve his species,
And wraps his body incessantly with spinning threads.
The seeds of his species come out the bud
Fluttering his wings.

And again for keeping the seeds
He opens the door looking outside the world,
Scattering on them the soft soil
And passes away into the fog silently.

- Tr. by Won Eung-soon

Bang Jung-sun/Korea

* Awarded new-poet prize from monthly "Literature and Arts" in 2001.
* Member of the World Poetry Research Institute.
* Address: 360, jaryong-ri, Sangha-myeon, Gochang-gun, Jeonbuk,
585-910, Korea
Tel: 010-6770-0481

누에의 일생

자연에서 나오는 밥을 먹고
자라며 한잠 두잠에 깨어나며
일생의 끝자락은 가까워지고
세월이 길지 않은
여정의 짐을 내려야 한다

종족의 보존을 위해
먹던 밥을 멈추고
시지 않고 풀어내는 실타래 속에
몸을 감싸 안고 날갯짓에
종족의 씨앗이 싹을 튼다.

그 씨앗을 보존키 위해
문을 열고 세상 밖을 보며
씨앗위에 고운 흙 뿌려 주고
말없이 안개 속으로 사라진다.

Red Maple Leaves at Yongmiri

Here the souls slumbered together
Upon some affairs left unsaid

The tree might have grown
Eating the tears shed by mountaineers

Beloved son died young
The bereaved Mother's distressed heart
Has soaked through the tree

Even now it is spring time,
The maple leaves are unusually red.

- Tr. by Choe Hong-kyu

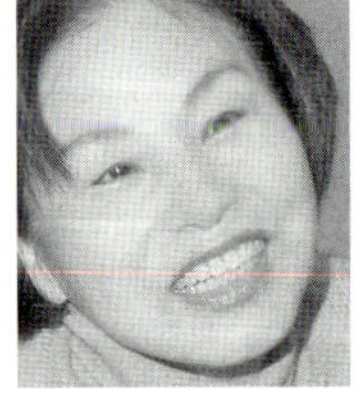

Bark Il-so/Korea

* Awarded a prize for a budding writer from the recommended writer's association
* A member of Korean Writers' Association
* Published joint literary work entitled 'In Autumn, I Want to like the tree'
* Poetic Anthology: The Mind's Mirror under the Flowers; A Letter Sending to Heaven; The Love of Young Years Blooming as An Aquarelle
* Address: 603, 101 dong, Jugong Apt, wolgye 2-dong, nowon-gu, Seoul, Korea
* Tel : H.P 011-9833-3154 * E-mail: barkiso@hanmail.net

용미리 붉은 단풍

못다 한 사연 두고
잠든 영혼들의 마음이 모여서일까

여러 산사람이 쏟고 간
눈물을 먹고 자라서일까

청춘에 잠든 아들
어미의 애타는 마음이
그곳에 스민 때문일까

봄인데도 용미리 단풍은
유난히 붉다

The Rose of May

Who said
That the rose is a seasonable queen!
You, looking abashed
Are the girl's adolescence of 18 years old.

Still pining for him,
But not convey her message,
Only bearing it deeply in mind,
She has thorns in heart,
The heart, dyed in red color
The moments
Worrying herself,

At last they are changed into hate,
Turning sulky and pushing them out,
O, unforgettable yearning!

Screwing up her courage again,
Thrusting out her slender neck over the wall,
O, longing, longing!
Being choked in heart.

Tr. by Won Eung-soon

Cho Keum-ja/Korea

* Started literary career through "literary movement & Trend" in 2005.
* Received the first prize at a prize contest for woman essay writer that seohai broad casting superintend.
* President of jeonbuk woman's tennis club
* Member of the world poetry research institute
* Member of the Balya literary club
* Chairman of Industrial Construction at Gochang County Assembly.
* Address: 191-15, Eupnae-ri, Gochang-eup, Gochang-gun, Jeon-buk, 585-807, Korea.

오월의 장미

계절의 여왕이라
누가 말했나!
수줍은 듯 들여다 보이는 그대는
열여덟 소녀의 사춘기 모습

그리워하면서도
전하지 못하고
가슴속 깊이 새기려니
가시가 돋고
빠-알갛게 물든 가슴
속만 태우는
순간순간들

마침내 미움 되어 밀어내고
토라져 봐도 파고드는
그리움이여

용기 내어 다시금
담장 너머로
가녀린 목을 내밀어 보지만
가슴을 찌르는
그리움! 그리움!

A Meeting on May

The May
Of the filial duty came.
Very happy
My love is enough to be brimful.

Looking at the window,
Now and then, I am so sick as yearning for you.
Buddha's eyes give a candle and a lotus
And carry Spring on a green frog's back.

The color's festival,
The morning sun scatters dust
And opens onset of Spring's blessing.

All things in the universe
Go to draw water on the cloud to Ilkwang temple.
It paints a quadrangle heart with pure paint,
That is the grimy world,
It vomits Chilbo mountain with a true devotion.
This is a "karma" with an uncle,
That means Buddha's love.

- Tr. by Won Eung-soon

Cho Ki-hyun/Korea

* Majored in Painting, at College of Fine Arts, Seoul National University.
* Retired from Middle & High School as a Principal.
* Prizes of Han Mak Literature, The Literary Trend, The Space of Literature, and The World Poetry Research Institute.
* Now A Critic, Poet, Essayist, Painter, and A Dancer.
* Address: 102, 5-dong, Hanjung villa, Chunchun-ri, Maesong-myeon, Whasong-si, Gyeonggi-do, Korea.

5월의 만남

5월
효도孝道가 왔다
반갑구나
내 사랑 가득하여라

창을 보고 이따금 그리워서 앓는다
부처의 눈 촛불과 연꽃을 주고
청개구리 등에 봄을 태우고 간다

색동 축제
아침 해는 흙을 뿌리고
입춘대길立春大吉을 연다

만유萬裕가 일광사로 구름 타고
물 길러 간다
때 묻은 세상 순결한 페인트로
사각형의 가슴을 칠하고
산도라지 정성으로 칠보산을 쏟아낸다
삼촌三寸과의 인연 불심이란다.

The Sad Dream

Suddenly
I look down the trodden ground.
As if it may be so many karmas(fate),
It is implanted as a shadowless seed,
Whirling space and fading away,

How can I help it, even if it was to come?
All of a sudden
When the lapse of time passed far off in its quick pace,
As if it recognized its vanishing shape,
It went away with leaving behind.

Fire of spirit to flow like falling star
In the sky brimful to be emptied
Erased its footmark according to the path of retreat
Tamed to the earth's revolution
By shrieks leaning as if it is turned upside down,

The clear sky
Is wide for a noble rumination,
But its hearing
Dies far away
Along the river carrying troubles of the world.

- Tr. by Won Eung-soon

Choi Byeong-ryun/Korea

* A member of Jeongeup literary club
* A member of jeonbuk writer's club
* A director of Baikya Literary men club
* A member of the World Poetry Research Institute
* Started literary carrier (poet) through "Literary Movement & Trend" in 2009
* president of jeongeup branch of Lions Club
* President of jeoneup agent of Hyundai marine insurance
* An adviser of the jeong-eup City Federation for Environmental Movement

비몽悲夢

홀연히
디딘 땅을 굽어본다
하 많은 연緣이련만
무영無影의 종자로 심어져
공空을 맴돌다 저버리다니

아니 옴만 못한들 어쩌랴
불현듯
세월은 바쁜 걸음으로 멀어지며
이지러지는 형체를 인식한 듯
그냥 두고 간걸

비어 가득한 창공에
유성처럼 흘러갈 혼불
공전空轉에 길들여진 퇴로를 따라
엎질러지듯 기우는 비명으로
발자국을 지우고

맑은 하늘은
고매한 새김을 위하여 넓건만
들림은
풍진을 나르는 강 따라
아득히 멀어지네

Dance of An Empty Space

The blue sky took off her clothes.
So aching beautiful figure,
Her purity,
With the beauty, she tempts me.

But
I
Can't meet her.

When I stand around you,
Giving up all secular desires,

You
Already
Would have gone far away to be a wind,
Like a bird of passage flying with a poor love,
Dancing a dance of empty space,
Meeting a lotus flower and going back.

- Tr. by Won Eung-soon

Choi Yong-kwang/Korea

* Born at Gangnung, Gangwondo, Korea.
* First debut as a poet and a critic from the Literary Movement and Trend.
* Teacher of National Language at Sudo Girls' High School Teacher.
* Chairman of the Literary Coterie of the Korean Poets.
* Member of the Korean Writers' Association.

허공의 춤

파란 하늘이 옷을 벗었다.
시리도록 고운 몸매
순수
그 아름다움으로 유혹한다.

그래도
난
만날 수가 없다.

세속의 욕망 다 버리고
그대 곁에 설 때쯤

그대
벌써
가난한 사랑을 안고 가는 철새처럼
허공의 춤을 추며
연꽃 만나고 가는 바람 되어
멀리 가고 없을 테니……

The Hovering Afternoon

The autumn grasses
Are warmed up
In the afternoon's sunbeam.

The late dragonfly
Is arranging its last day,
Dozing at the smell of dry perilla's stalks.

The wind
Shakes the autumn grass's stalks leisurely.

Did the singing birds at yard
Leave for anywhere
Preparing themselves for a journey?

At the age
The gray hairs always getting caught by the hands,

In the afternoon
The autumn rambles about.

- Tr. by Won Eung-soon

Choi Yun-seon/Korea

* Member of the Poetic Circle "Geul-Saem"
* Member of the Literary Association at Yangpyung
* Won a Prize of the Poetry Contest for Women's Arts of Kyeonggi-do(2012)

서성거리는 오후

가을 풀들이
오후 햇살에
데이고 있다

때늦은 잠자리
마른 들깻대 향내에 졸며
마지막 날을 정리하고 있다

바람이 한가로이
가을 풀대를 흔들고 있다

마당가에 조잘거리던 새들은
행장을 차리고 어디로들
떠난 것일까

흰 머리칼 자꾸
손에 잡히는 나이에

가을이
서성거리는 오후에

Flower and Life

The flower doesn’t select the soil
And lay blame on the sunshines and natural features.

The flower controls itself
By nature with its nature.

Its true shapes are the crooked backs
And the delicate palm of hands,
Even if they look as unexpectedly so small,
Which they stick their roots
More to the crevice of sloping rocks.

Choung Song-jun/Korea

*Born at Uijeongboo, Geonggido, Korea.
*Graduated from Dept. of Jungang Univ. & the Graduate School of Jungang Univ..
*Retired as a Principal of Jukjeon Middle School, Yongin, Geonggido.
*Recommended as a poet from the magazine, "Poetry and Poetics", 1962.
*Taught as a Professor of Han-Ra Univ..
*Taught as a Inviting Professor of Keonggi Univ..
*Representative Prof. of 'Gwangju Literary Art Collete'.
*Served as a Chairman of 'the Gwangju Forum', Geonggido.
*A Member of the Literary Men's Association of Korea.
*A Director of Freedom Poets Association of Korea.
*A Central Committee of the Modern Literary Association.
*Won the 'Great' Prize from "the Literary Movement & Trend ", (1998).
*Won the 'Original' Prize from the Freedom Poets Association, (2000).
*Poetic Anthology: <The Weight of Longing>, <The Silence of Wind>, <The Flower and The Wind>, <Drawing a Sound of Light>, <Living As What I am>, <Repetition of Longing and Love>, <The Wave of Nature and Universe>, <A Vortex of my Life>, and <The By-Road of My Life>.

The flower follows like a shadow
And only changes its generic character.

Don't say it has no new thing,
Even if all things have spent quietly
Breathe hard or weakly so as to be stifled,
Indeed, don't insist they aren't new ones.

Laying down obliquely with its shadow on,
The flower takes the smell of winds,
I and the sky leave its dewdrops behind.

The flower is always as it is.
It doesn't lay blame on either.
It only has its looks as it is.

- Tr. by Won Eung-soon

꽃과 삶

꽃은 토양을 가리지 않고
일조권이나 기후 풍토를 탓하지 않는다.

꽃은 본디 심성으로
스스로 조절한다.

비탈진 바위 틈새에 뿌리를 더 활착시키고
앙징스런 몸짓일망정
낮게 구부린 등덜미며
가냘픈 손바닥들이
꽃의 참모습이다.

꽃은 그림자처럼 따르며
자기의 속성을 바꿀 뿐이다.

꽃은 새로움이 없다고 말하지 말자
순하게 살아온 모든 것들이
어리석고 나약한 숨소리로 기가 꺾여도
정말이지 새것이 아니라고 우기지 말자.

꽃그늘을 베고 비슷이 누워
바람의 향기를 믿는다
나도 하늘도 꽃이슬로 남는다.

꽃은 언제나 그대로이다

그 또한 탓하지 않는다
꽃은 제 모습 그대로일 뿐이다.

The Lotus Flower at Gunja Pavilion

The lotus flower doesn't get dyed in the mud,
But blooms in lofty solitude like a man of honor
So the flower drops even a drop of sewage out of itself.

The lotus flower at Gunja pavilion has sustained for one thousand years,
Purifying the ditch water,
And a lover emitting its fragrance like the lotus,
Her merciful heart like Buddha.

All the lovers who come to the Gunja pavilion,
Become a Buddha with you and I, embracing the lotus flower
All become a man of honour.

- Tr. by Won Eung-soon

*Gunja Pavilion: It's a tangible cultural property in Jeonbuk Province.

Eun Hee-tae / Korea

* Pen Name: Seokcheon
* Poet &Essayist.
* Graduated from Dept. of National Lang.& Lit. of Jeonbuk University.
* Man of National Merit (Student Soldier in Korean War).
* National Medal of Moranjang.
* Taught as Teacher for 36Years.
* Received the 3rd Prize of Agricultural Literature.
* Address: 17-5, Aenggok-gil, Gobu-myeon, Jeongeup-city, Jeon-buk, Korea.

군자정 연꽃

진흙탕에서 물들지 않고
고고하게 군자처럼 자라 꽃피우고
한 방울 오물도 몸에서 굴러 떨어진다.

천년을 지켜온 군자정 연꽃
시궁창 물 정화시키며
꽃향기 품어내 연꽃처럼 사는 님
부처님처럼 자비로운 마음

군자정 오시는 님
연꽃 안고 너도 부처 나도 부처
모두 군자가 되네.

* 군자정君子亭: 전북유형문화재 133호

You Bloom as An Orchid(Flower)

Where do you bring a fragrance?
With having your green petals even in midwinter
After keeping silence to carry something,
You bring an aroma on the spring's sunshine.

Sitting on the cold veranda
Without appearing your face as you are,
Getting a rough tongue while you sleep
Tearing your tattoos and raising stalks,
You bring the fragrance.

The flower, that blooms leaning on your slender stalk,
Even though it's not beautiful,
The deep aroma
Carrying over,
Did you send it?

You, dropping your head yourself,
Due to your humble face,
Now coming into blooming as gentle an orchid
With the best fragrant mind,
Yielded by unforgettable loneliness,
You come nearer to me.

- Tr. by Won Eung-soon

Eun Yo-suk / Korea

* Completed the Dept of National Language and Literature in the Air and Correspondence College, Korea.
* Recommended as a Poet in Globe Literature.
* Served as Vice President of Baek-Ya Literary Institute.
* A Member of Literary Man's Association of Korea.
* Vice President of the World Poetry Research Institute.
* A Member of Editorial Staff in Traffic & Environment Newspaper.
* Poetical Anthology: "The Snail's Dream".
* Address: 1638-5, Sinlim Bon-Dong, Gwanak-gu, Seoul,151-029, Korea.

그대는 난꽃으로 피어

그대는 어디서 향기를 가져오는가요
한겨울에도 푸른 잎새를 두르고
무엇인가 가져오려고 침묵을 지키더니
봄별을 타고 향기를 가져오네요

추운 베란다에 앉아
얼굴 제대로 보이지 않고
잠들어 입에 혓바늘 돋더니
문신을 찢고 꽃대를 올려
향기를 가져오네요

가냘픈 꽃대를 잡고 피어나는 꽃
아름다운 모습은 아니지만
다소곳한 꽃에서 건너오는
그윽한 향기는
그대가 보낸 것인가요

예쁘지 않다고
스스로 고개 숙인 그대
이제 다시 은은한 난꽃 피어내
가장 향기로운 마음 지니고
외로움 못이겨 내 곁에 다가오는가 보지요

Autumn leaves

Mountain stained with red leaves;
Horse is running into the mount.
Forest, transparent air are
glittering in bright autumn leaves.

Drinking deeply
glow, fog, fresh air
The rider is running on horse back
tasting her tender skin.

The heart sprashing as a action cinema screen,
The earth is shaking, whirling in earth-quake,
Passing over the branches and the cloud,
wrapped up in violent quake.

Leaves shining in transparent sunbeam,
in trembling vein
The horse is running slowly .
on horseback
The rider is contemplating autumn leaves
around the mount.

- Translated by author

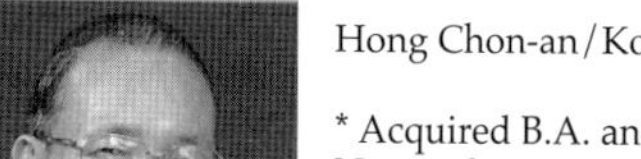

Hong Chon-an/Korea

* Acquired B.A. and M.A. on French Literature at Seoul National University, Ph.D. in Literature at Continental University. Former Ambassador to the Republic of Zaire, Republic of Congo, Republic of Brundi and Republic of Rwanda, Dean of National Unification Institute. President of Literary coterie "Roots".
* A member of P.E.N., Korea Modern Poetry Association.
* Adress: 118-2106, Dong-A Cheongsol Apt, Chang-4dong, Dobong-gu, Seoul, Korea (Tel) 02-902-4038 (H.P) 010-8447-4038

가을 속으로 들어가면

단풍으로 물든 산
말잔등에 앉아
가을 속으로 들어가면
나와 말과 숲과 투명한 공기와
가을 광채가 하나가 된다

저녁 노을과 새벽 안개와
맑은 공기 가득 마시며
말과 함께 달리면
부드러운 말의 피부와 하나가 되면

마음이 긴장하면
액션영화 장면처럼
온 세상이 흔들리면
옆을 스치는 나뭇가지도
뭉게구름도 깨닫지 못하고
격렬한 진동에 묻힌다

햇살에 나뭇잎들이 투명하게
빛나면
말의 달림이 부드러운 진동으로
바뀌면
진동이 나의 온몸에 파고 들면
말 위의 나는
가을의 산을 바라본다

A Poor Man's Possession

The water which flows down from the deep valley,
Is not all cascade's water.
The bird's song, wandering without possession,
And matching together with animals in the mountain,
They're the harmony to get along in the world, It's not hubbubs.
The remarks weighing the wise life
Flock together, and the poor man's feast begins,
Which has run into torrents of rains like a cinnamon tree.
How is beautiful today,
The walking man's world without any possession?
The world he lives in like a swan rising above the heavy burdens,
And the world in which he has run to far way
Like a music in a nice tone of getting nothing,
Is also a nice cellist's music.
Even to walk without any possession is a happy space,
The emptiness doesn't mean always poorness.
Non the less, happiness smiles in a waiting mind.

- Tr. by Won Eung-soon

Hong Yun-pyeo/Korea

* Poet, Sijo(A Tree-Verse Korean poem) poet
* Born in Dang-jin, Chung-nam, in 1950
* Graduated from Korea Open Univ., Kyong-hee Univ., Graduated from graduated school of Gong-joo (public administration M.A.,)
* Awarded Budding Writer through the literary magazine "Farmer", "Literary World", and recommended as a poet by "sijo
* Published Poetical books such as "Spending Winter", A Crane Village", "Like A Wind and Dew", To Bloom A Crane Village", The Flower of Salt", "Dreaming Grand Bridge of West Sea", Published Sijo poetical work "An Azalea in Ami Mountain"
* Wrote the words for the song such as "Spring in An-kook Temple", "My Love Firefly"(International Record: A Song in My Mind)
* Member of International Pen Club in Korea Headquarters, Korea Writer's Association, Korea poetry Association", "Korea Music Copyright Association" Korea Sijo(Korean style poem) Literary Association", "kyung-Hee Writer's Association"
* The present Dang-jin branch manager of Korea writer's Association
* Address: (Nuskin Dangin Center) 238-1, Eupnae-dong, Dangjin-si, Chung-nam, Korea. Tel: 041-355-3844, Cell No: 010-7434-3844

무소유

깊은 산 계곡에서 흐른다 해서
다 폭포수가 아니다
가진 것 없이 떠도는 새들의 노래
산짐승의 어울림
그건 살아가기 위한 세상의 조화로움이다
아우성이 아니다
어진 삶을 위해 헤아려보는 말들이
모이고 모여서 계수나무 같이
줄기차게 빗줄기 속을 달려온 빈자貧者의 향연
오늘도 가진 것 없이 걸어가는 몸
얼마나 세상이 아름다우랴
무거운 심신을 떨쳐 버리며 백조처럼
음악처럼 살아가는 무소유 선율로
먼 길을 달려도 세상은 고은 첼로음악이다
가진 것 없이 걸어도 행복한 발걸음
빈 몸은 언제나 가난함이 아니다
그래도 기다리는 마음 있어 행복하도다

A Dance of Mt. Nam

The dance of aromatic trees at Mt. Inwang
The soft dance of yellow soils at Mt. Nak,

The dance of clean water like a cataract at Mt. Soorak
The dance meandering like the pine wind at Mt. Dobong...

The dance like blazing fire, melting a metallic spot
At every peak of Mt. Kwanak for a hundred million years,
Is harmonized hotly as one,
Gets joined hotly together to be a moon,
And united hotly to be a sun.

The smell of earth, sweat, and deers...
The smell of water, and the smell of sweat, and bears...
A new millennium... an old millenniun... the smell of human beings...
The smell of love...
The smell of the millennium faith...
And the smell of cattle...

- Tr. by Won Eung-soon

Hwang Seong-ee / Korea

*Real Name: Hwang Hye-Ryun.
*A Director of Ehwa Alumnae Literary Society.
*A member of the International Pen Club, A Director of the Literary Women's Association of Korea, and A Committee for Materials Excavation.
*Poetical Anthology: "In the Mirror", "The Bird of Space", etc.
*A Poet Laureate at Los Angeles.
* Received An Honorary Doctoral Degree of Literature at Los Angeles.
*Recommended as a Proud Sook Myung Woman.

남산의 춤

인왕산의 향나무 춤
낙산의 황토흙 부드러운 춤

수락산의 폭포수 맑은 물 춤
도봉의 굽이굽이 솔바람 춤이...

일억 년 관악의 봉우리마다
쉿물 녹이는 꽃불춤이
하나 되어 뜨겁게 어우러지네
달님이 되어 뜨겁게 어우러지네
햇님이 되어 뜨겁게 어우러지네

흙 냄새 땀 냄새 사슴의 냄새...
물 냄새랑 땀 냄새랑 곰들의 냄새...
새 천년... 옛 천년... 사람의 냄새...
사랑의 냄새---
천년 믿음의 냄새...
소들의 냄새...

A Bamboo

A bamboo
Standing upright
Is vacant its inside.

If the human being
Is sad,
Could I define a wish?

Only once
Our life
Coming,
And passing away.

Filling up is a lonesome truth.

A sound of space
Puts on its wing's clothes
Thrusting through its body.

- Tr. by Won Eung-soon

Jang Eun-hae / Korea

* Made a Debut as a Poet from monthly magazine, 'the Literary Arts and Trend'.
* Won the Prize of 'the Literary Arts and Trend'.
* Member of the Literary Circle of 'the Korea Poets'.
* Mail Order Salesman.
* H.P. 010-4817-3926

대나무

바르게 선
대나무
속은 텅 비어 있다

인생
서러우면
소원 하나 세우랴

딱 한번
오고
가는 삶

채우면 허전한 진리

공간의 소리는
제 몸을 뚫어
날개옷을 입는다.

Um Tree*(A Kalopanax)

Whether it's "Um namu" or "Om namu"
I don't know its name well,
In spite of hearing it often,
I have always passed through it.

The dress you put on is tattered,
But you who are seen at rare intervals
In the fields of secluded mountains
Are the ancient looks.

You who are buried in the quiet country
Without applying to medicines
And cultivating help,
Are just a ginseng,
And a wild ginseng.

Jang Hyun-kyung/Korea

* Born at Yecheon, Gyeongsangbukdo* Poet, Essayist, Pen Name: Jajeong.
* Made his Debut as the poem " The Spring Cold with 2 other poems", 2006 and at the same year, issued an essay, "The Little Killing Field".
* Published the poetic Anthology of " When the Apricot Blooms Fully", 2008 and had a party in honor of its publication of the poetic book.
* Set up a Signboard of "Parolho Literary Village", 2008.
* A Member of the Literary Association of Korea.
* A Member of the World Poetry Literary Research Institute of Korea.
* A Chairman of the Cheonggye Literary Society.
* Won the Prize of Mul-Rye Literature, of the World Poetry, of the New Literature, and of Heo-nan-seol-heon Literature.
* Present Address: 40-3, Joongkog 2nd Dong, Gwangjingu, Seoul, Korea.

Though you are loved by the same kind
Calling you the fatsia shoots,

With the grim thorns
You drove away the foreign enemies,

Your soft leaves for boiling slightly,
Your fruits and stalks for cooking,
Your roots for fresh saps,
Roused the public interests.

- Tr. by Won Eung-soon

엄나무

엄나무인지 음나무인지
이름도 잘 몰라
많이 들어 봤지만
지나치기 일쑤다.

몸에 걸친 의복은 남루하나
산간벽지 들판에
드문드문 보이는 너는
태곳적 그 모습

약 뿌리지 않고
가꾸지 않아도
초야에 묻힌 의젓한 네가
바로 인삼이요
산삼이로다.

피가 섞인 내 동족이 두릅이라고
새싹으로 온갖 사랑 받고 있지만

험상궂은 가시로
외적을 물리치고

여린 잎은 데쳐서
열매와 가지는 삶아서
뿌리는 생즙으로
세인의 관심을 끈다.

5:30 A. M.(Five Thirty at Dawn)

Very occasionally I have opened my eyes about 5:30 at dawn,
Recently I've woke in spite of myself at that time every day.
At that time, what I have done, passes urine or not,
And before I am aware, how have I so advanced in age
That I can't fall asleep, nay, I wake up early?
Definitely, on my face wrinkled thickly.
The lazy kids of mine are irritable on my sleeping late,
But it meant that I was young and healthy, didn't I know it indeed?

One day, around 5:30 at dawn I opened my eyes in spite of myself,
If I only think of, I could do something,
I couldn't do anything for one or two hours
But lying in bed only to think looking up the ceiling,
And getting up barely on the sofa, staring at darkness absentmindedly,
And beginning to move for a whole day with such inconvenient morning hours,
I've no idea whether I live worth living, or not.

Jeong Ji-ahn/Korea

* Born in A-san city, Choongnam , in 1961
* Graduated from Dongguk Univ., Dept. of Ind. Eng. (BS)
* Graduated from graduate school of Dongguk Univ., Dep. Of Ing. (MS/Ph.D)
* Present: Assistant Professor at Shinsung College
* Address: Rm 207, 103-dong, Hyundai Green Apt., Sigok-ri, Dangjin-eup, Choongnam, 343-753, Korea

Day after day, drinking a cup of 'Soju' at that evening,
I have grown old, and so have we lived,
Though we've more penitent memories than good ones,
We all have lived such a life without exception, how can we do?
I might not have thought so, and so might not have been sad,
Only I wish I would not get up with the head ache the next day,
After drinking, and moreover wake from a long sleep for 30 or 40 minutes.

- Tr. by Won, Eung-soon

새벽 다섯 시 반

새벽 다섯 시 반경에 아주 가끔 눈을 떴는데
요사이 언제인지 매일 그 시간이 되면 눈 떠진다
그때 하는 일이라는 건 방광을 비우거나 또는 말거나
세월이 어느새 잠이 오지 않는, 아니 잠이 일찍 깨는
그 나이를 살아왔나? 하긴 얼굴 주름이 늘고 굵어 졌어
게으른 자식들이 늦잠 잔다고 성화를 했지만
그게 건강하면서 젊다는 것이었는데, 정말 몰랐나?

어느 날 정말로 모르게 눈이 떠지는 새벽 다섯 시 반경
생각하면 무엇이든지 할 수 있지만
그렇다고 무엇이든지 아무것도 못하는 멍한 두어 시간
잠자리에 누워 어두운 천장을 보면서 생각하는 것
겨우 일어나 소파에 앉아 아무 생각 없이 어둠을 본다는 것
이렇게 시작되는 불편한 아침시간을 갖고 하루를 살아보면
삶에 뭐 끈적이는 보람, 뭐, 어떤 것이 있는지도 모르겠다

매일 같은 날, 그날 저녁에 소주 한잔 하면서
지금 이 나이가 된 것 그리고 이렇게 살았다는 것
좋은 기억보다 후회스러운 서러운 마음 더 많겠지만
예외란 별로 없이 그렇게들 살아가고 있으니, 어쩔까?
그렇게 생각하지 말았으면, 서러워하지 말았으면
소주 한잔 한 다음날 머리 아프게 일어나지 말고
게다가 한 삼십 분이나 사십 분 더 늦게 눈 떠지기를

The Way Going Toward You

Look here...
Passing by the happiness in so full bloom,
The liberty in so brilliance,
And the nose's end
The smell of the blue wind
Is alive one by one,
Waving by the swelling life
Through the artery of the whole body.

Look here...
My heart throbs
With 'boom' 'boom' like a drum.
The new green buds are sprouting
In the grey heart hardened like a fossil.

I who gained a true freedom from you,
Taking the flower wine
Like honey in my lips,
Scattering the laughing sounds a little
That are resembled to the acacia aroma,
Into the dazzling sunbeams of the early summer
Toward you, becoming a new way for its light solely,
In raptures
I am walking so ecstatically like this.

- Tr. by Won Eung-soon

Jeong Ji-won/Korea

* Pen Name: Seo Woo
* Born in Jeonju, 1970.
* Made her Debut as a Poet in "the Literary Trend" monthly.
* Reciting Poet(Won the Great Prize of National Reading Meeting0
* A Member of World Poetry Literature & of Baek-Ya Literary Society.

당신께로 가는 길

보셔요...
이토록이나 만개한 행복을
이토록이나 눈부신 자유를
콧끝을 스쳐 지나
푸른 바람의 냄새가
한올 한올 살아서
온몸의 혈맥을 타고 파도치는
생명으로 넘실대고 있어요.

보셔요...
'쿵' '쿵' 북소리처럼
제 심장이 뛰어요
화석처럼 굳어버린 검은 심장에
푸릇푸릇 새순이 돋고 있어요

당신으로 하여 정녕 자유한 저는
입술에는 꿀처럼 달디단
꽃술을 물고
아카시아 향기를 닮은
자잘한 웃음소리를 날리며
초여름의 부신 햇살 속으로
오롯이 빛을 향해 새 길이 된 당신께로
황홀히
이토록이나 황홀히 걸어가고 있어요

Walking Along the River

I take a walk with my wife along the riverside road,
Where the green reeds are waving like their hairs
With a cool wind of the river,
And the white hawkweed flowers split their hairs.

A glow in the sky is embraced in the lover's mountain.
At the riverside path with rich chestnut flower's leaves scattered,
In the busy, busy river in order to hide its shadow,
Our couple are left alone.

Flowing endlessly, endlessly,
Along the lonely, lonely waterway,
Wandering, drifting here and there,
I wonder, the river has its families.

The stars glitter in the grey river.
It seems they make the way of their families.
After their sons and daughters have married,
They all would flow happily
Along the star's way in the river.

- Tr. by Won Eung-soon

Jeong Jin-su / Korea

* Born in Incheon City, Korea.
* Serving at the National Tax Office(Present)
* Graduate from Dept. of National language of the Air and Correspondence College
* Member of the Literary Circle in National Tax Office
* Member of the Association of the Literary Trend and Thought
* Member of the World Poetry Institute
* Won a Literary Prize from the World Poetry Institute
* Address: 4384, Singil 4-dong, Samsung Layan Apt. 106-301, Youngdeungpogu, Seoul, Korea.

강물 따라 걷다

시원한 강바람 따라
푸른 갈대 머릿결 출렁이고
하얀 조팝꽃 가르마 타는
강변길을 아내와 함께 걷는다

노을이 연인산 품에 안긴다
그림자 숨기느라 바쁘고 바쁜 강물속,
짙은 밤꽃 이파리 흥건한
강둑 길에 우리 부부만 남겨진다

떠돌며 떠돌아
외롭고 외로운 물길을
끝없이 끝없이 흐르는
강물도 가족들이 있는 걸까

검은 강물 속에서 별이 반짝인다
별들도 가족의 길을 만드는가 보다
자식들이 모두 출가한 후에라도
강물속 별길
따라 모두 함께 행복하게 흐르고 싶다

If Love Becomes Memory

If not to vanish, however hard we may sweep, sweep,
And not to forget, however we may erase, erase,
Is the retrospection, I would leave my love behind as a vernal landscape.

As if it doesn't follow the vernal hind heels,
Passing by with flowery rain scattering,
As if the returning spring
Was born in beautiful April as ever,

We, embracing the spring in heart,
If we go to a vision for a love not a separation,
I would flow without hesitation.

- Tr. by Won Eung-soon

Jeong Mi-na / Korea

* Born at Damyang, Chungbuk, Korea.
* Made a Debut as Poet from 'the Literary Arts and Trend'.
* Member of a Literary Circle, 'The Korean Poets'.
* Hand Phone: 010-4782-5881

사랑이 기억이 되면

쓸어도 쓸어도 사라지지 않고
지워도 지워도 잊혀지지 않는 것이 추억이라면
나는 봄날의 풍경으로 내 사랑을 남겨 놓으련다.

꽃비로 흩날리고 가는
봄의 뒷자락을 따라가지 않는 것처럼
다시 찾아오는 봄이
여전히 아름다운 4월로 태어나는 것처럼

봄을 품고 가는 우리가
이별 아닌 사랑을 향한 꿈으로 가는 것이라면
서성이지 않고 흐를 것이다.

A Sweet Home of Birthplace

Mother, binding a white skirt round her waist,
And cooking rice in the kitchen,

Grandmother, opening a sealed window,
And waiting for us to come back from school,

A detached room with peaceful sounds,
Filled with the father and mother's laughter,

A brother-and-sister sevensome
Lived happily laughing, sometimes crying together.

A cute black puppy
Wagging its tail,

The cute chicks, following their hen
That she makes them peck the chicken feed,

The scene of the lovable calf is vivid before my eyes,
Sucking cow's milk, chewing the cud,

Dyeing our nails red
With bloomed balsam flowers near our terrace,

The place where the persimmons hung in clusters with green fruits before our house,
And the flowers of apricot and cherry were in full bloom, is my sweet home. (After I have been to the home town in 2007)

- Tr. by Won Eung-soon

Jeong Soon-ja / Korea

* Pen Name: So-Yeun.* Born at Sooncheon, Jeon-Nam, Korea.
* Graduated from the Course of the Graduate School of Administration in Ewha Woman's University.
* Served as a Chairman of the Essay Literature of Ewha Woman's Univ., its Counselor(Present).
* A Member of the Literary Men's Association of Korea, International Pen Club, and a Director of Recommendation of Essayist Committee.
* Received the Prize of "the Jang-Han Mother", the Prize of Minister of Physical Bureau of '88 Seoul Olympic Game, of the Literary Art of Sooncheon Girls' High School, and of Essay Part of 'the Huh Nan Seul Heon' Art.
* Essay Anthology: "Tolling at a Mountain Temple", with other 2 Vols.
* Address: 247-162, Seokyodong, Mapogu, Seoul, Korea.

고향 집

흰 앞치마 허리에 두르시고
부엌에서 밥 지으시던 어머니

봉창문 열어 놓고
학교 간 우리들 기다리시던 할머니

할아버지 아버지 웃음소리
화목한 음성 서린 사랑방

칠 남매 우리 형제
울고 웃으며 살았네

반가워 꼬리치며
재롱부리던 검둥이

모이를 쪼아주는 어미 닭을
따라 다니는 예쁜 병아리들

되새김질하는 어미젖을 빠는
귀여운 송아지 모습이 선하네

장독가 봉선화 곱게 피어
손톱에 꽃물들이며

집 앞 감나무 감 똘기 주렁주렁
살구꽃 앵두꽃 곱게 피던 고향 집

(2007년 고향 집을 다녀와서)

An Ode to the Moon of Poetry

To the place I quicken steps, crossing the field with a lantern,
It may be better for couple to fall in love with my throbbing heart,
But the falling rain is so unkind as to forget those days.

When going along with loneliness, that troubles the sweet sleep in darkness,
Sitting on a bare naked tree, I call old poet,
But Soul being far away from moment, all things can take in breath.

Longing for even hatred, evening clouds write a poem in the sky,
When being glow with the setting sun in a change of heart of joy,
The moon gathers tears pursuing the lover's steps.

- Tr. by Won Eung-soon

Jin Sang-soon/Korea

*Ex-Chairman of Writer's Association at Gimjae Branch
*President at General Society of Arts of Korean Painting
*Member of Literary Men's Association of Korea
*Vice Chairman of Kirin Literature at Jeon-Buk
*Member of Literary Men's Association of Jeon-Buk
*A Compilation Committee of A Dictionary of Modern Poets in Korea
*Received Prizes:
- Chosen Four Times at The Nation-Wide Arts Exhibition of Byok-Gol
- Won the Prize of new Poet from "The Han-Kook Poetry" monthly
- Won the Great Prize from "The Han-Kook Poetry" monthly
- Won the Prize of Culture of Gimjae Citizens
- Won the Prize of Nosan Literature
*Publication:
- An Extra Star, Hanging in the Sky, The Reason the Wind Sits on the Tree, Now and Then, On Such A Day, Long Letters of A Crane

시월詩月의 노래

들 건너 초롱불 밭길 가는 그곳에
마음 저며 꽃 피웠음 둘이도 좋으련만
야속타 추적되는 비 그 시절 잊으라 하네.

어둠은 단잠을 헤집다 외로움이 동행일 때
헐벗은 나목에 앉아 옛 시인을 부르다
영혼에 순간이 멀어 만물의 숨결을 고른다.

미움도 그리워서 하늘에 시 쓰는 석연
지그시 감기는 희열 회심으로 놀이 붉을 적
달님은 임의 발자국 따라 눈물을 줍는다.

Spirit (2)

Thou art a being of ontological existence because of no shape,
And a being of semantical existence because of thy perfection,
Which is a noun given as a concrete role.

Today, in the center of thy role
I have gone and come, and have stayed,
But thy art the power and the master of center of my life.

Though my life
Is in a hallucination,
In an ostentation,
And in all falsehood,

There exists a providing shelter for the soul
Of absolute guard,
Only the master of life.

- Tr. by Won Eung-soon

Jun Duk-ki/Korea

* A Member of the Literary Men's Association of Korea.
* A Director of the International Pen Club in Korea Headquarter.
* A Director of the Modern Poets Association.
* Poetical Anthology: <The Grassland without Dew> with other 10 vols.
* A Collection of Column: <Open Mind, the Blue Heart> with other 4 vols.
* A Collection of Essay: <Silvery Sands of My Life I Picked Up While Working> with other 2vols.

*The Selected Poems: <The Road to that Land> with other 3 vols.
* Address: 147, Dongsomundong 4ga, Seongbukgu, Seoul, Korea.

영혼 (2)

형체가 없기에 존재론적 존재
그 완전성에 의미론적 존재
구체적인 역할로 부여된 명사

오늘도 역할의 중심에서
나는 가기도 오기도 머물기도 하나
삶 중심의 힘이시오 주인이시라

착각 속
과시 속
온갖 허구 속 인생이지만

거기 절대적인 수호자
오직 생명의 주인
그 영혼 보살핌이 있음이라

A flower

Condensed energy after a floral axis,
spout from the roots.
How glittering it is!
How powerful it is!
By the way
That was just a moment.
That just had a pleasant while.
Who knows!
The truth that the flower fold a head,
fall down itself on the bare ground.

- Tr. by Ok-Im Jung

Jung Ok-im/Korea

* Poetical Anthology: Turning with the Vane.
* Adress: 5-305, Saneopin Apt., Gocheokdong, Gurogu, Seoul, Korea.

꽃

꽃대 차오르던 분수령
응축된 에너지
찬란하더라 힘차더라
그런데
그건 한순간이더라 한때더라
누가 알았으랴
스스로 고개 꺾어
맨 땅에 얼굴 묻을 줄.

The Bukhan River(Nami Isle)

Like a certain image of dawn, by chance,
The river, whirling round in a circle and disappearing,
Flows round silently,
And the isle keeps its own place tactlessly.

The flowing river becomes a waterway.
The man on a little ship is heading for somewhere,
And a white heron lowers her head feelingly,
Looking down at the old prow of the ship is staggering.

The white clouds,
Covering or floating on opposite mountains,
Are so busy in streaming out dreamy retrospects,

So soon the missing expression of that ship,
Whirling around the river
Returning back to the same place,
Resembles an evening twilight.

That is why the waterway of this river,
Which is unable to secede from a woman's steps
At sunset.

- Tr. by Won Eung-soon

Jung U-ha/Korea

* Majored in Korean literature
* Won Sulsong literary award
* Won the Gaya Gold Crown of the World Poetry
* Published poetical works entitled 'A Love Song of Fine Classics'
* Freelance writer, a guidance teacher for an essay writing

북한강(남이섬)

문득 동그랗게 맴돌다 사라지는
어느 새벽 연상처럼
강물은 빙둘러 앉아 말없이 흐르고
섬은 우직하게 제자리를 지키고 있었다

흐르는 강물은 뱃길이 되어 준다
배 위에 오른 인생은 어디로 밀려가는가
자꾸만 낡아 가느라 비틀거리는 뱃머리가 안쓰러운 듯
흰 왜가리 한 마리 숙연하게 고개 숙인다

앞산 허리를 휘감았다 풀어주는 흰 구름은
보일 듯 말 듯한 추억을
강물에 흘러보내느라 여념없는데

어느새 강물을 휘돌아
제자리로 돌아와 버린
저 배의 아쉬운 표정이
저녁놀과 닮아 있다

그것은 아낙의 해거름 발길 같은
이탈할 수 없는
이 강의 뱃길 때문이리라

A Body of Vocabulary

Is it the east for the sun to rise in the east?
As it is the east, does the sun rise?
Is it truth? is it cognition?
An undeniable consciousness
Pushes 'what it should be'
In the frame of the invariability.

The demonstrations of the flooded languages
Restrict the age's gap,
Trifle even the pure bedrooms
And violate it.

The weapons of unchecked languages
Display fully as much cicatrices and influences
As an internet in megabyte velocity of light
And exist actually before us like an idol of a goddess,
So must we accept and pass over?

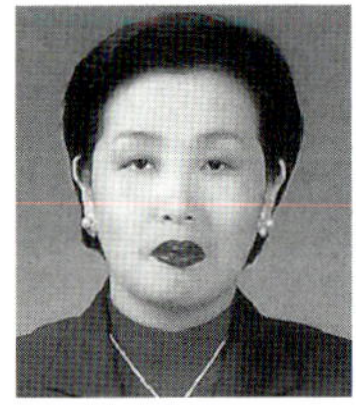

Kang Young-duk/Korea

* Start a literary career through monthly magazine 'Munhak 21' in 1998
* Put my name on a biographical dictionary in 2002
* Put my literary work on the biographical encyclopedia
* A member of "SGI literary man's association" "the world poet research institute" "kangnam literary man's club" "guro literary man's club" "millennium literary man's association"
* Joint literary work: A Clamor, A String of leaves, Yearning becomes flower by the expression in your eyes, The Wind that Bring Life

* Address: 1-202, Daehan apt., 381-18, Hwagok7-dong, Gangseo-gu, Seoul, 157-885. Korea
* E-mail: luxvia @yahoo.co.kr * Phone NO: 02-2604-8234/ 010-9970-8234

Even if they are violated by ultraviolet rays,
A piece of a new language, pushed out of the world,
May be a living spore with sucking force
By gestures of sunshine having official approval.
As it is the east, does the sun rise,
Or as it rises inside my heart, is it the east?

Today
The wind of consciousness
Hears heavily the pains of falling leaves
Getting out of the way,
From the street of a waste heart of the city.

- Tr. by Won Eung-soon

단어의 몸

해가 뜨므로 동쪽이 된 것인가
동쪽이므로 해가 뜨는 것인가
진리인가 인식인가
거부될 수 없는 의식은
불변의 틀 안으로
당위성을 밀어 넣고 있다

홍수가 된 언어의 시위들
시대 격차를 좁히며
순수의 침실마저도
농락하며 침범해 든다

초고속 메가패스 광속도의 인터넷만큼
더 많은 상흔과 영향력을 발휘해 내며
채반에 걸러지지 않은 언어의 무기
온전한 실상의 여신상처럼
우리 앞에 존재해도 되는 것인가

자외선에 유린당해도
세상 밖으로 밀쳐 나온 한 톨의 햇살박이의 언어
공인력을 가진 햇살이의 몸짓으로
흡인력을 지닌 살아 있는 포자이기를
동쪽이어서 해가 뜨는 것인가
내 안에 뜨는 쪽이므로 동쪽이 되는 것인가

의식의 바람은
오늘도

Korea/강영덕

황량한 도심의 거리에서
물러져 가는 낙엽의 몸살을
즐펵하게 이야기 듣는다

The Mother's Way

Thou art love incarnate(an incarnation of love),
Who embrace me softly and shake a cradle
Like the sound of beating rains,
Like the smile of sunlights.

Thou art a winner of faith,
Who help me to our feet by two hands when we fall down,
And embrace me hot when we shed tears,
And pray on her knees and push me dripping with sweat.

Wherever I am, whatever I do,
Thou art an ardent supporter of my life.
Wherever I exist, whatever I act,
Thou art an eternal pioneer of my life.

Love is le raison d'etre,
Love is the reason to keep on living,
Believing things that are not visible,
Expecting things that are not desirous.

Mother, the living days
Are all love's traces getting into someone's debt.

- Tr. by Won Eung-soon

Kim A-lang/Korea

*Published poetical works titled 'Adrg Leaf on the Earth', 'A plain', 'A gaze at a Thorny Bush',
* An auditor of Seongdo literary circles, a curator of Harvard school, a teacher at yeongje nursery
* A member of the blue sky club of an air force, member of the Korea Writer Association, member of farmer's literature club, and so on
* Address: 102-806, Chunggu Apt, shinbanpo, jamwondong, seochogu, Seoul, Korea
* E-mail: alangk@hanmail.net * Tel: 010-7470-4936

어머님의 길

두드리는 빗방울 소리처럼
따스한 햇살의 미소처럼
포근히 안아주고 요람을 흔들어준
당신은 사랑의 화신이죠

쓰러지면 두 팔로 일으키고
눈물지면 뜨겁게 감싸주고
엎드려 기도하고 땀 흘려 밀어주신
당신은 믿음의 승리자죠

어디 있든지 무엇을 하든지
당신은 내 생의 열렬한 응원자
어디 있든지 무엇을 하든지
당신은 내 생의 영원한 선구자

보이지 않는 것을 믿으며
바랄 수 없는 것을 바라며
사랑은 삶의 이유
사랑은 살아갈 이유

어머니, 살아가는 날들은 모두가
누군가의 빚을 진 사랑의 흔적이죠

A Middle-Aged Woman's Heart 1

Spring rain falls down on the dry land,
Due to energy stimulated the living power
The spring winds blow windingly without sound.

The loneliness, permeating into a middle-aged woman's heart
After passing the long winter's tunnel,
Flows like a river melted in the spring rain.

The hidden sprouts growing in exhausted life
Is a pressed sensibility of inevitable sadness
Opening up like new buds of a crack in the rock.

Sprouting up from the deep roots
Makes a young bud spring up in the middle-aged woman's heart
Irrespective of its aroma.

- Tr. by Won Eung-soon

Kim Baek-kyeong/ Korea

* Pen Name: Bobae
* Born in Goheung, Jeon-nam.
* Recommended as a poet in 'Munyechunchoo'.
* Issued such Collaborated Anthologies as 'The Haedong Literature', 'The Sinmunye', 'The Munhaksegye' and The Literary Movement & Trend, etc.
* Won the prize of 'International Culture and Art', of 'the Manree Literature', of 'the Hurnansulhan Literature.
* Present:
* Member of Literary Writer's Association.
* Manager of Cultural Exchange of Overseas in Korea.
* Official Director of Underwater Environmental Association.

중년의 여심 1

메마른 대지 위에 봄비가 내리네
생명력을 북돋우는 기운에
봄바람도 소리 없이 휘감겨오네

긴 겨울의 터널을 지나온
중년의 가슴으로 파고드는 고독이
봄비에 녹아서 강물처럼 흘러가네

삶에 지쳐도 자라나는 숨은 싹들
바위틈 새싹처럼 비집고 나오는
꼬집을 수 없는 비애의 억눌린 감성

뿌리로부터 펴 올리는 움틈으로
향기가 없어도 좋을 한 송이 꽃망울
중년의 여심에도 솟아오르네.

A Family Photograph

When we enter the house
They always greet us
With their sunny smiling face ,
Saying, "Welcome!".

Always as ever,
Equally to anyone,
Raining, or sun rising,
And wind blowing, or snowing,

All welcome and greet us gladly.
There are no my team, and your side
In that square world,
Only there is soft love for welcome with smiles.

As joyful as we look at the family photograph,
So if they are happy persons,
We shall be happy also.

-Tr. by Won Eung-soon

Kim Bok-nam / Korea

* Completed the whole course of study at Free Literary Univ.
* A member of Jeonbuk Free Poetry
* A chairwoman of the Twenty-fourth Yucho
* A member of a literary group which publishes a magazine "The Sound of a Leaf"
* A member of Baikja Literature
* A member of the World Poetry research Institute
* Address: 101-1205, Dongguk Apt, 1034-1, Jinbuk2-dong, Deogjin-gu, Jeonju-si, Jeon-buk, 561-782, Korea

가족사진

그 집 들어서면
환하게 웃는 얼굴로
"어서 오세요" 하고
반기네

언제나 한결같이
누구에게나 똑같이
비가 오나 해가 뜨나
바람이 부나 눈이 오나

모두가 환영하며 반겨주네
저 네모 세상에는
내 편 네 편이 없네
웃음으로 반겨주는 사랑이 있을 뿐

바라보면 즐거운 가족사진처럼
바라보면 행복한 사람들이면
참 좋겠네

Crying a Humble Cry

If I am humble, tears gush up.
Because it is a grudge cherished deep in my heart.
I can't meet sorrows face to face
Which come up to me round the corner of recollections.
Facing them with my body making up and my mind steadying,
I can perceive even walking with my eyes closed,
The joy of a scattered spring day
That is dispersing the flower's petals.
I find you shaking the loneliness
On a dreary autumn day
When fallen leaves walk secretly.
I must love you
In order to make me beautiful.
Then crying a humble together,
Our good relation
Will be an overflowing dam-water.
I will live for you sincerely
As if I wish the dawn of the sunrise.

- Tr. by Won Eung-soon

Kim Chong-ki / Korea

* Born in Sun Cheon city(1938~)
* Graduated from Goryou Universty majoring on Korean Literature, pre-principal of Suong Eui Girls High School Korean Literature, presbyter of Korean Presbyterian Church, made a debut as a poet by 'Christian Literature' 'Trend of Literature' 'Modern Sijo'
* Member of Korean Literature Association, member of International PEN Club in Korean Branch, awarded by Young Rang Literature Prize, Christian Poet Prize, Trend of Literature Prize and Epipodo Literature Prize
* Collections: As Sunrays in Vacant site (1991), Laugh Bunged up on End of Nose, Sorrow Always Living in My Mind, I'll Live Unreservedly and Gay-spiritedly, A star Alive in My Mind literary group magazine : High Jump Of Grasshopper, The clean person washing even though the tear
*Address: 621, Sanghadong, Giheunggu, Yongin City, Suwon-dongmaeul Ssangyong Apt. 303-1701, Geonggido, Korea.

겸비謙卑한 울음을 울며

낮아지면 눈물이 솟습니다.
가슴에 고인 생애 때문입니다.
추억의 모퉁이를 돌아 내게 다가서는
슬픔을 민낯으로 만날 수 없습니다.
몸단장하고 맘 가다듬고 대하면
꽃잎이 흩날리는 분분한 봄날의 기쁨을
눈 감고도 감지하며 걸을 수 있습니다.
가랑잎 사분대는 가랑가랑한 가을날엔
외로움을 흔들고 있는 그대를 발견합니다.
나를 아름답게 만들고자
그대를 사랑하고야 말 겁니다.
겸비한 울음을 더불어 울며
우리의 참 좋은 관계가
차고 넘치는 봇물이 될 겁니다.
일생 동안 해 뜨는 새벽을 바라듯
그대만을 위해 간곡히 살겠습니다.

A Dream

In an exuberant wood of summer
When a cuckoo cries sadly
Unbearable yearning carries me away
To the house of hometown,
But it dances hanging on the pine tree's branches
About its mouth of the town's garden.

Looking at the old mother from afar,
Who works with her stoop
And her hand hardened with rough work,
I wail bitterly folding a tree in my arms,
Because lacking a filial piety makes me hesitate running to mother.

Crying myself, when I turned my head,
The lovable rivers and mountains of home town are changed,
Being enveloped in darkness like despair,
I felt after my pillow that was soaked in wet
As if it was fully wet in flood.

Kim Don-young/Korea

* Pen Name: Eunro. Born at Youngkwang, Jeonnam, Korea.
* Graduated from the Air and Correspondence College.
* First Debut as a Poet through "the Sinchoon Literary Arts" and "Literary Movement & Trend".
* A Photo-Writer(Present).
*A Member of Literary Writer's Association of Korea.
* Poetic Anthology: "The Wind's Whisper"
* Address: 311-13, Bulkwangdong, Metrotower 2206, Eunpyunggu, Seoul Korea.

It was a dream.
Perhaps I dreamed such a dream
By weighing old mom on my mind,
She is my mom to love deeply in my heart.

- Tr. by Won Eung-soon

꿈

여름의 무성한 숲
뻐꾸기 애잔하게 울어
참지 못한 그리움 고향으로
고향 집으로 달려가나
동산 언저리 소나무 가지에 걸려
매달려 춤춘다

구부러진 허리로 일하시는 노모
굳은살 박힌 거칠은 손
먼발치에서도 보여
나무 끌어 안고 통곡한다
불효자식이라 쉬 달려갈 수 없어

울다 고개 돌려 바라보니
그리운 고향 산천 간데없고
절망 같은 암흑의 어둠만 휩싸여
더듬더듬 만져보니 베갯잇 흥건하다
장마에 흠뻑 젖은 옷같이

꿈이었다
생전에 불효한 게 마음에 걸려
보고파 보고파서 꿈꿨나 보다
내 심장 뜨겁도록 그리운 어머니.

In Celebration of New Myung Sung Church

1. After long hours,
The expecting doors of the church are widely opened.
The mountains and rivers shake in joy
And the sea dances.

From the far place
Over the horizon the great outcries are heard(audible),
Our beautiful church
Where the prayers of hope stay.

In hot passion
With shouting sound of "Hosanna", "Hosanna",
Our Lord, Jesus enters on a young donkey.

Kim Eui-shik/Korea

* Born in Sangju,Gyeongbuk. Grown up Chungju
* Now serves concurrently as a professor at Inha University
* A Visiting Professor at Incheon University
* A lecturer at the Juvenile financial education centre
* A director at Save zone I&C
* A director at Korea Production Society
* Started a literary career through Literary Movement & Trend
* Published poetical works entitled 'Becoming a root of a dandelion
* Literary work entitled 'Pull an Oar When the Wind Goes Down', Live a wealthy man till Die', Hold the World in Your Bosom' and ten others.
*Address: 328-7, Gildong 2nd-dong, Gangdonggu, Hanmaeum-Jutaek 401, Seoul, Korea.
* Caf adrees : Caf.daum.net/YesKim

2. Gathered are the meek in mind,
Sat up all night keeping the cornerstone,
And scattered seeds of their lonely tears.

The cedar trees, planted beside the well
Grow up the sky as pillars for the church,
And sing all for the young souls!

3. The unknown women! who broke a jade vessel,
Thou art really sacred.
We....,
Drop the anchor of the salvation,
And go forward to the land of refusal and of indifference!

The blue sky is higher for the prepared men,
The rich land waits for us,
Run for energetically the far place!

- Tr. by Won Eung-soon

'명성' 새 성전 입당

1. 오랜 시간들,
   기다리던 성전문 활짝 열린다.
   기쁨 속에 산천이 진동하고
   바다가 춤을 춘다네.

   저 멀리 아득한 곳
   지평선 너머 함성이 들려오고
   소망의 기도 머무는 곳
   내 아름다운 성전

   뜨거운 열정
   호산나 외치는 소리, 소리들
   어린 나귀 타고 주님 입성하신다.

2. 마음이 겸손한 자 다 모여
   모퉁잇돌 홀로 잡고 지새운 새벽
   외로운 눈물 사면을 적신다.

   우물가에 심겨진 백향목은
   하늘 향한 성전기둥 되어
   젊은 영혼을 노래하여라.

3. 옥합을 깨뜨린 이름 모를 여인들이여
   그대 진정 거룩하여라
   우리들....,
   이제는 구원의 닻줄내리고
   거절의 땅. 무관심의 세계로 나아가자.

준비된 자 푸른 하늘은 더 높고
기름진 대지는 우리를 기다리니
저 먼 곳을 향해 힘차게 달려가자.

The Autumn Dawn

Ar dawn, awakened from a cool breeze,
Long after giving an alarm whistle outside the window,
Lying in the room with only the sound of a wall clock,
From head to foot,
I fill the autumn dawn with one thought.

If I yearn to someone for my life
Getting a vague warm memory,
I've a reliable dream I should come across sometime.
The ice age(glacial epoch) of my years,
That has frozen in the deep valley of my mind,
Your beautiful smile, a finger, even a small gesture as they are,
When my heart becomes hot in some degree,
Could I melt the glacier to save your life?

If the beginning and the end of destiny(karma) are the same root,
I could meet even at the end of the street corner,

Kim Gui-rye / Korea

* Started a literary career through 'Literary Movement & Trend'
* Majored in Korean Language and Literature at Jeonnam University
* A announcer at MBC(Busan, Kwangju)
* A director of the gathering of woman(Kwangju Branch)
* Completed the course of a speech guidance teacher at Ewha woman University(Educational center), completed the course of an essay-philosophy at Ewha woman University (Educational center)
* A speech consultant, an essay teacher, completed the course of Free Literature University (with the class of 25th)
* President of a literary group 'Majungmul', A member of Jeonbuk free poetry recitation, A director of World Poetry Research Institute

Only once,
I should catch your warm hands,
Throbbing my heart,
At this autumn dawn
I am taking care of the mind core.

- Tr. by Won Eung-soon

가을 새벽

서늘함에 눈떠진 새벽
창밖 맴돌던 자동차의 경적도 멀어진 지 오래
벽시계 초침만 부지런한 방에 누워
정수리에서 발끝까지
한 생각으로 가을 새벽을 채운다

아롱이는 따스한 기억을 붙잡고
누군가를 죽도록 그리워하면
언젠가 마주칠 거라고 놓지 못하는 꿈
항상 오래 익힌 생각들이 만들어내던
네 고운 웃음과 손끝 하나 작은 몸짓까지
깊고 깊은 마음 골짜기에 그대로 얼어버린
내 세월의 빙하기
얼마나 이 가슴 더 뜨거워지면
너의 생명 녹여낼 수 있을까

인연의 시작과 끝이 한뿌리라면
길목의 끝에서라도 만날 수 있을 거라고
꼭 한 번이라도
너의 따뜻한 손 잡아볼 수 있을 거라고
다공질 가슴 다독이며
가을 새벽
마음의 뼈를 추스르고 있다.

A Jewel

It is longed for,
It is confidential,
And It is a jewel hided deeply.

A jewel glitters,
It is sparkling like a star at dawn
Shining alone even if you don't see it.

- Tr. by Won Eung-soon

Kim Hak-jin/Korea

* Born in Gochang
* Be on duty at Asan Hospital in Jheong-up
* Member of the World Poetry Research Institute
* Address: 346, Yonggye-dong, Jeongeup-si, Jeon-buk, 580-230, Korea
Tel: 063-533-9025 / 010-3950-9025

보석

그립습니다
비밀입니다
깊이 숨겨 둔 보석입니다

보석은 반짝입니다
그대가 봐 주지 않아도 홀로 빛나는
여명의 샛별처럼 반짝입니다.

A Palatable Meeting

That's right,
It's a mountaineering.

Going on my way when I see a wild flower,
I wink my eyes once,

Going on my way when I meet a small fountain,
I kiss it freshly to the heart,

When an oriole stops my step who is crying sadly,
For a moment,
I listen to her generously with clear mind.

At dawn that the poem is falling,
I have a composure to put words, ears, eyes, mouth,
And all ideas in tea cup, to spend out to the river.

There is nothing but poems,
Among whom I met on the way to the mountaineering.

To compose poems as if I click on 'searching for' joyfully
Is a palatable meeting with true poems.

- Tr. by Won Eung-soon

Kim Hee-soon/Korea

* Her Debut as a Poet in 'the Future Literature', 2004.
* Anthology of 9 Poets, "A Wind-Bell Sound".

맛난 만남

그래,
산행을 하는 것이다

가다가 이름 모를 들꽃을 보면
눈 한 번 꿈쩍이고

가다가 옹달샘을 만나면
가슴 시리도록 입맞추며

슬피 우는 꾀꼬리 발목 잡으면
잠시,
널찍한 마음 말그스레 귀 기울여 준다

詩 떨어지는 새벽에는
말, 귀, 눈, 입, 마음, 온갖 생각
찻잔에 우려 도도히 강물에 보내는 여유

가다가 가다가 만난 이,
詩 아닌 것이 없구나

즐겨찾기 클릭하듯 詩 짓는 것이야말로
진정한 詩와의 맛난 만남.

The Snow Island

A village, buried in the snow covered mountain
Lays its head on a new moon
Suspending on a pine tree,
And sunk in a deep bog.

A brushwood door is frozen,
No man is stirring,
And a wood and birds
Are hidden in the snow.

The old couples are linked with the coverlet
As if the yard and the roof become one,
Being confined in the snow island like a same fence,
Are waiting for the magpie's cries*.

* the magpie's cries: it means good news.

- Tr. by Won Eung-soon

Kim Hyung-chol/Korea

* Pseudonym: Dong Cho
* Birth place: in BuAn JeonBuk Province
* One of the literary men's Association. Work: But havent been hear a lovable saying
* A eulalia flower of Bong du mound. Prize: Korea poetry great prize
* Address : 351, Bonghwang-ri, Dongjin-Myeon, Buan-gun, Jeon-Buk, Korea

눈 섬

설산에 묻힌 마을이
소나무에 걸린
초승달을 베고
깊은 수렁에 빠졌다.

사립문 얼어붙고
오고 가는 사람 없고
숲과 새들도
눈 속에 숨어 있다.

늙은 내외 이불 몰아
마당 지붕이 한 덩이 된
한 울 눈 섬에 갇혀
까치 울음 기다린다.

Flowers fall down in the Rain of Flowers

Though the white magnolia over the window
In the garden bloomed its pretty flowers
In clusters splendidly, as if they lighted up,

The white flowers fall down in the night rain
Secretly with a little voice 'wududuk, wududuk',
So as to be white on the ground
And their clusters are strewn in the rain of flowers.

Though the flower blooms again
At the place, in next year,
Its bluish green petals like a season of May queen
Covered the place luxuriantly,
However,
However I
I miss the white magnolia so constantly, that my eyes
Stay at the garden over the window in spite of myself.

- Tr. by Won Eung-soon

Kim Il rye/Korea

* Born in 1955 in Seung-ju, Jeon-nam
* Graduated from Naju University
* Finished the graduate course of Jeon-nam Univ. (the course of woman leader)
* Finished the training course of Etiquette of Chosun Univ.
* Finished the course of Literary Creation of Kwang-ju Univ.
* Published a collection of essays entitled 'Even the humble has a potential for leadership' in 1996
* Published poetical works entitled 'The fragrance of Lilies' 'You and I are One Flesh' 'Qatar, Land of Blessing'

꽃비에 꽃 다 떨어지네

창 너머 뜰에 하이얀 목련화가
송이송이 아름다운 꽃들을
불 밝힌 듯 환히 흐드러지게 피웠건만

두고두고 보고 싶은 하~얀 꽃들이
우두둑 우두둑 몰래 온 밤비에
바닥이 하~얗도록 와시시
꽃비에 꽃송이가 다 떨어지네

내년이면 그 자리에
그 꽃 다시 피겠지만
계절의 여왕다운 5월의 청록색 이파리가
무성하게 그 자리를 이불처럼 덮고 있지만
그래도
그래도 나는
그 하이얀 목련화가 자꾸만 그리워서
나도 몰래 창밖 뜰에 눈길이 머무네

Under A Bush Clover Tree

A prophet, hiding under a bush clover tree,
Entreating to die being utterly worn out in discouragement and fatigue,
Today is lying everywhere to sleep with his head on a stone pillow in Korea.

When crying for it with his hands under the hot sun in a wilderness,
That he would rather end his life than live like this,
There is one who gives a dream even in a nightmare.

This is an angel, who wakes him up from sleep under the bush clover tree,
And gives the baked bread on rock and a bottle of water,
Makes him eat and drink, awakening him even if lying again.

The place he want to arrive at on foot day and night, for 40 days,
Where is it? that he can't find however he looks around,
Being exhausted with thread and loneliness at a corner of a wilderness,

The uncountable prophets, being harassed with intolerable debts,
Again entreats to pass away,
Not to give hope, bread and water from angel.

- Tr. by Won Eung-soon

Kim Jae-kyun/Korea

* Graduated from Dept. of Political Diplomacy of Jeon-Nam Univ., and from its Graduate School of Jeon-Nam University.
* Received Doctoral Degree of Politics(Ph.D.).
* Recommended As a Poet from 'the Sidae Literature'
* Poetical Anthology: <The Brier Under the Moon Light> with others.
* Received the Prize of Gwangju Literature.
* Selected Specially 5 Times at the National Art Exhibition of Korea.
* The chairman of Gwangju City Party, Democratic Party
* A Congress Man(Present).
* Address: 1357-2, Yongbongdong, I-House 2nd Floor, Korea.

싸리나무 아래

낙담과 피로에 지쳐 기어든 싸리나무 아래
죽기를 간청하며 누워서 잠이 든 예언자는
오늘 대한민국 도처에서 돌베개로 누워 있다

이렇게 살 바엔 차라리 목숨을 거둘실 것을
광야의 작열하는 태양 아래서 두 손 모아 외치는데
잠결에까지 따라와 가위 눌린 꿈을 주는 이

천사다. 싸리나무 그늘의 잠을 흔들어 깨우면서
뜨거운 돌에 구운 빵과 물 한 병 건네주는 이
다시 누워도 또 깨우면서 먹고 마시도록 하는.

이제 밤낮으로 사십 일을 걸어 이르고자 한 곳
그곳은 어디일까 아무리 둘러보아도 찾을 수 없는
사막의 한 귀퉁이에서 두려움과 외로움에 지쳐

다시 죽기를 간청하며 차라리 목숨을 거두실 것을
천사의 빵과 물을 주지 마시고 희망을 거두시기를
견딜 수 없는 빛에 시달리는 셀 수 없는 예언자들.

An Evening Twilight

An evening glow
Tinges the sky with rosy flush.

In the evening glow
There is a hamlet of my home town.

The stream
Murmurs with a sound 'jol, jol, jol' too,

In the blue sky
Like the floating thick clouds,

The thick, thick clouds
Are floating about in clam patterns.

In the evening twilight
Mommy, daddy

Laugh merrily
With hahaha, hohoho.

- Tr. by Won Eung-soon

Kim Ji won/Korea

* Graduated the Buddhist course at samsun Sung-ga univ
* Her position: the head priest of Kyonseong temple of the Buddhist-JogyeJong, Vicepresident of the Nam-Yang-Ju branch of the leterary mem's Association
* Works: "Cuckoo cryed the day When hometown left"
* Home town's rainbow, Yearing of the wild bird
* Prize from: Chung-Hon leterateur the art prize
* Address : Gyeonseong grotto, San 3 Songneung 1-ri, Jinkeon-eup, Namyangju-si, Gyeonggi-do, 472-830, Korea

저녁노을

저녁노을이
빨갛게 물들어 간다

저녁노을 속에는
내 고향 마을이 있다

졸졸졸
시냇물도 흐르고

푸른 하늘에
떠가는 뭉게구름처럼

뭉게 뭉게 조개무늬
구름도 흘러서 간다

저녁노을 속에는
엄마, 아빠가

하하하 호호호
즐겁게 웃고 있다

An Angel's Smile

The beautiful hands of her love, melted like a silk thread,
Makes the pains of the body and soul
Flow like water silently,
And the endless smile
Is now filled with a rainbow-colored soul

Her white smiling love
Hastens her hurried steps
To move to some place,
Toward the angel's love smile on her lips
I flow silently like fragrance,
Toward the white wing's feathers,
And toward painful minds under their diseases
The smile of a white love overflows from my soul.

By chance!
In fear of not giving the warm love to them,
Looking for the painful patients,
And in fear of giving the consoling love late for them,
The white angel is walking with hurried steps,
With the white smile.

- (At the Hospital of St. Carrolo in Suncheon Looking at a Nun's service of love)

- Tr. by Won Eung-soon

Kim Ji-yeul/Korea

* Graduated from The College of Chemistry in Joseon University.
* Finished The Graduate School of Jeonnam University(master of science) and that of Catholic Medical College(doctor of medicine).
* A professor of Jeonnam Medical College.
* The president of The Korean Nuclear Medicine Academy(1996~ 1998)
* Address : 160, Ilsim-ri, Hwasun-eup, Hwasun-gun, Jeon-nam, 519-809, Korea

천사의 미소

명주실 날처럼 녹아내린
그 아름다운 사랑의 손길이
영육의 아픔을
소리 없이 흐르게 하고
그 더없는 미소가
무지갯빛 영혼에 지금도 가득하다

하얀 미소에 잠긴 사랑
어디로인가
바쁜 걸음 재촉하고
입가에 가득한 천사의 사랑 미소
난 향기처럼 잔잔히 흐르고
그 하얀 날개깃에
병마의 고통에 젖은 이들의 마음에
새하얀 사랑의 미소가 넘쳐 흐른다

행여나!
따뜻한 사랑을 베풀지 못해
힘들어 하는 병자의 마음을 찾아
새하얀 미소로
어루만져 주는 사랑이
늦을까, 종종걸음을 재촉하며 가고 있다

―(순천 성가롤로 병원에서-수녀님의 사랑봉사를 보면서)

A Sinful Dress -A Dreadful Dress

The sinful dress,
Wrapped up in mind
The language,
The facial expression,
And the action
To hide,
To conceal oneself.....

The dreadful dress,
Wrapped up in mind
The conversation,
The facial expression,
And the behaviour,
Not to reveal,
Not to disclose oneself.....

- Tr. by Won Eung-soon

Kim Jin-soo / Korea

* Pen Name: Keun-Gil.
* Born at Namwon, Jeon-Buk, Korea.
* Graduated From Seoul National Univ., and the Graduate School of Jeon-Nam Univ..
* A Member of the Literary Men's Association of Korea, of the Essayist Association of Korea.
* Director of the World Poetry Research Institute of Korea.
* Poetical Anthology: <In the Your Truth & In My Truth>, etc..
*A Full-Length Novel: Literary Man.
* The Books: Essay Anthology & Selected Short Stories, etc.
* Address: 401, Chungdam Park View, 61-11, Chungdamdong, Gannamgu, Seoul.

죄악의 옷- 두려움의 옷

숨기기를
감추기를
말도
표정도
행동도
마음에 씌운 죄악의 옷......

드러날까 봐
알려질까 봐
말도
표정도
행동도
마음에 씌운 두려움의 옷......

An Unexpected Order

At Namdaemun market, at Euljiro(street)
The unseen dead persons are walking,
And forming in a line, they are going in haste,
As if it were a hope wherever they would go.

A death goes into the black cello
Unties its hair long,
And is looking out the world
Writhing its body with haggard eyes of doubt.

A group of white birds soared up between the thin branches of the trees
Keeping in a straight line long,
Are going dimly over the Han river.

A great deal of death went down by the river.

Laying one death below the green tree,
Snow flakes scattered from the heaven in the end.

- Tr. by Won Eung-soon

Kim Jong-hee/ Korea

* Born in Cheonju City, Chungbuk, Korea.
* Graduated from Dept. of English Lit. of Yonsei University.
* First Debut as a Poet through "the Poetics" monthly magazine(1982).
* A Member of Writer's Association of Korea, International Pen Club, and the Good Literature Club.
* A Committee for Guidance of Modern Poet's Association.
* Director of Member's Club of Poetics.
* Prize from "the Poetics" monthly magazine.

* Address: 337-36 Seokyodong, Mapogu, Seoul, Korea
* Phone: 02-335-0264(Home), 011-229-0264(Handphone)

예기치 않은 질서

남대문시장에서, 을지로에서
보이지 않는 죽음들이 가고 있다
일렬횡대로 줄을 맞춰 바쁘게 가고 있다
어디든 가는 것만이 희망이란 듯이

죽음 하나 검은 색 첼로 속으로 들어가
머리를 길게 풀어헤치고
몸을 말며 의심의 까칠한 눈초리로
세상을 내다보고 있다

실낱같은 나뭇가지 사이로 하얀 새 떼가 날아올랐다
일직선으로 길게
한강을 넘어 가물가물 가고 있다

대량의 죽음이 강을 따라 내려갔다

푸른 나무 밑에 죽음 하나 뉘어놓고
마침내 하늘에서 눈발이 흩날렸다

An Endless Echo of Love

Like a glittering star through darkness,
Like a rising moon brightly,
Sing a song of Love.

Sing a song of Love,
Who is beautiful and fragrant like a rose,
Who is brilliant and glaring like the sun.

Our Love will be forever,
Blooming in any season of spring, summer, autumn, and winter,
And even in hot and cold weather.

No matter what the poverty, pain, and an ordeal may come,
When we overcome them with frugality, theft, and mental activity,
The endless echo of Love will approach to us.

- Tr. by Won Eung-soon

Kim Joung-woong / Korea

* President of World Poetry Research Institute and World Poets Club, was born in Gochang, Korea, in 1938 as the 71st scion of King Kim Soo-Ro of Kaya. He is a Poet, essayist and columnist. He graduated from Dongkuk Graduate School, majoring in Public Administration. He received Honorary Doctorate Degree of Literature from the World University, Arizona, USA. He worked for the Far East Broadcasting Station as an announcer in Seoul for years. * He received awards such as Puwon Literature prize, Gold Crown World Poets Award, World Poetry Laureates from International Pen Club(1995). He is President of World Poetry Research Institute and World Poets Club, former vice president of World Poetry Research Institute and World Poets Club, member of Korea Literary Men's Association, member of Pen Club, former president of Moyang Literature Association, diretor of Moonyesajosa, director of Hanmaek Literature, former president of Galsoop Literature Association, Supervisor of Gochang Branch of Korea Literary Men's Association, etc.* He published his poetry books: Anna's Riverside; The Wind Sound of SeonWoon Temple; Pansori; The Hymn of Gochang; The Sun-Risen Time. He pubulished his essay books: Regarding The Subjects as Heaven and Upright Outcry. He published in a news paper; On The Exclusion of Political Parties From The Local Self-Governing Election. He has published four Anthologies Of World Poetry.

* Address : 192-67, Eupnae-ri, Gochang-eup, Gochang-gun, Jeon-buk, 585-807, Korea

영원한 사랑의 메아리

어둠을 반짝이는 별님처럼
휘영청 떠오르는 달님처럼
사랑의 노래를 부르자

장미처럼 아름답고 향기 짙은
태양처럼 찬란하고 눈이 부신
정열의 사랑을 노래하자

봄 여름 가을 겨울 어느 때나
더위나 추위나 계절 속에 피는
우리의 사랑은 영원하리

가난과 고통과 시련이 온다 해도
검소와 절약과 심기로 극복하며는
다가오는 영원한 사랑의 메아리

An Ideal Woman

- By the Lake

When the brilliant spring view hangs down
Beyond over the lake,
Your voice hearing on clearly,

When looking the silent lake
A missing image rising on its surface
Is a compassion of my throbbing heart.

Her eyes wetting like the lake
Say a significant warm feeling smiling secretly.

Picking up peach blossoms in dream every night,
And floating a few flower's petals on the blue river,
You and I fall in the rosy gulf.

Ah! I have to send the innocent woman far away,
With grudging to part her.

The throbbing breath
Behind her broadcast joining with her announcement,
Has been echoed in my heart clearly.

- Tr. by Won Eung-soon

이상향의 여인
—호숫가에서

찬란한 봄빛이 드리우면
호숫가 저편에서
선연히 들려오는 그대 목소리

잔잔한 호수를 바라보면
수면 위에 떠오르는 그리운 영상
가슴 설레는 지극한 애련

호수처럼 적시어 오는 그의 눈동자
넌지시 미소하는 여운의 온정

밤마다 꿈결 속에 도화 꽃을 따들고
푸르디푸른 강물에 한잎 두잎 띄우며
그대와 나는 장밋빛 심연에 젖어 있다

아! 그립고 아쉬움에
멀리 보내야 하는 청순한 그녀

어우르는 아나멘트에
방송의 뒤란에서 켕기는 그 호흡!
지금도 낭랑히 메아리 져 온다.

Your Smile

In this wide world
Among the many persons
You with smile flied to me silently
Became a light of hope
And a seed of love,
Bloomed the flower of happiness in my gentle heart.

Whenever, wherever, and whoever else,
Even in our delight, or in our sadness
The one who occurs to me first of all is only you.
Darling! when you began to sleep soundly
I stared your sleeping figure silently.

About your beautiful eye rims that the two letters
"Getting old" weren't suitable for you,
The year's medals are seen.
My heart was too full for words.

Kim Kye-yoon / Korea

* Graduated from The College of Medicine in Jeonnam University.
* Finished The Graduate School of Jeonnam University(M.D.).
* The president of the southern branch of The International Wise Man.
* Awarded the golden prize of Red Cross Philanthropy Prize.
* Debut through "Jigu Munhak" by essays.
* A member of The World Poetry Research Institute.
* Published a poetical works entitled "A Dreamy Hwangryong River"
* Address : Kim Hospital, 161-2, Daemin-dong, Dong-gu, Gwangju-si, Korea

Indeed, I had a dull pain in my heart.
Truly I wouldn't stop to speak out like this:
"Darling! I wish you to be healthy."

Since I was born in this world, and have been living,
If I say I found the one largest happiness,
It should be very you.
I was fond of you and
I loved you so much that
I have felt very happy owing to your favor.

- Tr. by Won Eung-soon

당신의 미소

이 넓은 세상 속에
이 많은 사람 중에
미소 품은 그대가 내게 사뿐 날아와
희망의 빛이 되고
사랑의 씨앗이 되어
잔잔한 내 가슴에 행복의 꽃을 피웠습니다.

언제 어디에서 그 누구라도
기쁜 일이 생겨도 슬픈 일이 생겨도
제일 먼저 생각나는 사람은 오직 당신입니다.
여보! 어젯밤 당신이 곤히 잠들 때
나는 그대의 잠든 모습을 가만히 보았습니다.

"늙음"이란 두 글자가 당신에겐 어울리지 않았던
그 고왔던 그대의 눈가에도
세월의 훈장이 보이더군요.
가슴이 찡했습니다.
참으로 마음이 저려왔습니다.
"여보! 건강만 해주세요." 라는
말이 입술을 타고 흐르더군요.

내가 세상에 태어나 지금까지 오면서
제일 큰 행복 하나 찾았노라고 말 한다면
그건 바로 틀림없는 당신일 겁니다.
그대를 좋아하고
그대를 사랑할 수 있었기에
나는 그대 덕에 참으로 행복했으니까요.

Swallowing A Glow of Sunset

I desired to go to the north, to the north,
Expecting you against the Imjin river.
If I've one red heart,
Can't I live even a frozen land of the north?
They persuade me to give up the heart silently,
Erecting the cock's comb of the south.
But, look at the rusty hedgehog around the Imjin river.
That is not the very problem of my own heart,
But perhaps the enduring mobile load against the turbid stream,
Wearing a crown of thorns weaved with 38wires.
You said that you liked more the heart than a triangle and a root,
Who had come and gone through the north and the south.
If you lead me to go the north taking my hands,
I would go to the place against the south.
As if roaming like the rusty Cupid's arrow,
Hanging about in the path, entering the woods,
And sleeping together with the trees being faint in verdant shades,

Kim Kyung-hee / Korea

*The 3rd Daughter of the Resistance Poet Kim Ak in Gwang-Ju City.
*A Member of the Literary Men's Association of Korea; of the Modern Poets Association.
*Vice Chairman of the Literary Movement & Trend; A Editor of Gangseo Literary Association of Seoul.
* Chief Editor of Eulji Publishing Corporation
*Received the Prize of Literature of the Literary Movement & Trend.
*Anthology: <The Beautiful Scolding>, <The Soul Sketch in Soul>, etc..
*Address: 1269, Guro-Bondong, Gurogu, Jungang Apt., 10-1901, Seoul.

I would desire to be an etranger with you.
If the angle of my heart is at an angle of 38 degrees,
Could it be possible? However, my shadow is dyed in black color
about the border line of fresh water of Imjin river,
What can I do?

- Tr. by Won Eung-soon

노을을 삼키며

그대 바라보며 임진강 거슬러
북으로 북으로 가고 싶었습니다
붉은 하트 하나만 있다면
동토의 북녘에선들 못 살겠는지요
남쪽 맨드라미 닭벼슬 곧추세우고
조용히 그 하트를 버리라고 타이릅디다
허나, 임진강 철조망 녹슬어 버린 걸 보세요
바로 그건 제 심장의 문제가 아니라
38줄로 엮은 가시면류관 쓰고
견디고 있는 저 탁류의 활하중活荷重 탓 아닌지요
남과 북 오르내리던 그대가
삼각뿔이나 루트보다 하트가 좋다 했습니다
그대가 손을 잡고 북으로 가자면
저는 남쪽을 버리고 갈 것입니다
녹슨 큐피드 화살이 헤매듯
길에서 서성이다 수풀로 들어가
녹음에 실신한 나무들과 혼숙하며
그대와 에뜨랑제가 되고 싶습니다
제 심장의 각도 38도면 되겠는지요?
헌데, 제 그림자가 민물 경계선쯤에서
검은 빛으로 물들어가니 어쩌면 좋지요

The Wind's Way

The wind rises in a gulf.
The wind, losing its way cuts to the quick.
It drives looking for the way,
Even colliding, falling down, and getting smashed,
Toward the way that we cannot stop,

Where are you going?

The heavy snowfall, inflating the mother earth
Like cappuccino's bubbles,
And your heart gets touched with even one snowflake,
Having much red liquid, gushed out from its scratch.

Whom are you looking for?

The overcoat, being stripped off by the wind,
The shoes, getting ripped(torn),
I contend against you standing in the raw,

Kim Mi-kyoung/Korea

* Born at Gangjin, Jeon-Nam, Korea.
* Graduated from Dept. of the National Language and Literature of the Air and Correspondence College of Korea.
* An Authorized Intermediary(Present).
* Recommended As a Poet from the Monthly 'the Literary Movement & Trend'.
* A Member of the World Poetry Research Institute

So the offended scratches are deep
Setting up the colder body than ice and mind.

Standing on the way of the wind,
Looking for me?
And from an inscrutable life
Looking for the way of the other shore?

The ice, covered with snow
The lake, covered with ice
And the deep silence under the lake
Are suffering from the recollecting seasons.

Even an ecstatic sadness stays on the way of the wind,
And you are sick on its way too.

- Tr. by Won Eung-soon

바람의 길

심연에서 바람이 일었다
길 잃은 바람은 폐부를 후빈다
길을 찾아 바람을 운전한다
부딪치고 넘어지고 깨어져도
멈출 수 없는 그 길을 향하여

어디로 가느냐 너는

카푸치노 거품처럼
대지를 부풀리는 폭설
눈송이 하나에도 마음이 부딪쳐 덜컥,
생채기에도 쏟아진 검붉은 액체 흥건하다

누구를 찾느냐 너는

바람에 외투가 벗겨지고
신발이 찢겨
맨몸으로 서서 너와 대적한다
얼음보다 찬 몸과 마음 대지에 세우고
덧난 생채기 깊어진다

바람의 길에 서서
나를 찾느냐?
불가해한 삶에서
피안의 길을 찾느냐?

눈 덮인 얼음
얼음 덮인 호수
호수 밑 깊은 정적이
추억의 계절을 앓는다

황홀한 슬픔도 그 길에 머물고
바람의 길에서 너도 앓고 있구나.

The Fantastic Picture

- Poem for an Appreciation of the Theme on Fantastic Pictures

The wire-netted bamboo pole hung on the roof is colored,
And disposed of distance and shading in many folds or single fold.
Viewing at the side, it looked like a bamboo wood with the wire entanglement,
And at the front, it is a figure painting of still life like one of Minerva Hermit.

Flashing it with optical lens,
The half-crossed thinking figure looks like sitting,
The Leaning Tower of Pisa looks like a triangular position in optical illusion.

Rise and fall of all natures
Uncertainty in time and space with distrust of Changes,
And man's body is linked with 5 essences of creation,
So what a longevity, a prosperity, and an attachment they are!

All things in the world
Is like a fantastic picture brought into practice.
Ah! how wonderful, or mysterious the providence of the Creation is!

* Minerva: A goddess of wisdom, industrial arts, and war in Roman mythology.

* 5 Essences of Creation: Color, Sense, Imagination, Action and Cognition.

- Tr. by Won Eung-soon

Kim Sang-hyun/Korea

* Pen name is Keum Gang.
* Born in Yang-ju gun, Gyeong-gi do in 1937.
* Graduated from the subject of literary art in Seolabol Art College.
* A member of The Korean Writer's Association.
* An executive of The World Poetry Research Institute.
* The president of 'Baek-ya' Literary Association.
* Poetry books : "A Beggar Who Sits on A Golden Cushion"(2003) "Anthology of Korean Famous Poems"(2003, collaboration)
* Address : 608-202, Hanguk Apt, 727-2, Sin-gok-dong, Uijeongbu-si, Gyeonggi-do, 480-787, Korea

환영화幻影畵
—환영 주제 미전 관람 감상시

철망 죽봉을 천정에 달아 채색하고
원근 명암을 다겹 단겹을 처리하였다
옆에서 보면 철조망 대나무 숲 같고
앞에서 보면 인물 정물화 *미네르바 신선도

광합 렌즈로 비추어 보니
반가좌 사유상이 정좌하고
피사탑이 정립 착시하다

영고성쇠 삼라만상은
무상시공 불신변이물不信變異物
인체 또한 *오온 연합緣合이어늘
장생 영화 애착 얼마나 가련한 일인가

세상에 모든 것
실상에 이기 체용 환영화이어라
아! 천지섭리 경이 경외여!

* 미네르바: 로마신화의 여신으로 지혜, 공예, 전쟁의 여신.
* 오온: 창조의 5요소로 색수상행식色受想行識

An Impromptu Poem (Beginning 7 Characters)

- It's a Great Prize Winner's Poem at a Literary Writing Contest

Jeon - In the deep dream, the previous night
Guk - A beautiful lover has been to me, in fragrance of a
chrysanthemum
Dae - At every curve round the High Hills named Daekwanryung
Pyo - The Floating Clouds Conspicuously
Ja - A proud old friend at Wonju province
Dae - Opening the great door, the high Chi-ark mountain's foot is
seen
Hoe - Greeting us with its complacent smile and its open heart
The aroma of the flowers is full under the sky of Wonju.

* The above poem is called an impromptu poem beginning the first letter of 7 characters, but I think it's not possible to translate the poem exactly. So I wish you to appreciate its contents only.

- Tr. by Won Eung-soon

Kim Sang-kyung/ Korea

* Pen name: Hyang Myung
* Born at Asan, Kochang, Jeonbuk, Korea
* Studied under the Poet, Shin Seok-jeong
* Made a Debut as a Poet from 'the Literary Arts and Trend'
* Vice Chairman of Yangcheon Literary Association
*A Defence Committee of Copyrights in Korean Writers' Association, and of a Member of the Modern Poets' Association.
*A Commander of Shinwol No. 2 District at Uangcheon Police Station
Address: 361-1 Hwagok 1-dong, Kangseo-gu, Hwagok Daelim Apt. 5-1504, Seoul
Tel: 010-6211-2100(H.P.)

즉흥 7행시

—32차 문협 전국 대표자대회 백일장에서 장원 수상작

전 - 전날밤 깊은 꿈 속
국 - 국화꽃 향기 속에 고운 님 왔다 가더니
대 - 대관령 굽이굽이
표 - 표표히 흐르는 구름
자 - 자랑스런 원주의 오랜 벗이
대 - 대문 열고 치악산 기슭
회 - 회심의 미소 띠고 가슴 열어 맞이하니
원주 하늘 아래 국화 향기 가득하네

A White Night

It is almost pitch black.
On the ground of the boisterous world
With grey clouds
Covered by darkness,
White snow flows down shuffling along.

Cover this stuffily hollow world
With the bright, golden colored one
And cover a human, the humans
Who have spoiled the brutal nature
Like sternness.

Bury it all,
This white night,
And cover the hearts that distort the truth.
And struggling frozen hard,
Return to life again as white snow.

Then,
It will come back home of the mother's breast again.

- Tr. by Won Eung-soon

Kim Seok-ki/Korea

* Pen Name: Il-Mook.
* Graduated from the Air and Correspondence College.
* Recommended As a Poet from the Literary Magazine of 'the Han-Wul Literature'.
* A Member of the Literary Men's Association of Korea; of the International Pen Club in Korea.
* A Member of the World Poetry Research Institute of Korea.
* An Official at the Health Insurance Corporation(Present).
* Address: 40-2, Jungangdong, Gwachun City, Geonggido, Seoul.
* E-mail: sksanai@hanmail.net

하얀 밤

칠흑漆黑 같다
어둠이 깔린
잿빛 구름 더불어
난무亂舞하는 세상
어그정거리며 흰 눈발
땅 위로 흘러내린다.

답답하고 어웅한 이 세상
밝은 생금빛 세상으로
덮고 또 덮어라
서릿발 같은 검붉은 야성野性
저지르는 인간, 인간들

이 하얀 밤,
모두 묻혀 버려라
진실眞實이 왜곡된 심장도 덮어라
꽁꽁 얼어붙어 몸부림치다
다시 하얗게 되살아나거라

그리하면,
젖무덤 고향으로 다시 돌아오리라

A Grain of Sand

There is time in a grain of sand
As a grain, a grain, pieces of time,
And mysterious pieces of all of the universe.

A grain of sand has the wind's traces,
The moon's sob,
The sun's strong footmark,
And even the sound of waves and of crying fishes
Has been recorded in a grain of sand.

Your pains and sobs
And a history of human being
Has been written in a grain of sand without saying.

That we see through a grain of sand
The universe and history.
A grain of sand, you have been valuable!

- Tr. by Won Eung-soon

Kim So-youb / Korea

* Recommended As a Poet from the Literary Magazine 'the Han Kook Literature'.
* A Member of the Modern Poets Association; of the International Pen Club; of the Literary Men's Association of Korea
* Director of the Woman's Literary Society of Korea.
* Chair Professor of Department of Creative Writing, Daejun University
* President of the Whole Christian Culture Art Association of Korea(Present)
* Poetical Anthology: <Thou Rising As a Star>with others.
* Collection of Essays: <The Green Color Life>with others.
* Address: 261, Chungsoodong ,Chunan City, Chung-Nam, Sunkyung Apt. 112-601.
* E-mail: kimsoyeop@yahoo.co.kr * Mobile: 010-2440-6615

모래 한 알

모래알에는 시간이 들어 있다
한알 한알 시간의 파편들
온갖 우주의 신비로운 조각들

모래알에는 바람의 자국과
달빛의 흐느낌과
햇빛의 강렬한 발자욱과
파도소리와 물고기들의 울음소리까지
모두 녹음되어 있다

모래알에는 너의 애통과 흐느낌
인류의 역사가 말없이 적혀 있다

모래알 한 알에서도
우주와 역사를 보나니
한 알 모래알이 얼마나 소중한가

A Star having a love in its mind

You are shining like a star having a love in its mind,
being tightly hugged in my bosom.

You are flying to a dream world "The Everland"
your two little twinkling hands, quickly toddling.
kissing a lot of wild flowers gently,
following a butterfly fluttering.

jumping up and down, clapping your little hands,
with seeing comely flights of white peacocks and all of the little birds in forest.
I hear you laughing with a silvery voice.

You are seeing sleeping lions with dangling theirs body,
slowly swimming penguins.
and eating your baby food at the cozy room.

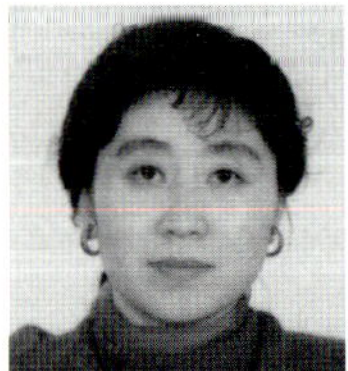

Kim Sun / Korea

* Born in Seoul
* Studied at Songshin Women's University,
Graduate School of Songshin Women's University,
Graduate School of Seoul National University, majored Piano.
* Studied at Korea National Open University, majored English language literature
* Debuted through Gigu Literature Journal
* Address: 301 Ho, 105 Dong, Joyparkvill, 139-6, NamSan-ri, PaengSeong-eub, PyeongTaek-Si, Gyeonggi-do, 451-803, Korea.

looking at yourself in magic glass,
sitting on the rainbow settee,
with toddling at the Secret Rose Garden.

smiling at a child your age each other,
with getting on a train and a merry-go-round.

dancing in your bare feet like a willow, through a fountain
like white flowers of buckwheat.

Our love is getting growing with touching your tender cheeks,
and Our shoulders are shaking when laughing.

You are shining like a star having a love in its mind,
being tightly in my bosom.

- Tr. by Kim Sun

사랑을 머금은 별

쏘옥 품에 안긴 너는
사랑을 머금은
별처럼 빛난다

두 손 반짝이며
꿈의 에버랜드
잰걸음으로 불러들여
팔랑대는 나비 좇아
다소곳이 무리져 핀 야생화에 입 맞추고
숲 속 새 하얀 공작새 무리의 우아한 비행
온갖 귀여운 새들의 날갯짓에
작은 손 마주치며 동동대는 두 발
귓가에 번지는 은방울 웃음

늘어져 잠자는 사자
유유히 수영하는 펭귄들
휴식 공간 오붓한 식사
장미 향 가득한 씨크릿 정원에서
뒤뚱뒤뚱 걸음마로
요술 거울 보며
무지개 의자 앉아 보고
한 바퀴 기차와 회전목마 돌며
또래 보고 웃음 짓고

하이얀 메밀꽃 같은 분수 새로
나부끼는 벗은 발들의 춤

Korea/김 선

까르르 웃음에 들썩이는 어깨들
살며시 젖어드는 사랑
마주치는 보드라운 뺨

쏘옥 품에 안긴 너는
사랑을 머금은
별처럼 빛난다

A Long Wait

Like a seeker after truth in solitude,
Seeming to pick up and swallow even the sound of winds,

Did I attain a spiritual state of self-effacement in a mountain temple?
Infiltrating through darkness in the night,

The loneliness
In a mute, dusky one-room,

When I lay myself down on bed alone,
Hearing by chance between being asleep and awake,

To the sound of falling leaves
In case it is a sweet heart,

I listen to it with throbbing.

- Tr. by Won Eung-soon

Kim Sun-chul/Korea

*Graduated From Kochang High School, Jeon-Buk.
*Served 25 years As a Civil Servant of Police.
*An Auditor of Kochang Branch of the Literary Men's Association of Korea.
*A Commentator of Culture Sightseeing in Jeon-Buk.
*A Member of the World Poetry Research Institute.
*Address; 489, Gesanmyun, Asanri, Kochanggun, Jeon-Buk, Korea.

기다림

바람 소리마저 집어삼킬 것 같은
적막 속에 구도인처럼

산사에서 무아의 경지에 이른 것인가
밤이면 어둠을 뚫고 찾아드는

외로움에
어스름이 묵기 어린 단칸방에서

홀로 누워 있노라면
비몽사몽으로 귓전을 스쳐가는

낙엽 굴리는 소리에
행여 님이련가

설레임으로 귀 기울인다

Psalms On Autumn 12

The sound of a clock, crying in the autumn night
Flowing in the river,
The far off sound, being deep endlessly,
Alarming again as melody in the grave,
And it's sound of revolving, and crying.
At the end of a yesterday's life
Coming drawn by the elastic string,
The deep blue spearhead
Crying in the autumn night,
The sad temple without a true Buddha
Running idle for nihilism,
Again, in this night standing and seeing,
Time at this side,
Time at that side, that we never go to
The sound of the clock on the head,
Alarming in the autumn,
Runs idle again and again-.

- Tr. by Won Eung-soon

Kim Sung-youl/Korea

*Born in Namwon, Jeon-buk
*Won a literary award in a field of shijo through 'Literary Movement & Trend' * Won a criticism of literature as a budding writer
*A member of Korean Writers' Association *A member of Korean Poem(shijo) poets' Association *A member of Jeonla shijo literary association *The chief vice-president of Literary Movement & Trend *An editor of the world of literature of Korean Nation in China *An editor of an the Korean Poetry Encyclopedia *An academic adviser at the social education department of Kongki University *An editor in chief of Literary Movement & Trend * Aon a prize of Korean Free Poet Association *Won the Kaya Gold Crown of the World Poetry *Literary work: Published poetical works entitled 'Mountains and Rivers dear to Me', 'Journal for Returning Home', 'The Flag of Farming'
*Address : room 611-1103, dongmoon good morning Apt, Supsokkil maul, dongpe-ri 1687, kyoha-eup, paju si, Gyeonggi-do

가을 시편 12

가을밤에 울고 있는 시계 소리
강물로 흘러와서
무덤 속의 선율로 다시 우는
먼－ 소리는 끝없이 깊어
돌면서 울고 있는 시계 소리
고무줄로 당겨서 오는
어제의 삶의 끝자락에서
가을밤을 우는
시퍼런 창 끝
무상으로 헛돌고 있는
구슬픈 적멸보궁
다시, 서서 보는 이 밤에
기어이 못가는
이 쪽 세월,
저 쪽 세월,
가을에 우는 시계 소리는
머리 위에서
자꾸만 헛돌고 있어－.

A Path of A Mountain Valley

The cosmos flowers at one side in the empty field
Getting wet in the rain,
And your looks shaking askew,
As if being drunk by the strong wind,
Are soaked to the loneliness.
With only wetness on its clothes
Hiding in that solitude,
Grazing as if it were someone's tear,
Your appearance, hanging around your walking steps
In order to cut your way through a rainy way,
Is haunted by.

- Tr. by Won Eung-soon

Kim Whoa-ja/Korea

* Poet. Born in Chungbuk, Korea.
* Graduated from National Lang& Lit. of Busan University.
* A Member of KBS Chorus.
* Director of Korea Woman's System.
* First Debut as a Poet through "Literary Movement & Trend"
* A Member of the World Poetry Research Institute, Baekma Literature, Daejeon Poets' Association(Present).
* Received the Literature Prize of the World Poetry Institute
* Address: 487, Sajeong-dong, Joong-gu, Woonamstawon 101-801, Daejeon City.

산골 길

빈 들판 한켠에
비에 젖은 코스모스
세찬 바람 위로 술 취한 듯
비틀대는 너의 모습
외로움이 스며 젖는다
저 속에 숨어 있는
누구의 눈물인 양 스쳐가는
옷깃에 물기만 남아
빗길 헤치는 걸음걸음에
서성이는 너의 모습
눈에 밟힌다

Han's Home Town

A starlight, keeping the galaxy
Over the hillock,
Where Genghis Khan was riding.

The soft garden of grass
With the ridges of Ural Altaic,
The carpet like the earth star.

Under the sun-shined heaven
And the earth,
The Khan, Ochirbat*
He is a servant of new nation.

The mother's blood,
Holding hand in hand
It's Mongolian speckle.

* Khan: leader, king.
* Ochirbat: The 1st President of Mongolia Democracy(1993).

- Tr. by Won Eung-soon

Kim Woon-jung/Korea

* Born at Euisung, Kyeongbuk, Korea, 1950.
* Graduated from Dept. of Business Administration, Hanyang Univercity(M.A. Degree)
* First Debut as a Sijo Poet through "the Literature Monthly", 2006.
* Director of Seoul Association of UNESCO Korea, and Member of International Rotary Club, district 3650, Namsol Rotary Club.
* A Member of the Literary Writer's Association of Korea, and of the Modern Poet's Association of Korea.
* Director of "Palbang Trading Company"(Present).
* Poetic Anthology: "Bound for the Earth"(2007), "Land, of Arirang"(2009), Fly Above the Cheonsan Mountain"(2010).
* Address: 529-159 Bupyungdong, Bupyunggu, Palbangsan, Incheon City, Korea.
* Telephone: 02-2631-4080, 032-504-4080/ 010-3080-8000(Handphone).

한韓의 고향

칭기스 말 달리던
구릉 너머엔
은하銀河 지킨 별빛.

알타이 우랄 등성
이고 잔 풀밭
지구별 양탄자.

햇볕 쬔
하늘 땅 칸*
오치르바트*
새 나라 새 머슴.

손에 손 마주 잡은
어머니의 피
몽골리안 반점.

* 칸: 지도자, 임금
* 오치르바트: 몽골(1993년) 민주화 직선 초대 대통령

To Thee

The prime of the youth
Matures redly like my longing,
On the day when one or two words what I want to say
Pile up like falling leaves,
I would enter the red mailbox,
To be a letter brought to you.

- Tr. by Won Eung-soon

Kim Young-hee/Korea

*Born in Chungju, Chungbuk, Korea.
*Member of a Committee for Writer's Rights and Interests, Korean Writers' Association.
*Member of a Committee of the Autograph Association of Korea.
*Columnist of The Chungju Newspaper(Present).
*Reporter of the Jungangilbo in Vancuber, Canada.
*Member of Chungju Writers' Association, and of Jungwon Literature.
*Published A Poetic Anthology 'The Moon's Lips'.

그대에게

푸르던 시간이
내 그리움처럼 붉어지고
하고픈 말 하나 둘
낙엽처럼 쌓이는 날에는
빨간 우체통에 들어가
그대에게로 가는
편지가 되고 싶다

On the Occasion of the Vega Festival

Before the Vega festival
The washing rain falls to wash their wagon,
Which the Altair and the Vega should go on together.
Good earth gets wet in the rain silently.

On the day of the Vega festival
The sudden shower falls down due to the joy's tears,
Which the Altair and the Vega shed tears in meeting.
Good earth gets wet in the tears silently.

After the Vega festival
The sudden shower falls down due to the sorrow's tears,
Which the Altair and the Vega shed tears in parting,
Good earth gets wet in the tears silently.

The drenched good earth
Swells up with a legend of love,
And our hearts are too full for words
With a dream to sprout our love.

- Tr. by Won Eung-soon

Kim Young-mi/Korea

* Pen name: Da-In
* A poet, an essayist
* A member of the Korea Writer Association
* A member of Pen Club in Korea Headquarters
* A director of the magazine "Literature & consciousness
* A chief editor of a quarterly magazine "Modern selected poems
* The chief director of the Image Literature in Korea
* Awarded] Heonan Heosol prize in 2006
* Awarded a distinguished service medal from the magazine "Literature & consciousness
* A thesis : A Strategy for self protection and existence, and so on
*Address: 9-405, Boram Apt, Bondong, Gurogu, Seoul, Korea.

칠석에 즈음하여

칠석 전에는
견우와 직녀가 서로 타고 갈
수레를 닦기 때문에 세차우가 내린다.
대지는 묵묵히 그 물에 젖는다.

칠석이 되면
견우와 직녀가 상봉하여 흘리는
기쁨의 눈물 때문에 쇄로우가 내린다.
대지는 묵묵히 그저 그 눈물에 젖는다.

칠석 다음에는
견우와 직녀가 이별하여 흘리는
슬픔의 눈물 때문에 또 쇄로우가 내린다.
대지는 묵묵히 그저 그 눈물에 젖는다.

촉촉이 젖은 대지는
사랑의 전설로 온통 부풀어
우리는 사랑을 싹틔울 꿈으로
마음이 벅차다.

Before *Nogaree

Nogaree smells of wind passing by the bed of a salt-pond.
It's the smell from my husband entering with his back in the moonlight.

The elastic body,
With its desire and moisture for existence being captured,
Practices of Zen meditation lying silently on the plate.
As if wiping out the polluted scars from the open life,
I put the liquor 'soju' into my heart filled with love and hate.
While my heated lips are licking, with unfilled thirst from within,
Its fins, sticked to its body, flap its wings.
While its heart becomes salted by the castrated dream,
The little pollack waves bounding up my wine glass,
Together with smell of salt and slime.
At last I didn't chew the 'Nogaree'
Due to the wave's sound whirling near the mouth like the undrinkable sea water,

---

Kim Young-mi/Korea

* Pen name: Sim-Jeon
* Born at Chung-Ju, Chung-Buk, Korea.
* Recommended As a Poet from the Literary Movement & Trend.
* A Member of the Literary Men's Association of Korea.
* An Auditor of Gwangju Branch of the Whole Art Federation of Korea.
* Director of the Publication of Gwangju Literary Men's Association .
* Poetical Anthology: The Trampled Earthworm Cuts the Paralyzed Past, etc.
* Address: 422-1 Sam-Lee, Gonjiam-Eup, Hyun-yeunrip B-dong, #103, Kwangju City, Kyunggi-do, Korea

Only I drink 'soju' with no appetizers,
Looking at my finger's tip breaking 'Nogaree's body.

Before the 'Nogaree' resembling the sea after emptying my hard life lightly,
The malicious tongue of mine dreaming the drinkable escape gets dry,
My desire's scale of no emptied scatters in the air.

From its dry eyes, with nothing wet in its bowels,
Why I see the sea continually?
Why does the heart's wound benumbed by alcohol,
Make sound of waves increasing its body?

* Nogaree: a kind of Alaska pollack, dried fish.

- Tr. by Won Eung-soon

노가리 앞에서

노가리에서 염전 바닥을 스치던 바람 냄새가 난다
달빛을 등지고 들어서는 지아비 몸에서 맡던 그 냄새다

탄력 있던 육체는
욕망과 생존의 습기마저 포획당한 채
가지런히 접시에 누워 참선중이다
구멍 난 삶으로 오염된 상처를 닦아내듯
애증으로 차오르는 가슴에 소주를 부어 넣는다
채우지 못한 내 안의 갈증으로
열기 오른 입술이 접시를 훑는 사이
몸통에 달라붙어 있던 지느러미가 날개를 펼친다
거세당한 꿈으로 가슴은 염전이 되는 동안
어린 명태들이 술잔을 튀어 오르며 파도를 가른다
짠내와 갯내도 일렁인다
삼킬 수 없는 바닷물처럼 입전만 맴도는 파도소리 때문에
난 결국 노가리를 씹지 못했고
마른 몸통을 툭툭 분지르는 손끝을 바라보며 깡술을 마신다
간도 쓸개도 버려야 했을 지아비 빈 가슴을 바라보면서

치열했던 삶 가벼이 비우고 바다를 닮아가는 노가리 앞에서
취기 어린 도피를 꿈꾸는 내 독설은 서서히 말라가고
비우지 못한 욕망의 편린은 허공으로 흩어진다.

창자 속까지 수분을 비워낸 마른 눈에서 난 왜 자꾸만 바다가 보이는 걸까
알콜로 마비된 가슴의 상처는 왜 자꾸만 몸통을 불리며 파도소리를 내는 걸까

Mt. Jiree

The soft love
Like mother's breast,
I don't know its depth.

It has been a pillar of our race
Which took its place deep inside the Korean peninsula.
It's a celebrated mountain,
Surrounded by range after range,

Mt. Jiree,
Holding out to the end without a shake

Is our pride
That has kept up our nation in any adverse situation
Even suffering uncountable human pains.
And it's our existing ground like a broken boat
Defending safely on its central axis.

- Tr. by Won Eung-soon

Ko Bang-kyu / Korea

* Born at Okjeri, Sungnaemyun, Gochang, Jeon-Buk.
* Graduated from Dept of Literary Art of Masan Changshin University.
* Retired from the Managing Materials of Changwon Factory in Han Hwa Group.
* Recommended As a Sijo Poet from the Sijo Literature, 2003.
* A Member of the Lierary men's Association of Korea; of the World Poetry Research Institute of Korea; the Literary Coterie ' Soorim'; of A Consultant of the New Age Literature.
* Poetical Anthology: <A Love As Rose Flower>.
* Address: 463, Okjeri, Gochanggun, Jeon-Buk, Korea.

지리산

어머님
품속처럼 포근한 사랑
그 깊이를 알 수 없습니다

한반도 깊숙이 자리한
민족의 기둥였습니다
명산!
겹겹이 둘러 앉아

흔들림 없이
버팀목이 되어준 지리산

헬 수 없이 인류의 아픔을 안고
역경 속에서도
한민족을 지켜낸 자존심입니다
반도의 조각배라는 우리의 삶터를
안전한 중심축으로

My Wife

My wife cries in autumn.
Going out to the mown field,
And recalling her gaunt father,
Without no doubt
She drops tears as big as the hen's eyes.

At the rice harvest
The father's eyes like a vine caterpillar's eyebrows
Staring the field
With eyes of the stranger's like those of Kafka
Laid his two hands
On this little daughter's shoulder silently.

Hues of a human being,
Poems of a patriarch
Are melted entirely over the field.

Being overcome by the affection between father and daughter
That has lived together for 50 years,
Today, my wife walks
And is walking again,
The yellow field along the boundless river.

- Tr. by Won Eung-soon

Koo Ja-cheol/ Korea

* First Debut as a Poet(2009)
* Member of the Poetic Circle "Geul-Saem"
* An Auditor of the Literary Association at Yangpyung Writers
* An Executive Secretary of the Literary House of Hwang Soon-won at Yangpyung

내 아내

내 아내는 가을이면 운다
벼 베인 들판엘 나가
마른 몸의 아버지를 기억하며
여지없이
닭똥 같은 눈물을 떨군다

벼 베일 즈음이면
송충이 눈썹의 아버지의 눈은
카프카 같은 이방인 눈빛으로
들판을 응시하며
키 작은 딸자식의 어깨위에
가만히 양손을 올려놓으셨다

한 인생의 색채,
한 가장의 노래가
이 들판에 고스란히 녹아 있다

오십 년을 지내온
부녀의 정 다 못 새겨
만경강가 금색가루 수놓은 벌판을
아내는 오늘도 걷고
또 걷는다

A Notion in the Rain

Whether the sky makes its wry face looking at me,
Or I frown my face looking at the sky,
When the rain comes
On the grey cloudy day,
A long way off
An unknown bird alone
Takes her way for the nest
Fluttering on her wings,
Crossing the space of the broad sky.
A notion,
Where did it hide,
Sticks her face out gapingly.

Kuk Mi-na / Korea

* Made her first debut, receiving a prize for a new Poet from 'the Literary World of Korea'(2007), and receiving a prize for a new Essayist From 'the Kukbo Literature(2007).
* Member of 'the Korean Poets', and of Cheonan Literary Association.
* Literary Works: Essay Anthology, 'Whispering Between Rain and I'.
* Hand Phone: 010-6799-3949./ E-mail: kuk8989@naver.com

빗속의 상념

하늘이 나를 보고 찌푸리는 것인지
내가 하늘을 보고 찌푸리는 것인지
회색빛 흐린 날
배가 내릴라 치면
멀리서
이름 없는 새가 홀로
날갯짓하며
넓은 하늘 허공을 가로질러
둥지로 향한다.
상념想念은
어디에 숨어 있었는지
빠끔히 얼굴을 들이내민다.

Disinterested Beatitude

Have you ever heard
The secret sound when the red sun is setting,
At the west sky?
The world
Is beautiful even its fadeaway,

Have you ever seen
The wind waving branches
Passing and shaking by a wind?
Even the passing is missing,

There are many things
For me not to be heard,
Not to be seen
In the world.

- Tr. by Won Eung-soon

Kwak Byung-soo/Korea

* Pen name: Su-Am
* Won a Great Prize of 'the Modern poetry'
* Vice president of the Literary Circle of Seoul City
* Director of 'Seoul of Poetry'
* Finished Course of Creating Poetry at Hansung University
* Served as a Civil Servant
* Chief Director of Kyung-Hee Construction
* Poetic Anthology: <The Grave of Mind>, <Thou, Wake up>
* Address: 1704-102dong, Deokhyeon Apt, 808, Gyomun2-dong, Guri-city, Geonggi-do, Korea.
* E-mail: KBS3161@hanmail.net

무심

서쪽 하늘 붉은 노을
해 넘어가는 은은한 소리
그대는 들어 보았는가
세상은
사라지는 것조차 아름다운데

바람에 흔들리는 나뭇가지
스치며 흔드는 바람을
그대는 보았는가
지나가는 것들도 그리운데

세상에
들리지도 않고
보이지도 않는 것이
나에게는 너무나 많구나.

Looking at Craypas

Perhaps it was we were living extremely poor,
when I was a 4th grade primary school boy.
I made a picture using my crayons
Similar to the colorful candles sparingly.
One day, I painted a picture entitled 'night',
Which was sauce crocks lying aside,
At that time I became a foolish boy in public,
Believing the crocks at night to sleep.
Since I had lost the chance to make an excuse for the fact clearly,
I suppose I have grown up as a man,
Who had not made a drawing,
Satisfying as proxy of appreciating other man's pictures
In spite of my ardent desire of arts.
When I find present pupils to use fine colorful and various crayons rashly,

---

Lee Byeong-chang/Korea

* Born in1952
* Graduated from wonkwang Univ. specialized in Korean literature
* Graduated from a theological school of the Presbyterian denomination church, graduated from a theological school of Mokwon Univ. (Th. M)
* Get my education from Hanshin Univ.
* Started a literary career through the news paper of Christian
* Made a debut in letter again through 'Literaturer & Consciousness'
* The chairman of the just society of clergymen in Jeonbuk
* A general manage of the society of the Christian in Jeonbuk
* Occupied the chair of the Korean Christian
* A pastor in charge of Jindalrae Church
* President of Green Cross of Korea in Jeonbuk headquarters
* Address : 462, Shindeok-ri, Shindeok-myeon, Limsil-gun, Jeon-buk, Korea
* Phon No: 063-644-1551, 016-608-6941

I don’t know why I am so worried about it.
Looking at the craypas's pieces,
Being discarded, thrown away
The painful outcry of the painter,
Vincent Van Gogh seemed to be heard:
“I will pay your debts for them. If not, I will give my soul instead”
I wonder whether nowadays there is such a teacher as teaching,
‘The mountain has to be painted green color’,
‘The sky has to be blue color’,
And ‘the tree has to be tree-color, or not.

- Tr. by Won Eung-soon

크레파스를 보면서

초등학교 사학년 때였을 거야
그때는 무척 가난하게들 사는 때였지
색깔 있는 양초나 다를 바 없는 크레용을
그나마 아껴가면서 그림을 그렸지
어느 날 밤이라는 제목으로
장독 항아리들을 옆으로 누인
그림을 그렸는데
그날 나는 공개적으로
밤이 되면 장독이 누워 잔다고 믿는
바보가 되고 말았지
그렇게 표현할 수밖에 없는 진실이
무참하게 짓밟힌 그날 이후
나는 그림을 그려 본 적이 없이
성장한 거 같아
미술에 대한 열망을 남의 그림을 보는 것으로
대리 만족하면서.
요즘 아이들이 색깔 좋고 다양한 크레파스를
함부로 다루는 걸 보면 왜 그렇게
마음이 안 좋은지 몰라
버려져 나뒹구는 크레파스 조각마다
'돈은 꼭 갚겠다. 안되면 내 영혼을 주겠다' 고
절규한 고흐의 음성이 들리는 것 같아.
산은 녹색
하늘은 파란색
나무는 나무색으로 그려야 한다고 가르치는
그런 선생님이 요즘도 계신 건 아니겠지.

Green Mountains

The green mountains on March are pregnant with auspicious signs.
The last winter was so cold to have hard time,
That the babe grasses shiver pitifully from cold.

Are the rivers and mountains on April warm?
The profiteering scoundrels are very brazenfaced,
Making an excuse of the nation's matters, they commit theft.

We have enjoyed the democratic politics and only promoted lots of skills of theft.
Quit! Political profiteers, at first it's our country, next it's people.
Hold off the parliamental politics, govern the profiteers.

The blameless angels emigrated from this nation
Being sick at their hearts, the day will come before long,
That will be filled with many kinds of vulgarians.

The master left his house empty, if the stranger became a master,
Why don't you know the colonial period of Japanese, and continue to commit theft!
Oh! Heaven, bless our country to be an honest world.

- Tr. by Won Eung-soon

Lee Chang-hwan/Korea

* Pen name: wolin
* Published 26 volumes of poem-collections.
* Primary Ph. D and doctor of literature. Doctor of chinese medicine.
* The 28th Director of Sungkyunkwan
* Executive chairman of Traditional Culture Promotion Society inc.
* Member of "Korea Literary Writer Association", "International P.E.N. Club" and "World Poetry Association"
* Address : 176-3, Seobu-Dong Yeongyang-Eup Yeongyang-gun Gyeong-buk 764-800, Korea. Tel.(054) 682-7788

청산青山

삼월 청산은 서기 충천瑞氣衝天하다
지난겨울 너무 추워 고생했다고 애기풀이
야들야들 떨어 애처롭다

사월 강산은 따뜻한가
치정배治政輩들 간신肝腎이 큼직큼직 하구나
나랏일 핑계로 적도賊盜만 하는구나

민주방식 즐기다가 아이어른 적술賊術만 키웠네
아서라 치정배들아, 나라 있고 백성 있네
의회치법議會治法 없애버리고 적도賊盜부터 다스려라

죄 없는 천사들 간 쓸개가 썩어서
이 땅에 살 수 없어 이민 가고 잡종雜種 색깔
이 땅 덮을 날 얼마 남지 않았다

주인은 집을 비우고 나그네가 주인 되면
왜놈시대 다시 오는 것 왜 모르고 도적질이여
오호 하늘이시여, 정직히 사는 세상 내려 주소서

Waiting

I look at the sky,
Leaning over the window,
Holding a cup of hot coffee.

If that wind ceases,
Could he come?

At once my mind
Runs after you already,
And only the white clouds is floating high up,

The yellow flowery rain comes down in the sky,
Carried on the wind.

Though the silks and satins like throbbing
Are dazzling so soon at a junction of the street,
It seems as if you would not come yet.

- Tr. by Won Eung-soon

Lee Chung-hee / Korea

* Made a Debut as a poet from 'the Global Literature'(2003)
* Member of the Korean Writers' Association
* Member of Guro Literary Association
* Member of "Ye-sarang" Literary Circle
* Member of Korean Race Writers' Association
* Completed the whole Course of Writing Novel
* Won the Best Prize of Literature from the Korean Race Writers' Association
* Won the Golden Prize of Heonanseolwon Literature
* Poetic Anthology: 'The White Yearning'
* Joint Poetic Works: 'A Stepstone', 'Temtation of Winds', 'Corner's Path of City', 'A Yard of Literature'
* Novel: 'Novel's Nativity', 'The Golden Feeler(Antenna)'

기다림

진한 커피 한 잔 들고
창가에 기대어
하늘을 본다

저 바람 멎으면
그대 오려나

이내 맘은 벌써 그대를 쫓아
달음질치는데
흰 구름만 두둥실

바람결에 실려
하늘에선 노오란 꽃비 내리고

길목엔 어느새
설렘의 주단이 눈부시건만
그대는 아직도 아니 오시는지

Thanks to you, I am

The reason I still adore the sea is
because I'm in love with you.
The reason I still worship the sun is
because I'm in love with you.
The reason my eyes are open everyday is
because your figure is reflected in my pupil.

The reason I eagerly write poem is
because your figure is alive.
The reason I sing endlessly is
because your name is alive.
The reason my ears are open everyday is
because your voice is alive.

Thanks to you,
I realized the existence of the earth and the sky.
Thanks to you,
I realized the meaning of love and life
I am
thanks to you.

- Tr. by Lee Deok-Sang

Lee Deok-Sang / Korea

* Graduated from Korea University
* Started a literary career through " Literary Movement & Trend" (Poetry, Criticism)
* Literary works : The Name Called Waiting " etc.
* Awarded The Best Literary Ward from "Literary Movement & Trend "in 2010
* A writer & Translator
* A vice-president of " Literary Movement & Trend "
* President of 114Translation Company, President of 114 Call Center
* Address:Trade Center 816, 1107, Bisandong,Dongangu,Anyangsi,Gyeonggido
* TEL :031-385-4114 FAX: 031-385-0989 * Mobile: 010-3045-8291

난 너로 인하여

내가 여전히 바다를 흠모함은
널 사랑하기 때문이다
내가 아직도 태양을 숭앙함은
널 사랑하기 때문이다
내가 매일 눈을 뜨고 있다는 것은
너의 모습이 동공에 맺혀 있기 때문이다.

내가 열심히 시를 쓴다는 것은
너의 모습이 살아 있기 때문이다
내가 하염없이 노래한다는 것은
너의 이름이 살아 있기 때문이다
내가 매일 귀를 열어놓고 있음은
너의 목소리가 살아 있기 때문이다.

난 너로 인하여
땅과 하늘의 존재를 알았어라
난 너로 인하여
사랑과 인생의 의미를 알았어라
난
너로 인하여.

An Attachment

The love's secret words, not falling fast asleep
In my deep heart as the valuable retrospection,
Were really heartache yearning.

You, wandering always in my mind
And like a moon not leaving from heaven at dawn,
Were really heartbreaking sadness
As thick and heavy as rain.

You, for whom I pine and long,
Like stars of the Milky Way in the quiet night sky,
Stepping into the shadow of trees,
Were really my heartache love.

You, the field flower bloomed lonely in the deep valley of the mountain,
Who should endure as an old pine tree
Standing(Rooting) lonely at a crack(crevice) of rocks ,
Were really my solitude(loneliness).

- Tr. by Won Eung-soon

Lee Eun-hyeop / Korea

* Graduated in atomic energy course from Hanyang Univ.
* A principal of Ilsan Baikseok high school
* A chairman of Goyang Educational Society
*A member of Korea Writer Association
*Published a religious book: entitled 'Practical Theory of Prayer'
*Poetical anthologies: "I'll Go over that Mountain" with other 4 Vols.
* Prize: awarded 2 prizes from the Minister of Education, 2 prizes from the Minister of Science and Technology, the Order of National Service Merit, and so on.
*Address: 6-4, Daejo-dong, Eunpyeong-gu, Seoul, Korea.

미련

소중한 추억으로 마음 깊은 곳에
오래 잠들지 못하는 사랑의 밀어
가슴 아픈 그리움인 줄 몰랐습니다

새벽하늘 떠나지 못하는 달처럼
때도 없이 내 마음에 떠도는 그대
굵어지고 무거워지는 빗물 같은
내 애련한 슬픔인 줄 몰랐습니다

나무 그림자 속으로 천천히 걸어 들어온
고요한 밤하늘 은하의 별들처럼
그립고 보고 싶은 마음 가득한 그대
내 아픈 사랑인 줄 정말 몰랐습니다

깊은 산마루 홀로 핀 들꽃 같은 그대
높은 산 바위틈 홀로 서 있는 장송長松처럼
견뎌야 하는 내 고독인 줄 몰랐습니다

A Snow-flower Love

You are
The snow flake,
Who run as an arrow in the snow,
Is stuck in a target of my heart.

I am
The bosom of fire spark,
Dashing to you in a white horse strained by its manes.

It is
A snow-flower love,
Brought up by the influence of the hot and the cold,
Having fire and ice together
Between bosom and bosom.

- Tr. by Won Eung-soon

Lee Ji-young/Korea

* Hyosung University of French Literature, Member of Korean Society for Literature, Member of International PEN Club in Korea Headquarters, Member of Millennium Literature Society, Vice President of the Association of Korea National Literature, Vice President of the Society of Free Poets, Received of the Korea National Literature Prize, Received of the Literary Movement & Trend Literature Prize
*Books : 'Running in grief and Want to wet like a moonlit' 'A diary on Wet day' 'A Dreaming Confidential Talk' 'The one who is easy of access and the one that discourages friendly advances' 'Holding a Mountain in one's arms" and others
* Address: Rm 1002, 311-Dong Donga Apt Dream Town, Pyeongchon-dong, Dongan-gu, Anyang-si, Gyeonggi-do, Korea

눈꽃 사랑

너는
눈 속을 살로 달려와
내 가슴 과녁 삼아 꽂히는
눈꽃송이

나는
갈기 세운 백마로 너에게로 달려가는
불꽃 가슴

가슴과 가슴 사이
불과 얼음 함께 있어
뜨거움과 차가움의 입김으로
키우는
눈꽃 사랑.

The Reason

An alarm clock,
I am the alarm clock
Turning round in my room of thinking cave today,
I am an alarm.

At dawn,
The vitality of heaven and earth is beating,
The falling star of that sky
Along the brown ridges of Mt. Bukhan
Is passing just now.

An innocent love of mine!

He is the last height of my sincerity,
The chastity devoting to my fatherland,
And my fidelity.

Lee Kyeong-hwa/Korea

* Pen name: Lee Dok-mil
* Born at Sokcho, in Kangwondo, Korea.
* Graduated from Kangnung Girls' High School, and Dept. of Aeronautical Control in Incheon Technical Junior College.
* Announcer at Korean Airport at Kimpo.
* First debut as a poet from 'the World of Poetry', 1995.
* Poetic Anthology: The Rest Days (2007), The River Flowing Endlessly (2009), The Pearl (2010)

The pledge
That he and I made secretly,
And he,
Leading a tiny thinking boat of mine
In a favorable wind,
Is my fatherland,

An innocent love of mine,
The fatherland!
Vowing pity and royalty to him,
By resembling your kindness,

I,
Always waking,
A clock of fatherland,
I am an alarm clock.

- Tr. by Won Eung-soon

이유

자명종
나는 자명종
사색의 동굴 나의 방에
오늘도 쉬지 않고 돌아가는
나는 자명종.

천지의 정기가 박동하는
새벽이면
북한산 보랏빛 능선 따라
바야흐로 넘어가는
저 하늘의 유성

순결한 나의 님!

지성至誠의 마지막 고지
조국에 바치는 나의 정절貞節
나의 휘델리티(fidelity)

그분과 내가
남몰래 맺은 언약
위태로운 내 상념의 쪽배를
순풍으로 인도하시는
그분은
그분은 나의 조국.

순결하신 나의 님
조국이여!

나도 어진 그대 닮아
자비와 충성을 다짐하며

항상 깨어 있는
나는
조국의 시계
나는 자명종.

Tan-Heo*, A Great Buddhist Master

Through the Avatamska Sutra in one hand,
And the Chu Book of Changes in the other hand,
The great master, predicting the affairs of our country,
Earlier grew up in the family of an independence movement.

He was a philosophical monk and a studying one,
Comprehending and affirming all things in nature,
And being well versed in Confucianism, Buddhism, and the Zen,
He, taking a chalk in his hand, saying in front of the blackboard,
"Come and ask me, all intellectuals in the world!"
Was a great master in O-Dae Mountain.

The way we should go toward,
Getting out of the gorge of dashing this way and rushing that,
Is to reconcile and to cooperate with the sound Left and the rational
  Right,
And gives a hope to our people,
And it is a historic choice and a surviving way each other,
Which has already begun a posteriori Creation.

* Tan-Heo: A great monk of O-Dae Mountain in Korea.

- Tr. by Won Eung-soon

Lee Sang-jin / Korea

* Born in 1941.
* Entered upon literary career through the monthly magazine "Literary Movement & Trend"
* Served the Governor of the World Poetry Research Institute.
* Serves concurrently as professor of a school of law at Dongguk University.
* Address: #306, Hangjin Building, 2478, Hwanghak-dong, Jung-gu, Seoul. 100-871, Korea

탄허呑虛 큰스님

한 손에는 화엄경을
다른 손에는 주역을 부려서
나랏일을 예견하신 큰스님
일찍이 독립운동가 집안에서 성장하신 어르신

삼라만상의 변화를 포용하고 긍정하면서
유불선儒佛仙에 통달하신
철승哲僧이자 학승學僧이셨던 스님
백묵을 들고 칠판 앞에서
"천하의 지식인이여 와서 물어보라" 하시던
오대산의 선사禪師

우리가 가야 할 길
이제는 좌충우돌의 협곡을 벗어나
건전한 진보와 합리적 보수의 화해, 협력을!
우리 국민에게 희망을 주는 일
역사적 선택, 상생의 길로
후천개벽이 이미 시작했음을.

VANCOUVER

It is a far northern harbour
Where it lives with a poem.

The iced snow of Mt. Rocky binds the severe wind hard,
The wood of fir trees is soaring to the sky,

So beautiful the flowers are,
And an indigo lake,
So blue and wide river are,

It will sink you.

O, Vancouver with rocky mountains and cold water,
Pouring out over the warm sea!

(In Canada Conference of Korea Writer's Association, 2012. 6. 12)

- Tr. by Won Eung-soon

Lee Sang-mok / Korea

*First Debut as a Poet through "The Korea Writers", & as an Essayist through "the Korea Essay".
* A Licensed Tax Account, Yonsei MBA.
* A Member of Korea Quarters of International Pen Club, & of Korea Writer's Association.
* Writing Books: "High Tax, Low Voice", "Living Tax". "Late Confession," etc.
* Address: 954, 2nd Floor, Dogok-dong, Seoul, Korea.

밴쿠버

먼 북쪽 항구
시詩와 같이 사는 곳.

록키Rocky의 얼음 눈은 칼바람 꽁꽁 묶고
전나무 숲은 치솟는데

꽃이 아니 고울까
쪽 빛 호수에
너른 강 푸르러

그대 적시리

따스한 바다 위로 쏟아지는
바위산 시린물 밴쿠버!

King Solomon and Queen Siba

- At the Organ Recital of Hong Sun-kyung

The queen crossed the garden boldly,
Making a plan, 'I will tempt him'
That she should save her country being in peril,
What?
The queen Siba will come to see me?
His soldiers might get exhausted from a long walk on foot,
And be short of military provisions, nevertheless, come to see me?
I know. Come as much as you like.
I came here to extend my territory crossing the sea,
How could I retreat gently.
Suddenly the dark clouds are cleared off in the sky,
And the sun began to shine, the flowers to bloom, and the birds to
sing.
The queen, Siba
Appeared in the fragrant wind,
Where could the passion come to melt the iceberg?
Where did the nation go?
The King Solomon, being ever victorious
Was turned round her little finger,
The sword he drew, melt down of itself,
It was of no use controlling his mind.

- Tr. by Won Eung-soon

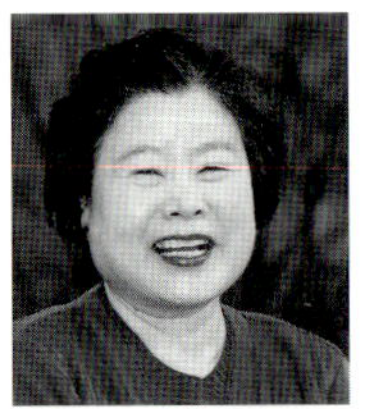

Lee Sin-kang/Korea

* Graduated in Korean literature from Sookmeong Univ. in 1968
* Started a literary career through Poetry Literature
* Won the third green poetry literature
* A director of Poetry Literature association
* A manager of the board of excavation for historical material of the Korea Writer Association
* A member of International Pen club in Korea Headquarters
* Published poetical works entitled 'A Man Who Has Been Living in An Uninhabited Island' and four others
* Address: 108-4, dunchon 2dong, kangdonggu, Seoul, Korea

솔로몬과 시바의 여왕
—홍선경 오르간 연주회에서

여왕은 위기에 놓인 나라를 구하기 위하여
'솔로몬을 유혹하리라' 는 계획을 세우고 과감히
정원을 가로질러 갔다.
뭐라고?
시바의 여왕이 나를 만나러 온다고?
먼 길을 오느라 병사들은 지치고 군량미도
바닥이 났는데 나를 만나러 온다고?
알았다, 얼마든지 와라.
내가 바다를 건너 영토를 넓히려고 왔는데
순순히 물러날 수는 없지.
갑자기 하늘에 먹구름이 걷히고 햇빛이 빛나면서
꽃들이 피어나고 새가 노래하기 시작했다.
향기로운 바람을 타고 나타난
시바의 여왕
빙산을 녹이는 뜨거움이 어디서 왔을까
나라는 어디 갔나
백전백승을 자랑하는 솔로몬이
그녀 앞에서 장난감이 되고
품었던 칼이 스르르 녹아내렸다
마음을 묶으려하나 소용없구나.

My Sweet Heart, Uhwha Dungsil

In a pictural fold screen, a cuckoo cries,
The moonlight flows in through the window,
The rosy cheeks blush shyly.

With lips like mussel flesh
Drinking a few cups from the gourd bottle,
The affection starving after austerity springs out.

The slender waist, a skirt in 12 width(pok) of joined parts,
A couple of love birds(mandarin duck) flying up on wings,
Together with 12000 peaks of the Mountain
Bearing deep love and hatred, seem to be real not a landscape painting.

My sweet heart, Uhwha Dungsil,
A moonlight of the flaming affection,
With a friend of clouds shines lively,
Making blind
A safe lamp.

- Tr. by Won Eung-soon

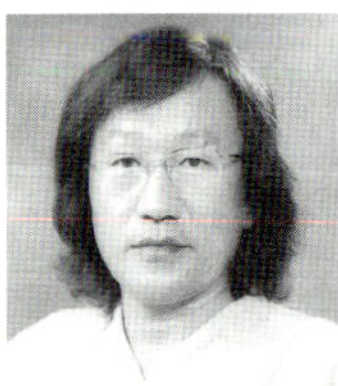

Lim In-chol / Korea

* Pen Name: Jee-Seok.
* Born at Onyang, Chum-Nam.
* Graduated from Jungang University.
* Recommended As a Poet of the Literary Movement & Trend.
* A Member of the Pen Net Literary Society in the Literary Movement & Trend Association.
* Representative Director of Han-Pel Ltd. (Present).
* Poetical Anthology: <As the Wild Flower>.

*Address: 707-1003, Mokryun Woosung Apt., Beomgyedong, Dongangu, Anyang City, Geonggido, Korea.

내 사랑 어화둥실

화병畵屛 속 두견새 울고
달빛 창에 새어드니
취한 볼 달아오르네

살조개 입술
호로병째 몇 잔 들이켜니
춘궁에 주린 정 동맥 치솟네

열두 폭 치마 가는 허리
원앙 한 쌍 활개쳐 오르니
일만 이천 봉 깊은 정한情恨
포개어진 산수화인가

내 사랑 어화둥실
불사르는 운우지정
달빛도 살아 오르니
보안등
마저 끄자꾸나

The Fire Festival

-A Sweating Bathroom of Fire

Opening the door and going in,
The falk paintings hang attractively on the yellow soil wall,
The sweating bathroom with the mugwort in a straw-thatched house
Is the fire festival removing public pollutions.

After counting thirty times hasty from one to ten,
Even counting seven times again
An effective temperature of the little sandglass
Rising to the heaven continually,

The 18 months granddaughter's loveable mouth,
Standing with 7 year old big kids
Tumbling at an outing place for the infants
Without falling down -twice so as big kids-,
Gestures jumping lightly with her dancing steps.

No Jung-ai/Korea

*Poet, Essayist
*Graduated from Graduate School of Jungang University
*Member of Korean Writers' Association
*Director of the World Poetry Institute
*Received the Prize of Kaya Golden Crown
*Received the Prize of President of the Korean Mothers' Society(Meeting)
-For Writing of an Impression on "Demian" by Herman Hesse
*Poetic Anthology: "The Earth is Indisposed (Unwell)"
*Essay Anthology: "Patchwork Wrapping Cloth"
*Address:142-8 Daehyun-dong, Seodaemun- gu, Seoul. Korea
*Tel: 02-362-6332/ 010-4762-6331 *E-Mail: nja6332@hanmail.net

Her wide eyes
And dimples
Lowing her head on the slide,
Getting to slide sensibly
And finishing so well as to be off.

You and the yellow soil room,
A winnow,
The soybean malt hanging on the wall
And an iron kettle, king of gluttons.

A Pyramid, the energy of the universe,
'A room of experience' for vitality,
The various wall pictures,
And even the architecture of Ramses,

A herb sauna
And the jade green quartz,

It is a healthy fire festival,
Attracting the energy
And pushing all pollutions out.

- Tr. by Won Eung-soon

불의 축제
—불 한증막

문을 열고 들어서면
황토벽 민속 민화들 정겹고
초가집형 쑥불 한증막
공해 모아 몰아내는 불의 축제

성급히 하나 둘 열까지
삽십 번 세고 나서 일곱까지 세고 나도
쬐고만 장구 모래시계
체감-온도 계속 하늘로 올라올라

영 유아嬰幼兒 놀이터
덤블링 일곱 살 큰애들과 서서
넘어지지큰애들만큼 두 번 넘어짐 않고
콩콩 뛰며 춤사위까지
손짓하는 18개월 손녀의 단정한 입

미끄럼틀에서 엎디어
요령껏 미끄러져
떨어져 마무리 하는
땡그란 눈이랑
보조개

너와 황토방
키,
벽에 매달린 메주
먹색 왕 무쇠솥

우주의 원기 피라미드
기氣 '체험실'
다양한 벽화와
이집트 람세스의 건축학까지

한의韓醫 사우나
비취색 차돌멩이들

기氣 모아 온갖 공해
떨궈 내는
편안한 불의 축제

A Mountain

The mountain of spring calls us shyly like virgin,
With its soft green "dress on".

The mountain of summer tempts us "powerfully"
With its abundant dressiness.

The mountain of autumn invites us "luxuriously"
With its maples on.

The mountain of winter gives us crystal smile,
"Dressing itself clearly" with its white attire.

When we feel our life get tired out,
And also feel languor of life,
It's good for us to climb up the mountains.

- Tr. by Won Eung-soon

Oh Jin-hwan/Korea

* Born in Suanbo in Chung-ju
* Graduated from Han-yang Univ., Dept. of Eng
* Graduated from the Dep of business administration of Yeon-se University
* Member of Korean Writer's Association
* Member of the International Association of Writers in Korea Headquarters
* Vice secretary general of the World Poetry Research Institute
* President of literary association 'An Annual Ring'
* Awarded the prize of the monthly magazine 'Literature 21'
* Awarded the prize of Tam-mee literature
* Awarded the prize of cultural exchange between India and Korea
* Awarded the Medal of Nokjoguenjeong
* Poetical Works: "A Persimmon left for Magpie" "In the bosom of you after becoming A Crane" etc.
* Literary Works: A commemorative work, "A fisherman who puts a bait for a man".
* Adrees: 2-202, Kyeongnam Apt, 1-8, Banpo-dong, Seocho-gu, Seoul, 137-765, Korea

산

봄의 산은 연한 초록빛의 “옷을 입고”
수줍은 처녀처럼 부른다.

여름의 산은 풍성한 옷차림으로
“힘 있게” 유혹한다.

가을의 산은 단풍으로 성장하고
“화사하게” 초대한다.

겨울의 산은 순백한 옷차림으로
“깨끗하게 단장하고” 맑은 미소로 던진다.

삶이 지치고 생에 권태를 느꼈을 때에는
산에 오르는 것이 좋다.

A Vision of Diaspora

With the withered bowels,
Running ahead for the future in their sand shoes,
Though the windflower, blooming in the head,
'let's rest a little',
A compass needle lost its way.

In the middle of desert,
Was not there an oasis all along?
The mother's face signals to the sky
Which the sun dried their souls,
But the Diaspora's present residence,
That they couldn't return or stay any more
At the place they went by mistake,
Was despair itself.

The illegal entrants, written in scarlet letters,
The strange plants rooted in the waste land,
Were they really a species who never remove to plant?

The Diaspora
Who the good Samaritan turns his head,
And dreams a dreadful dream alone.

- Tr. by Won Eung-soon

Park In-ae/Korea

* Debut as a New Poet from the Literary Trend and Thought
* Recommended as a Poet form the Third Literature
* President of the Korean Writer's Literary Circle at Dallas
* Columnist of the News Korea
* Manager of the Third Literature
* Member of the Korean Writers' Association
* Recorded as a Poet in 'the Great Encyclopedia of Korean Poetry'
* Joint Writings: The World Poetic Literature, The Dallas Literature, etc.
* E-mail: nadainae@naver.com

디아스포라의 꿈

쪼그라든 창자
모래가 든 신발로 앞만 보고 달렸는데
머리에 피어나는 바람꽃이
좀 쉬어가자 하지만
나침반이 방향을 잃었다

사막의 한복판
오아시스는 처음부터 없었던가
태양이 영혼을 말린 하늘에
어머니의 얼굴이 손짓하는데
떠나온 곳으로 돌아갈 수도
잘못 온 곳에 더 이상 머물 수도 없는
디아스포라의 현주소는
절망

주홍글씨로 새겨진 '불법체류자'
척박한 땅에 뿌리를 내리던 낯선 식물
결코 옮겨 심을 수 없었던 종種이었을까

선한 사마리아인은 고개를 돌리고
혼자서 무서운 꿈을 꾸는
디아스포라

Being grateful on my parents

Being a child of my parents is great honor in this
world and being a human in this world is great
fortune rather than a animal or plant.

Being human is result of lessons from parents. I am
grateful on my parents with the happiness and the
value of existence. It was from the lessons that make
me love others and make me frugal.

It is lessons of my parents that make me respect my
parents, love my family and succeed to ancestor's wishes

- Tr. by Park Keun-hoo

Park Keun-hoo/Korea

* Birth Place : Gimje-si, Jeonbuk
* Scholarship: Senior School of National Teacher's College of Jeonju-si. Seoul Music College.
* Career: Principal of Dongsin Elementary School of Jeongeup-si. Dean of Elder's College(Present)
* Authorial Career: Member of PEN
* Member of Korean Writers' Association
* Member of Jeonbuk Writers' Association
* Member of Jeonbuk Essayists' Association
* Member of Yunghonam Literature Association
* Member of World Poetry Association
* Member of Jeonbuk Poets' Association
* Writings: People of Many thoughts(Essay) and 7 other Books. Unconcluded Story of Two Life(Poetry) and 3 other Books.
* Address : 449-4, Sang-dong, Jeongeup-si, Jeon-buk, 580-801, Korea

어버이 자식인 것을 감사드리며

수십억 지구촌 사람 중 내 어비이 자식으로 태어난 것을
영광으로 여기며 자연의 황홀함과 눈부신 태양
하고많은 생명 중 초목이나 동물이 아닌
사람으로 태어난 것을 천우신조로 여깁니다

사람다운 흉내라도 낼 수 있음은 어버이의 가르침이며
땀 흘려 얻어지는 보람과 살아있음의 행복 속에
존재의 가치를 알고 모든 것을 사랑하고
근검 절약하는 사람 되어 더불어 살 수 있게 하시어
감사합니다

부모님을 존경하며 가족을 사랑하고 선영의 유지 받들어
후손에 부끄럽지 않는 사람답게 살 수 있음은
어버이의 가르침입니다

An Artist, Kim Yu-joon

Under Mt. Mudeung
While Mr. Kim Yu-joon always as a boy
Had made friends with perilous mountains and rivers,
One day he turned into a mountain,
A flower, a splendid twilight,
And a huge sea with shining brightly in various colors,
Like a strong snipe flying alone over the boundless sky,

He caused the mountain's ears to be washed,
The mountain's eyes to be washed,
And even its body to be washed all,

Park Moon-jae/Korea

* Poet, Pen name: Jook Hyun
* Boarn at Seondu-ri, Munnae-myeon, Haenam-gun, Jeon-Nam, and brought up at Woosuyoung, Haenam.
* Completed Dept of literary Creative Literature, Art College, Jung-Ang Univ. and graduated from Dept. of Language Education, Graduate School of Education, Yon-Sei Univ.
* Retired as an ex-teacher of Middle & High School.
* Prize Winning Work as "Falling Snow" at a Literary Contest in Spring in the Kwangju Newspaper, 1963.
* Recommended as "Fog and 4 other Poems" in the monthly magazine "the Modern Poetry", 1980
* Published <Winter Orchard> as Children's Verse in "the Critical Children's Literature", 1981.
* A Director of Yangpung Literary Men's Association, and A Vice Chairman of the Kangnam Men's Association.
* A Member of the Literary Coterie 'Eung Si'.
* A Member of the Literary Men's Association of Korea; An Executive Committee of the Poets Association of Korea; A Chairman of the Reading Poems at Kangnam District.
* Received "Kosan Literature Award"; "Seaoul Great Literary Award"; "Young Rang Literature Award".
* Published the Poetical Anthologies entitled <Voice of the Winter Tree>, <Moran Day>, <An Abnormally Warm Winter>, <Sonnet of the Light of Grass>, <Passing by the Wood o White Birch>, and <Tamberly's Autumn> and <A Study of the Influence the Ballad Exerting on the Children's Rhyme> as a Critical Essay, etc.

Now he stripped even its bosom,
Getting intoxicated with all its energy for 365 days,
Playing at housekeeping all day long,
With a long pole out of his town's entrance,
And juvenile's crocks,
Turning into a stone Buddha
In the time of memory
Now very good man's man
Of southerns,
The artist, Kim Yu-joon,

- Tr. by Won Eung-soon

김유준 화백

무등산無等山 아래
만년 소년 김유준金裕俊이
주야장천 험준한 산천山川과 동무하다가
어느 날 산이 되고
꽃이 되고 현란한 노을이 되고
오색영롱한 한 마리 거대한 바다가 되어
구만리 장천을 홀로 나는 힘찬 도요새처럼

산의 귀를 씻기고
산의 눈을 씻기고
산의 몸뚱어리까지 다 씻기고 나서
이제는 산의 가슴속까지 벌거벗겨
일년 삼백예순날 산의 정기에 흠뻑 빠져
동구 밖 솟대와
유년의 사금파리와
진종일 소꿉놀이하는
이제는 시간 기억記憶 속에서
돌부처가 다 되어 버린
썩 괜찮은
남도의 사내,
김유준 화백畵伯.

A Rose

You!
As yet
Crying for a wisdom tooth,

From this morning
The wriggling is serious,
How about cutting the wisdom tooth?

At this Sangchun festival
For me to replace
In the empty sunken place,

- Tr. by Won Eung-soon

Park Youn-ki/Korea

* Pen Name: Chosan.
* Born in Andong, Kyeongbuk, Korea
* Graduated from Cheonsong High School.
* First Debut as a Poet through "Literary Movement & Trend"
* Recorded as a Poet in "The Encyclopedia of Korean Poetry"
* A Member of the Association of Literary Movement & Trend.
* Address: 322-90 Chosan-ri, Habuk-myun, Yangsan City, Kyung-nam, Korea

장미

아직도
사랑니 붙들고 우는
그대여!

그 몸짓
아침부터 벅찬데
사랑니 뽑으면 안 될까

이 쌍춘절雙春節
움푹한 그 빈자리에
내가 들어앉게.

A Life

There is no formula of life, and no right answer,
Even though some one teaches it, it doesn't be correct,
And though I try to search for it
There is no one to explain,
So I make the formula for myself,
I have to find it out,
Perhaps find it out earnestly.

I am not going to its way as it being the way of life,
The way is open because I go to it,
In order to cut through the way,
I have to suffer a lot of hardships and pains,
Therefore somebody says the life is a penance of life.

Even desiring to give it up
Many times, it is not life only for me,

Seo Jeong-il/Korea

* Vice Chairman of Institute of the Juvenile Literature of Korea.
* Chairman of Kyeonggido Branch Juvenile Literary Society.
* A Committee of Excavation for Literary Materials in the Writer's Association of Korea.
* A member of Association of Children's Songs & of Juvenile Literary Society of "the Grass and Flower" & of "New Buds" Club.
* Novel: The Star as Being a Mirror.
* Juvenile Poetical Anthology: 'Mother's Nagging'; 'A Babe's Cloud'; 'The Story of Little Trees'.
* Collection of Children's Songs: 'A Narrow Path'.
* Received a Prize: the 2nd Korea-Chinese, "Ongdalsaem" Juvenile Literature; the 32nd Writer's Award of Juvenile Literature of Korea; Excellent Writer's Award of Korea Newspaper.

But as being a lover to live with,
I have to make the way of life
Even facing death under a hard adversity.

- Tr. by Won Eung-soon

삶

삶의 공식이 없고 정답도 없으니
누가 가르쳐준들 답이 맞을 리 없고
정답을 찾고자 해도
설명을 할 사람이 없으니
내 스스로 공식을 만들고
정답을 찾아야 하니
열심히 찾아야겠지

삶의 길이 있어 가는 것이 아니라
내가 가니 길이 생기니
그 길을 만들기 위해서는
많은 시련과 역경을 겪어야 하니
그러기에 누가 삶을 고행이라 했나

몇 번이고 몇 번이고
포기하고 싶지만 나만의 삶이 아니라
함께하는 사랑하는 사람이 있기에
힘들고 어려운 역경 속에서 삶의 길을
죽어 가면서도 만들어 가야 한다.

The Wayfarers

We are the wayfarers,
After we slept,
Again the destiny we are bound to depart for,

For(To) the mountains and the fields
Passing over the crossroad,
The fate we are bound to follow the signals,

The mountains to pass over,
The rivers to cross over,
So, today and tomorrow,

Where can we meet
The wayfarers to go with
Through the dark road at night?

- Tr. by Won Eung-soon

Seo Jeong-nam / Korea

* A member of Korea writers' association
* A member of Korean modern poetry writers' association, a member of international pen club in Korea headquarters, second chairman of Seocho literary men's association, chairman of Chongda literary men's association, chairman of Korea psychology counsel association, an honorary Doctor of Literature and so on.
* A poet, a pastor, a judicial scrivener, a counselor of psychology and so on
* Address: 145-3,Docheongmyeon, Buangun, Jeon-Buk, Korea.

길손

우리는 길손
자고 나면 다시
어디론지 떠나야 할 명운命運,

건널목을 지나
산으로 들로
신호등 따라오는 순명順命,

넘어야 할 산
건너야 할 물
오늘도 내일도 그렇게

어딜 가면
어둔 길 함께 갈
길동무 만날 수 있을까

The Field in Rain

The affable drizzle
Tickles, tickles the dry land,
And incites torrents of a shower
To have a round of love-play.
In reaping a harvest season,
The farming land will produce big and lots of fruits
Like seed potatoes of ridging field

After the torrents of rain came and passed,
By chance, the cumuli in clouds followed to use magic,
The excited flogs, calling their mate,
A white heron circling over the green rice paddy
Perhaps is searching for the nest to settle with her love.

The water sound flowing down
From this valley and that valley,
Will make my ears be deafened,
Because at the shallows flowing with peach flowers
I came back leaving my ears behind there.

- Tr. by Won Eung-soon

Shin Dong-myeong/Korea

* Born in Seoul
* Started a literary career through the magazine 'Literary Movement & Trend'(essay)
* Started a literary career through the magazine 'Literary 21'
* Member of the international Pen Club in Korea Headquarters
* Member of Korean Woman Writer's Association
* Member of Modern poetry association
* Member of Korean essayist Association
* Won the Kaya Gold Crown of the World Poetry, etc
* Published poetical works: The Will of Wings'. A Short and Long Story.
* Published literary jottlings: From Han River to Senue
* Stray notes: A Watercolor Painting in the Picture
* Address: 601, Hyundae Apt, 171-61, Bulgwang2-dong, Eunpyong-gu, Seoul, 123-042, Korea
* E-mail: sdm1445@hanmail.net

비 온 들녘

붙임성도 좋지 보슬빈
메마른 땅 간질간질 간지럼 태우더니
발기한 소낙빌 꼬드겨
사랑놀이판 한 번 푸지게 풀어보누나
추수 땐
주먹덩이만 한 자식들 쓰윽 쑥 퍼질러 낳겠지
발두둑 씨알감자

장대비 마실 왔다 돌아간 뒤
뭉실뭉실 마술부리는 뭉게구름
행여 질세라
짝꿍 부르는 물오른 맹꽁이들
초록 논배미 위를 선회하는 하얀 해오라긴
어디쯤 연인과 보금자리 차릴지 물색 중인가 봐

이 골골 저 골골
콸콸 흘러가는 골창 물소리
한동안 내 귓속 먹먹하겠다
복사꽃 흐르는 개여울에 내 귀를 두고 왔으니.

A Soyo Mountain's Sonnet

At the station of throb
On the way of the human life,
Waiting for the life partner at my age of 23 years,
Just at that time,
I met you.

When we spread Love's wings,
Built our nest under Soyo mountain,
And I was embraced in your bosom,
I can confess
That I have felt happier than anyone in the world.

Love
Is the world only two men are making.
Always stay the place as you have done.
Only you
Are l'raison d'étre.

- Tr. by Won Eung-soon

Son Soon-ja / Korea

* Born at Pocheon, Geonggido.
* A Member of the Literary Men's Association of Korea.
* A Chairman of 'the Soyo Literature'.
* Received the Original Prize of the Space Poets Association of Korea.
* Received the Prize of Excellence of the Pure Literature.
* Poetical Anthology: <A Love Song of Soyo Mountain>.
* Collection of Essays: <A Happy Woman>.

* Address: 178-2, Sangyeon 1st-dong, 25 Setgolgil, Dongdoocheon, Geongigido, Korea.

소요산 연가戀歌

인생길
설렘의 정거장에 서서
동반자를 기다리던 스물 셋
그때,
그대를 만났습니다

사랑의 날개 펴고
소요산 아래 둥지 틀어
그데 품에 안겼을 때
이 세상 누구보다
행복에 젖었음을 고백합니다

사랑은
단둘이 해야만 하는 것
언제나 그 자리 머물러주세요
그대만이
살아가는 이유가 됩니다

A Spine in the Flesh

A feeler which searches for water,
Stepping on the vocal cords of birds
If one reckons her color sense in the breast
It reaches at twenty eight thousand

Those things are seeds of a male's mural,
Picturing in the flesh

Those things are seeds of a male's mural,
Picturing in the flesh

Those things are seeds of a male's mural,
Picturing in the flesh

Those things are seeds of a male's mural,
Picturing in the flesh

A chorus of water,
Marked the gap of time

A red morning mellows
On the wet flesh full of water

- Tr. by Su Jyahn Ahn

Su Jyahn Ahn/Korea

An artist of Western painting, poetess
A member of International Rotary club 3690 district
* Literary works: poetical works entitled "February"
* English grammar entitled "Hey, you are nothing peculiar"
* Wrote poems in serial form on "the magazine of A woman's dress "Crocodile, Chatelaine"
* Wrote poems on the Grand Korea Poetry Encyclopedia
* A member of a literary group "P&E"
* A member of the World Poetry Research Institute
* Awarded a grand prize for 2007 Korea Recitation

살 속의 가시

새들의 목청을 밟으며
물을 찾는 더듬이
가슴팍에서 그녀의 색감을 산술하면
이만 팔천 개

살 속에 그려지는 숫놈의 벽화
씨앗이다

시각의 틈새를 그은
물들의 합창이라

홍건히 젖은 살에
붉은 아침이 익는다

An Address Makes You

There is an address in thinking too.

In the same field, at the same day,
I buried potatoes, planted tomatoes, and transplanted peppers.

The potatoes with plump fruits under their roots,
The tomatoes with chubby fruits at their trunks,
And the peppers with red and green things,

The sun supplied its lights in free distribution evenly,
They are exposed to the rain and wind evenly,
And they enjoyed my warm helping hands.
So what makes my palate feel different?

Their names and seeds are different,
Nay, the flowers are different,
Butterflies and bees are not equal,

No, they are not.

Because they have their own address of different number in thinking,
Where was the address of my thinking placed?

- Tr. by Won Eung-soon

Tae Dong-chul/Korea

* Recommended As a Poet from the Literary Movement & Trend.
* A Member of the Literary Men's Association of Korea.
* Vice Chairman of the Guro Branch, of the Literary Men's Association of Korea.
* An Executive Secretary of the Academy of Literature.
* Address: 741-7, Oeri, Youngheungmyeon, Ongjingun, Incheon Metropolitan City, Korea.

주소는 너를 만든다

생각에도 주소가 있다

같은 밭에, 같은 날
감자 묻고, 토마토 심고, 고추 모종했다

뿌리에 토실토실 알이 든 감자
줄기에 몽실몽실 열매 단 토마토
가지에 울긋불긋 물건 키우는 고추

햇살은 무상 배급 똑같이 분배하고
비, 바람도 함께 맞으며
손길도 같이 누렸다
헌데 무엇이 내 미각을 다르게 할까

이름과 씨가 다르잖아
아니, 꽃이 틀리잖아
나비와 벌이 같을 수 없지

아니다

번지수가 다른 생각의 주소 때문이다
나, 생각의 주소는 어디에 자리 했나

A Stone

In the beginning, a stone
Appears from heaven,
Rolling down
By an inertia of silence,
Cuts and weighs down the trees and grasses.
Again forming a group of the other stones,
Boring the mountains to make a path,
Going into waters to make a lake,
And plants a heaven.

- Tr. by Won Eung-soon

Won Eung-soon/Korea

*Poet, Ph.D. Emeritus Prof. of Kyung Hee Univ.
*Chief Editor of The Christian Literature of Korea(Quarterly Magazine)
*Manager & Editor of the Professor's Newspaper
*Elder of Dongsoong Presbyterian Church

돌 하나

태초에 돌멩이 하나,
하늘로부터 나타나
침묵의 관성으로
아래로 굴러 내리며,
나무들과 들풀들을 꺾고 짓밟는다,
또 다른 돌들과 한패를 이루며
산을 뚫어 길을 내고
물속으로 들어가 호수를 만들어
하늘을 심는다.

An Hour doing it by Oneself

Everyday
I
Write a letter
About the undelivered story,
About the unseen matter.
Thinking if my life is short,
I think the end of my life.

In a day,
With a dark sky on my head,
Putting my tears together like a pearl,
I say so,
'I have loved
To the wind,
To the tree,
And to all things'.

-Tr. by Won Eung-soon

Yang Ah-rim/ Korea

* Member of 'the Korean Writers' Association'
* Committee for Development of Policy in 'the Korean Writers' Association'
* Seoul Member of 'the House of Literature'
* Vice president of 'the Poetical Literature Circle'
* Journalist and Director of 'the Hanguk-Munin'
* Vice President of Writer's Circle for Recommendation in 'the Hanguk-Munin'
* Won the Prize of Literature in 'the Hanguk-Munin'

홀로 하는 시간

날마다
나는
편지를 쓴다
보내지지 않는 사연
보여지지 않는 사연
내 삶이 짧다면 생각하고
내 삶의 마지막을 생각한다

어떤 날엔
밤하늘을 머리에 이고
진주처럼 내 눈을 모두어
바람에게
모두에게
사랑했다
그렇게 말한다

The Wave of the Tamjin River

The full moonlight like a girl's shame,
At early evening, the last month of the year
Stays above dimly the eastern mountain
Over the far, far horizon,

She drowns her cares,
Falling down softly on snowflakes,
Scattering like white petals,
Sitting down plump at ferry point covered with grasses of ferryboat,

When a shadow, hardened by the north wind
Bearing the traces of perseverance
Over the railing of the Mok-Ri bridge,
Embraces the splendid reeds tightly,
Hugging passionately.

The glimpses of the Tamjin river
Fluttering with brilliant moonlight,
Are the secret whispers of the river's waves.

- Tr. by Won Eung-soon

Yang Chi-joong/ Korea

*Born at Kangjin, Jeonnam, Korea
*Made new Debut as a Poet from the Literary Movement and Trend
* Graduated from Dept. of Creative Writing & Arts of Kwangju Education College
* Received the Prize of Poets Laurel Literature(6th, 2003); the Great Prize for Poetry of the 21 Century Korea Literature(11th, 2006); the Prize of Jeonnam Literture(31st, 2008); and the Prize of Kangjin Literature(1st, 2010) * Chairman of Onnuri Society of Literature
* Chairman of Kangjin Branch of Korean Writers' Association* Director of Jeonnam Writer's Association(Present)
* Vice President of Jeonnam Poets' Association(Present) * Cooperative Committee of Korean Writers' Association(Present) * Member of Haenam Literature(Present)
* Poetic Anthology: "A Crane Flying For A Millennium"
* Joint Literary Works: "An Invitation to the Green Land of Jeon-Nam" "Narrative Story of Jeon-Nam", etc. * Address: 13 Sudong-gil, Daegu-myun, Kangjin-gun, Jeon-Nam, Korea
* Tel: 010-8758-3027 * E-mail: ycjpoet@hanmail.net

탐진강 물결

아스라한 지평선 머문
희부연 동녘 산위에
소녀의 부끄럼 같은
섣달 보름 초저녁 달빛

하얀 꽃잎으로 흩날리는
눈발 타고 사뿐히 내려와서
초지草地 농선農船 나루터에 주저앉아
시름을 달래는데

인고의 손때 묻은
목리 다리 난간에
삭풍으로 굳은 그림자 하나
흐드러진 갈대숲 끌어안고
뜨겁게 포옹할 때

현란한 달빛 파닥이는
탐진강 편린들
강 물결 흐르는 조용한 속삭임.

I am you and you are I

- A meditation for our one Global Village

Some find only small things with their eyes
Wide open, but we can see things great
Even with our slits of eyes;
We are one in which
I am you and you are I.

A tree rooted in erath
May live its life alone;
Grow alone and
Prosper by itself.

But how can moving lives,
Especially a human being, the master
Of lives on earth among them,
Live his life alone?

Yeo Han-kyung/Korea

*Born in Munkeong, Keongbuk
*Graduated in Korean literature from Andong National University, Yeongnam University
* Resigned from a teacher at Cheonggu high school in Daigu
*Decorated with an national medal and a presidential citation
*Member of Daigu Literary Association, Korea Modern Poetry Association, etc.
* A vice-president of Daigu Literary Association
*Published several books
*Address: 505, wubang town 5dong, 240, hwanggeum 1dong, suseong-gu, Daegu city

We give and receive from each other;
Care for each other with
One heart of love and bloom it
into a flower of wisdom, peace,
And happiness......
This providence of nature

Are we not able to learn from clouds
Passing over the sky or from brook
Waters that keep singing, flowing down,
Through the hills to the sea

To find we are one
In which I am you
And you are me
And
all the creations are the one too

- Tr. by Yeo Han-kyung

나도 너이고 너도 나이고
―한지구촌을 위한 명상

눈을 크게 뜨고도 작게만 보는 사람 있듯이
눈을 작게 뜨고도 크게만 본다면
우린 하나다
나도 너이고
너도 나이고

땅바닥에 뿌리박은 나무들이야
홀로도 자라고 홀로도 번성해
세상을
홀로도 버티어 간다지만, 어디
살아서 움직이는 것들이야, 특히
만물의 영장인 인간들이야
그 어찌
세상을 홀로만 갈 수가 있다더냐.
주고받고 서로가
보듬으며 서로가

사랑으로 하나 될 때, 거기에
지혜가 꽃피고
평화가 꽃피고
기쁨이 꽃피고, 이것이 섭리라고

사방팔방을 살피며 하늘을 떠가는
흰구름이 말해 주지 않더냐.
계곡을 조잘대며 바다로 나아가는
시냇물이 말해 주지 않더냐.

우린 하나다
나도 너이고
너도 나이고
아니
삼라만상이 하나다

Cleansing Rusty Spectacles

Getting up in the morning,
Watching my glasses carefully in spite of myself,
Their rims are rusty in blue color
Between the shining gilt rims.

My spectacles are my other self(alter ego),
In which my warm blood flows .
And are the frosty glass growing dim
When returning back from walking in a snowdrift.

Through years
As if the flower blooms
When spring season comes,
It's very hard for me to cleanse my rusty glasses' rims.

Should I stop to cleanse them,
And again cease to cleanse?
Should I wear the rusty spectacles
And whistle as they are left rusty?

- Tr. by Won Eung-soon

Yoo Hee-bong/Korea

* Recommended as a Poet from the 'Hyundae Poetry' in 1993.
* Poetic Anthology: Published 6 books with 'the Flower of Language'.
* Essay Collection: 'The Happy Spring Well'.
* Art of Writing Creative Poetry: 'To Create Poetry Is To Write Future'.
* Director of Poetry in National Movement Center of Clean Contents, Korea.
* Present: Lecturer of Hoseo Univ., Suwon Univ.(Ph. D. of Business Management).
* Tel: 02-6412-0702/ 010-6412-0702

녹슨 안경을 닦으며

아침 일어나
무심코 내 안경을 눈여겨보았더니
반짝이는 도금 사이사이
파랗게 녹이 슬어 있다.

안경은 나의 분신
따스한 피가 흐르고 있는
눈보라 속을 거닐다 돌아오면
뿌옇게 흐리어져버리는 유리.

세월 속에서
계절이 오면 꽃이 피듯
녹이 슬어버린 안경테
이젠 닦는데도 힘이 겹구나.

그만 닦을까 봐.
다시는 닦는 일 그만둘까 봐
차라리 흐린 그대로
녹슨 그대로 끼고 휘파람이나 불까 봐.

The Black Vinyl Envelope

The hungry person's backs
Returning to the corner after the demonstration
With candlelights in their hands, waver before eyes.

The false cloud's smile erasing out of walls
Like the bivouac men staggering into a waiting room,
Is the black vinyl envelope flying to inflate its empty inside,
By memory filling its inside fully
How far should it go to make fixed?

Even burning their rage
Persons who was not cremated,
Scatter the fire sparks in the empty air.

When the cold winds draw lines on a music book
And choose to tune its thymes over the chips of high walls,
if a cat approach to the corner for the serene life,

Concentrating her eyelight, like the hungry rats
That rummaged in an ash can,
There are some persons confronting a precipice.

- Tr. by Won Eung-soon

Yoo Hee-Jeong/Korea
* Born in Gochang, Jeonbuk
* Entered a literary career through Munyeundong(Literary Movement)
* Finished 2Years' Specialist Course of Graduate School of Arts, Jungang University.
* Published book entitled "The Fragrance of green fruits of a Primrose"
* Studied fashion design at F.I.T in New York
* Graduated from the Air and Correspondence College (Open University)
* A member of Korea Writer Association , Mokwol Literature Forum
* Address : 104-405, daerim Apartment 57, umyeon-dong, seocho-gu, Seoul, Korea

검정 비닐봉지

도시의 골목으로
촛불을 들고 시위하다 돌아가는
허기진 등이 펄럭인다

담벼락에서 지워지고 있는 허망한
구름의 미소
역사 대합실 속으로 비틀거리면서 들어가는 노숙자처럼
텅 빈 속을 부풀리며 날아가는 검정 비닐봉지
어디까지 가야 정착할 것인가
속을 가득 채웠던 기억으로

분노를 태우고도
재가 되지 못하는 사람들이
허공에 불씨를 뿌려놓는 밤

찬바람이 높은 담장 사금파리 위에
악보의 줄을 긋고 음률을 고를 때
안주할 곳을 찾아드는 골목으로

고양이가 눈에 빛을 모으며 다가오면
쓰레기통을 뒤지던 배고픈 쥐처럼
절벽에 마주 서는 사람들

Morning of a Mountain Temple

On the place passed scratching the camellia wood,
Crossing the stone bridge of a thousand years old temple,
The shadow of a round moon is suspended looming.

The old temple sends by the postcard, carrying the water sound
From the deep valleys like tear's traces
That the gate-post of the bush clover was pressed by the liverworts,

The rumbling of a mountain
By a cuckoo's crying at the nutmeg's nest,
Has been worn out to echo around the valleys in Cheontae mountain,

The temple's bell sound at dawn,
The wood block's beating of Jeongsu temple
Flow on the waves of Gukangpo.

- Tr. by Won Eung-soon

Yoon Hyoung-soon / Korea

* Born at Daegu-myun, Kangjin-gun, Jeon-Nam, Korea
* Graduated from College of Agriculture, Jeon-Nam University
* Served at Ministry office of Agriculture for 20 Years, and at National Agrecultural Co-operation Federation for 13 Years
* Manager of the Kindred Society of the Haenam Family "Yun"
* Received the Prize in Literary Contest for Poetry under the Auspices of Jeonnam Daily Newspaer(1965)
* Member of the World Poetry Institute
* Address : Hyundae Prime Apt. 207-501, Sinjeong-maeul, 2-dong, Pungdeokcheon, Suji-gu, Yongin City, Gyeonggi-do, Korea

山寺의 아침

천 년 사찰 돌다리 지나
바람이 동백숲을 할퀴고 간 자리에
덩그란 달그림자 걸쳐 있네

싸리나무 문기둥이 이끼에 눌려
패인 눈물자국 깊은 골 물소리 낙엽에 싣고
산사의 소식 엽서에 띄워보네

비자나무 둥지 소쩍새
울음 토한 산울림
천태산 골짜기에 울다 지쳐버리고

여명을 알리는 새벽종소리
정수사 법당의 목탁소리
구강포 물결위에 흘러 보낸다.

All Extol *Haengdang(1512~1577)

Haengdang had clean and fragrant fruits in his demeanor,
That its root was inherited down to Dasan Cho-dang.

Haengdang was so clear and sensible that the village people asked him to remain in office,
His root and stalk has been continued deep and hard.

Again we realize his profound meaning of what he had done,
That he sent his grandson by his daughter to a village, Kyul-dong and made him stay there intentionally.

Even though Dasan's disciples did not say of it after all,
Haengdang's favors and benefits have come true.

Yoon Jae-myung/Korea

* Born at Gangjin, Jeon-Nam, Korea
* Graduated from Dept. of National Language of Korea University
* Served as a President of the Modern Criticism
* Served as the 7th, 8th, 10th of a Congressman in Young-Am
* Served as a Chief Director of the Association of Korea Classical Music & a President of Si-Jo Unions of Korea
* Served as a President of Haenam Yoon's Pedigree(Gosan Yoon Sun-do) in Central Clansmen of Korea
* Served as a President of General Unions of Educational Institute of Korea & Now serving as a Counselor
* Now serving as a President of the Association of Friendship between Korea and Japan(Founded in 1976)
* Now serving as a President of the Plan of Operation for Haeng-dang
* Now serving as a President of a Commemorative Events for Haengdang Yoon-Bok

Again,

Sungho Lee-ik called Toe-gei as '*Ja' in praise of him,
Dasan wrote the fact in the book "the meditations on Dosan".

A piece of gravestone has undergone rain and wind of Time,
Nowadays we attended on him in the tablet house.

At times reminding him, I have written his poem,
And only I am reciting Hangdang's song of farewell.

Clouds are cleared off and Dasan's thatched house, as it has been,
Shall we see the "book of the adore on Haengdang" someday?

* Ja : It means the same level as Confucius(Kong-ja)

* Haengdang(1512~1577) : His name is Bok. As 13 generations of Haenam Yoon's family line(Gosan Yoon Sun-do is 16 generations, Ingang Yoon Jae-myung, 27 generations), while he was in office, Toe-gei and town's people begged him earnestly to remain in office, even in the 60th birthday feast of his father in law, after drinking a cup of wine he departed the feast owing to the governmental duty, For lots of years he expounded about the doctrines of Chu-Tzu, associating with Toe-gei.

\- Tr. by Won Eung-soon

輿頌 杏堂(1512~1577) 행당 여송

仁康 尹 在 明

杏堂有潔馨佳實 행당에 깨끗하고 향기로운 열매 맺고
承託根茶山艸堂 그 뿌리는 다산초당으로 뻗어 이어졌네

故明哲輿頌願留 총명하고 사리에 밝아 고을사람들은 칭송,
유임을 청원했으며
深結根固蔕保存 뿌리는 깊게, 꼭지는 단단하게 이어져 왔네

也哉知杏堂深意 또한, 알겠노라 행당의 깊은 뜻
故遣外孫遊橘洞 일부러 외손을 귤동에 보내 머물게 한 것을

茶山群英終不言 다산의 제자들은 끝내 말하지 않아도
杏堂恩光必有事 행당의 은광은 틀림없는 사실이네

又 또

星湖記李子粹語 성호 이익(星湖李瀷)은 퇴계를 자(子)라 존칭했고
茶山陶山私淑錄 다산은 도산사숙록을 썼네

片石路傍風雨秋 한 조각 돌비석 비바람 겪어 왔는데
昨今成碑閣安置 요즈음 비각을 조성해 모셨네

腦裏時時待句寫 이따금 생각나면 얻은 시구를 얻어 적고
哦杏堂作送別只 다만 행당 시 송별을 읊을 뿐이네

雲初起艸堂依然　구름 걷히기 시작하고 다산초당 그대로인데
何見杏堂私淑錄　언제쯤 '행당사숙록'을 볼 수 있을까

* 杏堂(中宗七~宣祖十): 諱 復 海南尹氏十三世(孤山 尹善道十六世 仁康 尹在明 二十七世) 安東府使在任時 退溪等輿頌願留 聘父壽筵時不可留纔飮一盃辭去發職官遂行 杏堂退溪數年交驩講質朱書

* 행당(1512~1577) : 이름은 복(復). 해남윤씨 13세(고산 윤선도는 16세, 인강 윤재명은 27세)손으로 안동부사 재임 때는 퇴계 등 고을 백성들이 유임을 청원했고 장인 환갑잔치 때에는 관직소임 때문에 겨우 술 한 잔을 마시고 하직하고 떠났으며 퇴계와는 여러 해 동안 사귀면서 주서(성리학)에 관해 강론 질의했다.

Joy

Here and there
As all things have laid in good order,
They are all joys as ever.

The broken clayware
Has been preserved fully,
And it is also joy.

A stone, stumbled over a tiptoe,
Which is acting cute,
It is also joy.

The flowers wither,
The rising stars are seen,
And it is also joy.

Over the levee which man left
A narcissus, blooming lonely,
It is also joy.

- Tr. by Won Eung-soon

Yoon Sang-hyun / Korea

* Born at Gangjin-gun, Jeon-nam, in 1930
* Employer of Hanulnae Plantation(Farm)
* First Debut as a Poet with a Prize for the new Poet through 'the Korea's Poetry'
* The Founder of 'the Duryun Literature'(1959)
* Member of the Association of Korean Writers
* Published serially poems in the Korea's Poetry for 6 years
* Won the Great Prize of Literature of 'the Korea's Poetry'(2005), and the prize of 'Nosan Literature'(2010)
* His Writings: <A Blood Vessel>, <Fragrant Greenness>, <On the Plain of ripen Dream>, <Original Residence>, <A Green Color's Love>, etc.
*Address: 713 Sungsa-dong, e-Pyeonhan-Sesang 117-1301, Deokyang-gu, Goyang City, Kyunggi-do

기쁨이란

여기저기에
놓여 있음으로
모두가 하나같이 기쁨이어라

깨어진 질그릇이
오롯이 있으니
그것 또한 기쁨이라

발부리에 채이어
재롱이는 돌 하나
그것 또한 기쁨이다

꽃은 이울어지고
뜨는 별 보느니
그것 또한 기쁨이라

떠나버린 강둑 너머
따로이 피운 수선화
그것 또한 기쁨이라

Going Together

An eyebrow moonlight above the blue sky shines dimly,
And a way is an endless course.
That is a dew way of grass-leaves in the fog,
Searching for it, but in vain.

Rolling in a wave of one glass,
It's a way of going together with a sweet life.

The way carrying cloudy flowers from this side,
The way bringing flower aroma from that side,

The soil and pebbles soaking wet in light of grass,
Shake on the end of sleeves,
And scattering like a jade,
They become a way of water-spray mixed with flower fragrance.

A white dress, shined in the round moonlight
Comes near to the jagged path of flower on the cliff,
And hides in the song of 'the flowing time'.

- Tr. by Won Eung-soon

Yun Hae-Kyu/Korea

* Born in Haenam
* Member of the Korea Writers' Association
* Organized Eulji Publishing Company in 1981
* Published an encyclopedia of a shijo(a kind of short lyric Korean poem) in 1985
* Started a literary career after publishing an encyclopedia of Korean poetry in 1988
* Published with additions of Korean Poetry in 2002, Published with additions and up-to-date corrections of Korean Poetry in 2002
* Adress : 394-81, Seogyo-dong, Mapo-gu, Seoul, 121-840, Korea

동행

푸른 하늘 눈썹달빛 희미해지고
가는 길은 끝없는 길
가도 가도 찾지 못하는 안개 속
풀잎 이슬 길

한 잔 파도에 출렁이며
그리운 삶 함께 걷는 길

이쪽에서 꽃구름 싣고 가는 길
저쪽에서 꽃내음 싣고 오는 길

흙도 자갈도 풀빛에 젖는
휘휘 저어도 소매 끝
옥구슬 부서질세라
꽃내음 어린 물보라 길

하이얀 드레스가 둥근 달빛에 비춰
벼랑에 선 꽃의 톱니 사잇길로 와
'가는 세월' 노래 속에 스며든다

The Sea Cries under Waves

The sea, grasped its bruised breast
Against the giggling laughter of the rice paddy,
Becomes a serious Rodin.
It was a windbreak forest lining along the dike
That he offered silt at an estuary as a bribe and was granted.
The feeling guilty presses on him
For making crabs and gastropod as the 'fire-field' farmers,
In order to set a wind-wood? with the ribs without pieces of meat.
It made an iced mountain between the poor and the rich in vain,
And raised the blood pressure between the towns upper and below,
Increasing an objective number of "the sons and bitches" sniffing
  at a foul smelling
Its disgusting smell is attenuated.

Yun Mu-jee/Korea

* Born at Haenam, Jeon-Nam, Korea
* Graduated from Kwangju High School and from Dept of Civil Engineering, Hanyang Univ.
* Served as a Public Servant of Seoul City for 32 Years and Retired under the Age Limit
* Member of Korea Engineers' Association
* Director of the Cultural Exchange between South and North Korea
* Vice President of "Hyang-Woo Meeting" at Kwangju, Jeon-nam(Present)
* President of Haenam Yoon's Central Pedigree(Present)
* A Director of the World Poetry Institute, and of 'the Nature Literature'
* Address: 202-705 Yulgok-Ro, Yonkron-dong, Jaeil Office-Tel, Jongno-gu, Seoul
* Office Tel: 02-741-1019/ H.P: 010-5232-1979

The waning moon has deformed.
What on earth is this the cost of her giving flesh?
The sea wind defied, behaving capriciously at all times,
Even the fog of the small mountain grumbled about its narrowed ground.
He himself was very hateful, who granted the troublesome reclamation works.
He, who pushed down helplessly with being cut off his heart,
Feeling himself abominable,
Sat crouched under the high waves,
Today, the sea cries at any time.

- Tr. by Won Eung-soon

바다는 파도 밑에서 운다

논배미 벼이삭 킬킬대는 웃음소리에
멍든 젖가슴 움켜쥔 바다는
심각한 로댕이 된다
갯벌을 하늘에게 상납하고 하사받은 건
둑방에 줄지어 선 방풍림이었다
살점 떼어낸 갈비뼈로 바람숲 세워주느라
게와 고동을 화전민으로 만든
죄책감이 밀려온다
괜스레 가난과 부자의 얼음산 만들어
윗마을과 아랫마을 사이 혈압만 높아졌고
땅 냄새 킁킁거리는 개새끼들 객체수만 늘렸다
비릿내음 희석시키다
하현달은 기형이 되어 버렸다
살을 떼어준 대가가 이런 것이란 말인가
해풍은 수시로 변덕을 부리며 반항하였고
작은 산 안개조차 품이 작아졌다며 불평해댔다
말썽거리 간척을 허용해준 자신이 미웠다
심장을 도려내고 힘없이 걸어 내려간
허한 자신이 미워
높은 파도 밑에 쭈그리고 앉아
바다는 오늘도 시도 때도 없이 운다

An Ivy

With the deep blue heart beating,
And the sun light and wind embracing all over body,
Over the '88 Olympic Highway,
With which time and space have kept in contact endlessly,
Being pressed down under the realistic weigh,
Do you rise up still,
With creeping shape with difficult?
Now,
You have missed your way even to return.
With your gaunt skeleton exposed,
Between the sunburnt leaves
Stopping the blood's circulation,
You have been suntanned with difficulty
To the cliff's end of the strange world.

- Tr. by Won Eung-soon

Yun Su-a / Korea

* Born at Chon-An, Chung-Nam, Korea.
* A Reciter of Poetry
* Recommended as an essayist winning the prize from the "Literary Movement & Trend"
* Editorial staff of magazine "Literature 21"('97-'98) & Jigumunhak('98 ~'01) & Chief of Administration of "World Poetry Reserch Institute"
* Meantime, Chief of Administration of "Korean Literature Institute" & Editorial staff of "Literary Movement & Trend"
* Address : 115-902, Hyundae HillState, 155, Onsudong, Gurogu, Seoul, Korea

담쟁이

아직도 오르고 있느냐
짙푸른 심장을 파랑波浪이며
햇빛과 바람을 온몸으로 끌어안고
시간과 공간이 끊임없이 충돌하던
'88올림픽 도로
현실의 무게에 짓눌려
힘겹게 기어오르는 모습
이젠
돌아가는 길마저 잃어버렸구나
앙상한 뼈마디를 드러낸 채
검게 익어버린 이파리 사이에서
피돌기를 멈추고
벼랑 끝 낯선 세상으로
힘겹게 타오르고 있구나.

I Am a Seed of Eternity

I am a seed of eternity.
Here, on the earth
I found my terrestrial body
With a heavenly soul.
Wandering around this world
I composed my endless song
With a special design.
Looking at this design
The eye finds a contour
Of snow-covered mountain peaks.
The heart finds
The summer's heat there.
Goodbye, my hospitable home,
Where I've spent the best moments
Of my life, where inspiration
Was frequent guest!

Dr. Adolf P. Shvedchikov / Russia

* Russian Scientist, Poet and translator
* Born May 11, 1937, Shakhty, Russia.
* Graduated from Moscow State University.
* Senior Scientific worker at the Institute of Chemical Physics, Russian Academy of Sciences, Moscow.
* Chief of Chemistry, Pulsatron Technology Corporation, Los Angeles, California, U.S.A.
* Member of World Congress of Poets; of International Association of Writers and Artists; of Associazione Letteraria Italo-Australiana Scrittori(Melbourn, Australia).
* Address: 4317 Petit Avenue Encino CA 91436-3516, U.S.A.
* E-mail: adolfps@gmail.com

God Gave us as a Gift a Piece of Eternity

God gave us as a gift a piece of eternity.
We may use it as we like.
We may soar among sunny clouds
if you have enough forces to fly up into the sky.
God gave us as a gift a piece of eternity.
Transform this gift for a benefit of everyday life.
Save the diamond of your soul
To illuminate your path.
God gave us as a gift a piece of eternity.
Deliberately use this gift
For the good words and useful deeds,
And the thankful offspring will remember you.

Sitting on Pebbles at the Beach

Sitting on pebbles at the beach
Looking at the rolling wave
I know I cannot reach,
I know I cannot save
That mystery hidden inside
Of your depths, oh, rebellious sea.
How long do we have to abide
Solving that puzzle who are we?

The old House With an Attic

I remember the old house with an attic,
The small garden, the flowers.
I hear the languid sound of a piano,
I see the colored Chinese tea cups.
I remember your birthday
And glasses full of Georgian wine...
Your precious name, *Nina*,
Became my bright star forever!

Be Talkative, Trembling Wave

Oh daughter of the sea,
Be talkative, trembling wave
And sing me your tender songs.
Don't run away, stay with me,
Make this world a little better.
Those who only once
Were your captives,
Will never break your chains
And will sink forever
Into the depths of your love!

Reset Humanity

Restart by darkness
of time,
by the mud left out
by the falling star
and reconstruct
the whole world.

Reset humanity
without the illusion
of the paradise
with its delicious fruits
watched by the devil.

Restart by the essence
of the thought as a chip
incrusted in the soul
of the first tiny roundworm
called caenorhabditis elegans.

Teresinka Pereira/U.S.A.

* Dr. Teresinka Pereira, President of IWA
* Member of the American Civil Liberties Union
* Member of the Council for Secular Humanism
* Member of the United Nations Assoc. USA and the Business Council for the United Nations Ambassador at Large of the International States Parliament for Safety and Peace IWA Representative at Unesco: Emeritus Dr. Francis Dessart IWA Ambassador at UNESCO and UN: Dr. Jorge Alberto Costa e Silva
* Address : P.O.Box 352048 Toledo, OH 43635-2048, U.S.A.
* E-mail: tpereira@buckeye-express.com

Wall $treet

Concerned citizens
generate the rally
against Wall $treet greedy.
Rich clients get scared
but nothing else changes...
People are still camping
The police came and defended
the establishment.
People are still camping
People on the street
need to make more noise,
more movement,
more aggressiveness,
more determination,
more people
to strike right on
Wall Street with millions
of main street people.
Our goal is to close out
the Wall $treet
of the rich gamblers
and open the everybody's
working and savings
possibilities on Main Street.

Gliese 58/C

If you don't like this Earth
go to planet Gliese 58/c
which orbits
the Red Dwarf Star.
However
you have to hurry
in order to arrive there
before USA astronauts.
In the abyss of the universe
there are still unlimited places
in which to live in peace,
but only until
the Wall $treet gamblers
manage to buy them.

If I May Ask...

When time is slow
and the abyss of the distance
erodes our dreams

When we stop listening
to the commands from the heart
avoiding a rhyme
with ardent words

When silence pierces the soul
like a sharp knife

I ask myself
if I can truly love
or if my feeling are just
flashes of lightning
which come and go
while time is passing
by my day-by-day life routine.

세계시문학 제30집(2012)

인쇄 2012년 11월 5일
발행 2012년 11월 9일

편저자 | 김 정 웅
펴낸이 | 윤 해 규
주 간 | 김 효 열
편집장 | 김 경 희
펴낸곳 | **을지출판공사**

등록번호 · 제 2-741호
등록일자 · 1985년 2월 14일
주 소 · 서울시 마포구 서교동 394-81 홍익B/D 3층
우편번호 · 121-840
전 화 · 02) 334-4050, 334-4090
팩시밀리 · 02) 334-4010
E-mail : ejp4050@hanmail.net

값 20,000원

ISBN 978-89-7566-141-9 03810

세계시문학회
전북 고창군 고창읍 읍내리 192-67
☎ 063-564-4248, 010-6318-4248
585-807